The Paralympic Games: Empowerment or Side Show?

This book is dedicated to:

Anne (Africa), **Caja** (Oceania), **Caroline** (Europe) & **Tamsyn** (America)
Our Global Children

DISABILITY & SPORT

Series Editors

Keith Gilbert
University of East London

Otto J. Schantz
University of Koblenz-Landau

This book is the first in the series which aims to highlight the relationship between disability and sport. The series is based in the Centre for Disabilities, Sport & Health at the University of East London and does not specifically relate to any one discipline but aims to develop new research in cross disciplinary perspectives. The editors have both worked in disability and Paralympic sport and are dedicated to the development of the area so that students, academics and individuals can learn from a variety of interdisciplinary dichotomies. In short, we are questioning what the relationship between disability and sport is, and how the lives of disabled people are changed by their involvement in sport. If you wish to contribute to this series, please contact either of the two editors.

Keith Gilbert & Otto J. Schantz (Eds.)

THE PARALYMPIC GAMES:
EMPOWERMENT OR SIDE SHOW?

British Library Cataloguing in Publication Data
A catalogue record for this book is available from the British Library

Keith Gilbert & Otto J. Schantz
The Paralympic Games: Empowerment or Side Show?
Maidenhead: Meyer & Meyer (UK) Ltd., 2008
ISBN: 978-1-84126-265-9

© 2008 by Meyer & Meyer (UK) Ltd.
Adelaide, Auckland, Budapest, Cape Town, Graz, Indianapolis,
Maidenhead, New York, Olten (CH), Singapore, Toronto
Member of the World
Sport Publishers' Association (WSPA)
www.w-s-p-a.org

Printed and bound by: CPI Wöhrmann Print Service
ISBN: 978-1-84126-265-9
E-Mail: info@m-m-sports.com
www.m-m-sports.com

ACKNOWLEDGEMENTS

Our text is a culmination of ideas to create a book which developed the narratives of individuals working in the sport and disability fields and in completing this task to include both practitioners and academics in a text which supported the development of new and exciting research directions for the Paralympic arena. At the outset it must be clearly understood that we believe that this book would not have been possible to deliver if it were not for the kind support which we received from the authors of the various chapters. We are also proud to say that these authors are now friends and colleagues who we admire greatly for their ability to stick to the task at hand and never waver from their perceptions of the truth. We wish to give particular thanks to the following friends. Trish Bradbury, Jane Buckley, Brendan Burkett, Peter Corr, Anne Dinel, Mojca Doupona-Topic, Allan Edwards, Donny Elgin, Barbara Emener, Donna deHaan, Brent Hardin, Marie Hardin, Peter Horton, Mary Hums, Iris Lutz, Marilyn Kell, Peter Kell, Pamm Kellett, Katrin Koenen, Normazan Abdul Majid, Margie McDonald, Roger Noutcha, Chris Nunn, Lisa O'Keefe, Abdul Hafidz bin Haji Omar, Barbara Petri-Uy, Nathan Price, Frédéric Reichhart, Karen Richards, Heather Ross, Louise Savage, James Skinner, Kristine Toohey, Cesar Torres, Jo Winfield, and Eli Wolff. We would also like to take this opportunity to thank Hans Meyer and Thomas Stengel from Meyer and Meyer for their ideas and guidance through the development and editing process of the book. Finally, we would like to thank Eva and Yuen Ching for their support, love and borrowed time throughout the publishing process of this book.

CONTENTS

Section 3 Olympism Versus Paralympism?

Section 4 Cultural Diversity at the Paralympics

Section 5 Future Directions of Research on the Paralympic Movement

1   RECONCEPTUALIZING THE PARALYMPIC MOVEMENT

Otto J. Schantz & Keith Gilbert

'When normal and stigmatized do in fact enter one another's immediate presence, especially when they there attempt to sustain a joint conversational encounter, there occurs one of the primal scenes of sociology'.   *(Goffman, 1963,13)*

In July 1948, when the Games of the XIVth Olympiad opened in London, the neurosurgeon Ludwig Guttmann organized at Stoke Mandeville hospital in England a small sports competition for 16 World War II veterans with spinal cord injuries. His vision was that "one day the Stoke Mandeville Games would achieve world fame as the disabled men and women's equivalent of the Olympic Games" (Guttmann, 1949, 24). Indeed, this humble contest grew to become the second largest multi-sports event in the World. Despite the fact, that the Paralympic movement is rather young compared to other sports movements, it has undergone tremendous changes in the last twenty years, as have the social treatment of people with disabilities. Interestingly, there have been sports competitions for people with different disabilities since the end of the 19th century, which occurred at the same time as modern sport began spreading from England to Europe and North America. However, competitions for people with physical disabilities often resembled freak shows rather than serious sporting events (Schantz, 2006). The first disability groups to organize sport activities were the people with sensorial disabilities (visual impairments and deafness). Apart from some rare exceptions, it was only after World War II that the war heroes with physical disabilities were allowed to enter the stadium to then become sports heroes. For a öong time physical activities for people with disabilities were merely seen as a means of rehabilitation and adapted physical activities had been part of the medical field for quite some time. There is, we believe, still a big influence of the medical paradigm within the Paralympic movement, but disabled sports whether as a leisure activities or as formal competition have meanwhile been widely accepted, and recently universally promoted under the human rights umbrella. People with disabilities in almost all cultural spheres in the world have become emancipated and the disability sports movement has somewhat followed this evolution. However, the question needs to be raised as to whether the Paralympic Games really contribute to the emancipation and empowerment of people with disabilities? Do they aid the struggle for justice and equal treatment towards persons with disabilities?

Empowerment or side show? The provoking question utilized as the title of this book will probably remain unanswered. However, we believe that this book brings together a variety of perspectives: personal experiences, descriptions, analyses and scientific papers which go some way towards answering the question. Of course, none of these chapters gives a definitive answer to our question which is clearly rhetorical in nature. Some chapters tend to indicate that the Paralympics could empower the position of persons with disability in the sports movement and across global societies in general. Still others are much more critical and consider the Paralympic Games as second class Games, or as a subtle form of exclusion which keeps sportspeople with disabilities at the margins of mainstream sports. Nevertheless, it is not the purpose of the book to give a clear cut response or to take a particular position for one or either of these opinions. We consider this volume of selected writings as a modest starting point which hopefully will open the way to new horizons in the form of innovative and probing questions in various research programmes within academic disciplines such as anthropology, philosophy/ethics, sociology, cultural studies, gender and disability studies. We understand that the medical and life-sciences paradigm is still largely predominant in this field; however there is an enormous lack of solid, independent, and critical research in all other relevant disciplines. Therefore we hope this book will act as a source for quality research to be conducted outside of the medical paradigm.

Many of the comments which appear in this book have been made to stimulate discussion, are often written from a critical perspective, and are designed to challenge preconceived thoughts. Nonetheless, they are in no way written to discredit others but to offer new opinions, which we are happy to have challenged, so that we can open up the debate regarding the Paralympic movement and not just offer a viewpoint which satisfies Paralympic organizers.

So much for the opening statements which by their very nature are designed to provoke discussion and debate and as such we hope that many of the chapters in this book will provide a similar logic and also assist in the support of the athletes, coaches and managers who work within the movement.

A large number of the following chapters are concerned with the development of the Paralympic movement over the past years. They contend that we are living in new times and that the athletes who are growing up in this century are very different from those twenty years before and that there is a growing need for accountability and enlightenment of the Paralympic movement in order to keep in touch with the grass roots of the Paralympics.

More importantly, this book came about principally because of our previous work with disabled individuals and Paralympians. It has been put together in response to a growing need for more information about the effect that the Paralympics and sport has on the lives of individuals with a disability. Indeed, we argue from the outset that we know little of Paralympians lives and the manner in which they became disabled either through birth or through accident. All the public sees is the athlete – the wheelchair – the disability and their countries uniform. They know nothing of what it takes to get the athlete to that level of competition or nothing about their struggles in life or the courage and money that it has taken for them and their families to get to this position in life together. For example we asked two Australian athletes what being in the Paralympic team meant to them personally and how this helped them in life and to conquer their fears and support them through the tough times. *The responses are more important than anything written elsewhere in this book.* They are personal as the athletes are sharing themselves with the rest of the world in order to make people understand their struggles. So we begin with a snapshot of Donnys Elgins life:

REFLECTIONS ON A LIFE WITH RESTRICTIVE DISABILITY

Try growing up missing a leg. Try having operations on both hands because one thumb is missing and all your fingers are joined together. Try open-heart surgery. Try teasing and humiliation at school then add the constant pain from ill fitting artificial legs, and now you have a big part of my childhood.

To be honest, I would love to have grown up with two legs to be able to run around with my 'normal' brother and my three 'normal' sisters but this was never going to be the case. However, if it were not for them and the rest of my loving family I would have achieved nothing in life. Indeed, for me to run was a far cry from what I was once able to physically achieve, as I had a hard time just being able to walk. I knew that I was always going to need artificial legs and worried about this constantly. However, now I am happy today to state that having two legs doesn't really give you that much of an advantage in life and believe that most of the advantage which I feel I possess comes from my positive way of thinking.

As a kid being born without the lower 1/2 of my leg there was no way that you could convince me that it was ok or vaguely similar to other children. I clearly remember the day when I was teased so badly at school that I told my dad I didn't want to live any more. I remember sitting down on a box and crying, uncontrollably sobbing until my dad approached me and asked what was wrong. I told him that it's not fair. Why, why did I have to have one leg, why did I have to be the one to get teased, why couldn't it be my brother or even my sisters? Why were they all ok and not I. It's just not fair? Thankfully my dad was really smart and caring and had the ability to convince me that I was a good person even though I only had one leg. I will always be indebted to my father for his support and encouragement over the years. He was a good person for this role because he had a good attitude and a good sense of humour. My Dad also told me that the world is full of people that are the best in the world at something and it was up to 'us kids' to work out what that something is. He also showed me the other side of the tough times; he showed me that life could actually be worse and that I was actually one of the lucky ones.

By the same token you don't forget the times you walk down the street in shorts and have every single person take a look at you because you are different. Then there are the ones that just keep looking and then staring because you are not normal, you are handicapped, you are disabled, you are whatever the word of the day is to describe you being anything but the same as everyone else. Also, you never forget the days when the other children at school would call you names and not play with you. Some days you just want to reach out and punch them in the face, and then there are some days you do! There are the absent days at school, and the missed sports carnivals, I loved sport and missing these days was a really sad time for me. I hated no going on the excursions and the other the fun days because often I had to go and get a new leg made. This was a traumatic time for me and my Dad and I would get up at three a.m. so that we could be in the city by 6 a.m. and sit in a waiting room for hours, then eventually see the man that was going to draw on my stump, make a plaster cast or let me walk on this robot looking thing and then after hours of waiting and testing go home tired and saddened by the day's events.

The realization that a good leg makes all the difference to your whole day doesn't come that early in your life, mostly because your parents kept telling me that is the way life is and they argued that sometimes I just had to put up with a bit of pain. Over a childhood of hearing this and other comments and dealing with ill fitting legs I never quite got used to their comments because pain is just that, it is pain and pain is difficult to deal with. What happens however, is that you learn to deal with it, that's not to say that it goes away, you just don't make a noise about it. You learn to deal with it.

Then there were times when I experienced 'phantom pains', and the easiest and clearest way to describe 'phantom pain' is that it feels like somebody sticking pins into the bottom of your stump. The problem about 'phantom pain's is 'figuratively speaking' they totally have a mind of their own and you don't know when they are going to come and more so when they are going to go. Often they would start when you are relaxed, sitting in a classroom, at home watching the television or having dinner or whenever I am tuned into whatever is happening at the time - they hit you as if coming from nowhere with excruciating pain, right in the bottom of my stump, normally my first reaction is to take the leg off, though this does nothing to stop it. Often I just kick or stamp the leg as hard as I possibly can to try and rid myself of the pain. As you could imagine, when I was younger, this type of outburst was not all that welcome in a relatively subdued classroom or at home watching the television with my family.

Then there were the days that I would have to go to school on crutches wrapped in plaster after an operation and spend my day telling all the other kids what it was this time. I hated having to do this as it prolonged the agony and made me think more about the problems which I had in comparison with able bodied children. Indeed, how can I forget always coming second, third, fourth and last and then being told, 'oh, don't worry it's not your fault, you have got one leg, your disabled, if you had two legs you might have won'. Comments and problems like this become compounded until you get an opportunity to see other people that are different, and they actually appear the same. I began to notice that these people with other disabilities were the same as me and when you see them you realize that you are not different after all. These people were all involved in sport which saved me from myself and saved my life. However, there were some problems which I had to overcome.

The first barrier that I faced in my quest to become a Paralympian was not the competition and the tough training regimes but getting my parents to allow me to compete with other disabled people. My parents attitude was based on the theory that if you are disabled then you can't do a great deal in life which was most definitely the stereo type of people with disabilities in those days, thus there was 'no way' that they thought that their kid was disabled or going to have anything to do with disabled people. In their opinion they were convinced that their boy was normal, but just missing a bit of his leg.

Nevertheless, after speaking with some people involved in the disability sport area and constant nagging from me, they allowed me to compete at the state championships. This was clearly the turning point in my life for both my parents and I. Initially, the training and sports were tough as most of the athletes were good, but above all, from my point of view, I was now on an even playing field. I had defeated my personal demons and thus the journey began for the most important part of my life thus far - to become a Paralympian.

These comments by Donny drove us forward and enthused us to put together this edited text. We were principally interested in combining some academic work with practitioners on the ground who often see and experience things which the public or academics would not understand and who have also never had the opportunity to put their stories down on paper. This text is therefore a combination of methods and individuals who have come together much like the multicultural nature of the Paralympics themselves to provide an awareness of their talents and to bring new insights to the academic and practical field. More importantly we have asked athletes to become involved in this process and what follows is another example of the quality of person that we are dealing with in this text. The following scenario was written by Louise Savage who in her own right was one of Australia's greatest ever athletes. Louise gave us another perspective which is highlighted by her own snapshot of life with a disability and as a Paralympian.

LIFE REFLECTIONS

I was born with my disability and really don't know any different. I was introduced to sport at the age of 3 through swimming and have never really looked back. Initially the swimming was a form of rehabilitation, a way to build up my upper body strength and a lot of fun. It was not till I was 8 that I was introduced to wheelchair sports and I suppose that was an enormous window of opportunity that opened for me. I competed in every sport they had on offer and loved it. As I child I never dreamt of representing Australia or going overseas to compete. It just never really occurred to me.

My first international competition in 1990 was the turning point in my career as a wheelchair track and road racer. At those World Championships I really got a taste for what my sport was about. I had the chance to witness the best in the world which inspired me to want to be the best. From those games I decided I wanted to be a professional athlete.

2000 would have to be one of the biggest highlights of my career, not only on the sporting field but off. It was the first time I had competed in my home country at such a level and had my friends and family to witness my ultimate, winning gold. It was not only about the winning, but the way in which the games were held. It was such a celebration of life and celebration for people with disabilities. The people of Australia supported and enjoyed the games like no other. I was so proud to be Australian and to have such a magnificent sporting event in my own backyard. The Sydney 2000 Paralympic Games will be one of my most treasured memories forever.

I have now retired after winning two silver medals at the 2004 Paralympic Games in Athens. I left behind an amazing career record which saw me compete at four Paralympics (1992, 1996, 2000 and 2004) and win a total of nine gold and four silver medals. I also competed at three Olympic Games in the 800m wheelchair demonstration race in Atlanta, Sydney and Athens winning two gold and one bronze medal. At the IPC World Championships in 1990, 1994, 1998 and 2002 I won a total of 12 gold and 2 silver medals and at the IAAF World Championships I represented Australia in 1993, 1995, 1997, 2001 and 2003 winning the 800m wheelchair exhibition event on each occasion. At the 2002 Commonwealth Games I won silver in the 800m. Along the way I have broken at one stage or another every world record on the track from the 100m to the 5000m. Although now do not hold any individual world records.

For me it has been the most unbelievable experience to be involved in sport and compete at such a high level, to see the change in the recognition, understanding and acceptance of people and athletes with a disability all over the world. I would not have wanted life any other way. I now want to still be involved in my chosen sport so I am coaching and hope to bring through future champions and help create some golden dreams for them too.

Louise then was also an inspiration to us as her words were humbling and her achievements in elite sport have been simply amazing. The two athletes then were the inspiration behind this book for us. This book is seminal in that it introduces and opens up new and important information regarding aspects of the Paralympic Movement and in particular provides information about athletes, coaches and managers which has not previously been researched or written about. The main idea of the book is to provide a mix of theory and practice consequently chapters have been written from academics and practitioners alike. This blend and weaving of theory and practice into the text provides an informed look at the intricacies of the development of the Paralympic Movement, of some of its idiosyncrasies and shortcomings and some interesting ideas which should be explored and researched further in order to provide researchers and the public with insights into the world of the Paralympics.

With the thoughts of Louse Savage wringing in our ears we argue that the book rests on the assumption that an examination of the relationships between the personal, social and theoretical experiences of the Paralympic movement are influenced by many factors which are as yet un-researched and which may have important implications for the ways in which we conceptualize the disability sport and the nature of the direction and development that we construct for the Paralympic movement, Paralympians, coaches and managers in the 21st century.

This collection of chapters contributes to scholarship by providing an informed research based discussion of topics that are at the core of the Paralympic movement. Basically, its development and the ways in which we regard the Paralympic movement have changed minimally over the last two decades and it will be contended (as previously mentioned) in this book that a reconceptualizing of its development is required in the 21st century. Also, the book complements the basic discourses by extending the discussion in a critical way so that it is not just a description of what we can do to make the Paralympic movement more relevant but also an examination of some of the fundamental issues and discussions raised by the authors and the disability phenomenon that is often suppressed in the university environment. The bigger picture issues around globalization, the notion of empire building and social justice and equity issues which must be considered when thinking about the Paralympic movement and its role in society are all tackled in some manner. In short as supporters of disability sport we believe that this text provides answers to some important questions and develops further questions to be researched.

The following chapters take into consideration the perspectives of different Paralympic actors: athletes, coaches, managers, volunteers and journalists and spectators. The dissimilar approaches, writing techniques and styles emphasize and illustrate the diverse point of views: narrative texts and journalistic articles are willingly mixed with scientific papers and theoretical comments. We make no apology for this as each individual author chose their own method of developing their own voice and telling their own stories.

The first section 'Public and Media Perceptions' deals with the interaction between the Paralympics and the media and the way in which the event is perceived by spectators and others. There are several chapters which highlight the interactions and offer ideas for further research in the area. The chapter by Karin Richards on the Paralympic Games ceremonies provides some excellent examples of further research projects in line with those that have been previously completed in the Olympic context. The notion of the 'supercrip' is paramount in the work of the Hardins and of significance to the relationship between spectators and the Paralympics per se. This is added to significantly by the chapter of Reichart et al. who develop the theme of spectatorism at the 2004 Paralympic Games and raise the question whether sometimes these Games resemble a side show. They further enhance the themes developed by Hardin & Hardin by providing further research topics to be conducted at future Games. A highly interesting chapter is the one by Margie Macdonald who insisted on writing it in the style of a journalist so that we could understand the nature of the tasks which she undertakes at the Paralympic Games. It is a remarkable perspective and highlights the differences which we have attempted to incorporate into the development of this book by allowing individuals other than academics to put forward their viewpoints and argue in the development of new and innovative research ideas within the Paralympic arena as we believe that the informed laypersons voice is equally as strong as the academic voice. Schantz and Gilbert have a chapter in this section which deals with the way the print media construe and misconstrue Paralympic Games and ideals. They compare French and German media coverage of the Paralympic Games. The final chapter of the section by Barbara Emener argues the case for strong marketing perspectives to be taken when developing a marketing profile for the Games. It provides sound support for those who are thinking of the marketing aspect of disability sport in the future.

Section two 'Inside the Paralympics' takes a close look at some important aspects of the Games as they relate to individuals who have worked in several Paralympics. It is in fact an insider's viewpoint of the Games from the perspectives of coaches, managers, researchers, Otto Bock employees, classification experts and a solid look into the equestrian discipline which has rarely been written about or researched. Jane Buckley who is an expert in classification provides us with some valuable insights in to the processes and practices of classification within the context of disabled and more importantly Paralympic sports. Chris Nunn offers a critical chapter which is highly relevant and to the point, in that, he discusses in depth the relationship between administrators and coaches in the Paralympic movement. We endorse this chapter because it offers many new avenues for the possibility of further research and development in the area. Brendan Burkett, himself an ex-Paralympian, and champion swimmer provides a thorough understanding of some of the aspects of sports science which impact on the Paralympians and offers ideas for further research in specific sport science disciplines. The chapter by Peter Corr is perhaps one of the most authentic in the book as it is truly a piece of art where he brings an understanding of the intellectual disability area to the book and provides us with a deep understanding of the limitations and enjoyment of coaching such athletes. It is a heartfelt addition to the book, poignantly written and offers an interesting yet critical perspective to the Games and Paralympic sport. Katrin Koenen has spent a number of years working at different Paralympic Games for Otto Bock which is the well respected company that works during the Paralympic Games period to keep the athletes running, cycling and racing in their chairs by repairing equipment. She gives a distinct insight into the Games from an outsider's perspective and provides some important insights into the work of the Otto Bock organization in keeping the Games alive. It makes for interesting reading and delivers ideas for future research directions in all sport science disciplines including sports management as Otto Bock is a classic example of a company developing a strong corporate responsibility to the Paralympic community. The final chapter of section two is written by Donna deHaan, a PhD student from the University of the West of England who is interested in developing novel research in the area of Paralympic equestrian sport. This chapter is the first of its genre and should be viewed as an invitation to social scientists to research in this area as there is little work done. Also the chapter provides some interesting insights into the integrating potential of equestrian sport.

Section three 'Olympism and the Paralympics' is quite controversial. The first three chapters argue for the Paralympic athletes to be recognized as Olympians. On the other hand Lisa O'Keefe provides a good example of an introspective look at the 2000 Sydney Paralympics and Olympics. In this chapter she develops the notions of elite sport, doping and other problematic during Games time. These arguments are strong and further developed intellectually by Kell et al. and Wolff et al. who make some wide ranging assertions regarding the relationship between the Olympics and Paralympics on the local and world scenes. The final two chapters in section three concern the notion of volunteerism (Kellett & Ross) and prospect of terrorism (Horton & Toohey) within the Paralympic sphere of influence. Both chapters highlight aspects of the Paralympic Games which have not previously been researched and open up innovative ideas for the future of research in the areas. Although we ourselves argue that this section is controversial in its delivery we acknowledge that without controversy there is little interest and without controversy there cannot be progress in the field of social sciences. We hope that these chapters will engender impartial research groups or individuals to further study the phenomena in question.

Section four as the title suggests reviews some of the cultural and political diversity within the Paralympic movement and analyses different systems which have been put into place by some sporting nations in order to develop as fully fledged National Paralympic Committees. The first chapter of this section Trish Bradbury offers an interesting overview of the development of disabled and Paralympic sport in New Zealand, and as a former Assistant Chef de Mission responsible for Games Operations at the 2000 Sydney Paralympics she provides us personal interpretations and experiences to supplement her description of events. Of particular interest in this section is the chapter written by Barbara Petri Uy where she presents the geo-political situation of postwar Kosovo and argues for a Paralympic Committee in the new state of Kosovo. Mojca Doupona describes and analyses the steps made towards the organization and recognition of disability sport in Slovenia. The other chapters highlight and analyze developments of Paralympic movements in different non-Western cultures. Roger Noutcha studies the constitution process of the Black Africa Paralympic movement from a postcolonial perspective. In the same manner, Abdul Hafidz Omar and Norazman Abdul Majid describe and discuss the place and the structure of sport for people with disabilities in the Malaysian society.

This book then is the first of its genre incorporating both [practice and theory] and we are pleased that those authors who wrote for us did so understanding that there would be the poignant mix of theory and practice within the contents of the text. We trust that the reader will understand the nature of the task and assist us into providing actions which will shake the very foundations of Paralympic sports and reshape the approaches and structures of future research projects which are of both a practical and theoretical significance to the athletes and the movement.

REFERENCES

Guttmann, L. (1949). The second national Stoke Mandeville Games of the Paralysed. *The Cord*, 3, 24.

Goffman, E. (1963). *Stigma – Notes on the Management of Spoiled Identity*. Englewood Cliffs, NJ: Prentice-Hall.

Schantz, O. J. (2005). Leistungsentwicklung bei den Paralympischen Spielen (pp. 74-89). In Burger, R., D. Augustin, D. Müller, N. & W. Steinmann (Eds.). *Trainingswissenschaft. Facetten in Lehre und Forschung*. Mainzer Studien zur Sportwissenschaft Band 23. Niedernhausen: Schors.

SECTION 1

PUBLIC AND MEDIA PERCEPTIONS

This section highlights some of the important aspects of the Paralympic Games and Paralympic Movement as viewed by the public and the media. It is concerned with providing some insights into the multipart and controversial issues which surround the Paralympic athletes, the Paralympic Games and the Paralympic Movement itself. It raises concerns regarding the staging of the opening and closing ceremonies, how Paralympic athletes relate to the media, what happens during a Paralympics Games from the medias and spectators perspective and what its like to market the phenomenon called the Paralympics.

2 THE FIRE WITHIN: THE SYDNEY 2000 PARALYMPIC GAMES OPENING CEREMONY

Karen Richards

INTRODUCTION

Over twelve years ago in 1995 I was involved in the initial planning stages of the Sydney Olympic Games 'Opening and Closing' Ceremonies. Throughout this time period it seemed as if everyone wanted to be part of the planning of the Olympic Ceremonies and I felt honoured to be a part of the process. The first task of the Olympic Ceremonies team was to produce the Handover Ceremony for Atlanta. However, it was little known in Sydney at the time that there was the need to produce a handover ceremony for the Paralympic Games. Indeed, while planning was well on the way for the Sydney Olympic Handover Ceremony it suddenly become obvious that someone was needed to produce the handover for the Paralympic Ceremonies. As there were so many people wanting to work on the Olympics it was possible for me to add a more creative space onto the footprint of the Paralympic Ceremonies. However, at this time my commitment to the Paralympic Games was only perceived as short term as I intended to produce the 'Handover Ceremony' then return to the Olympic Ceremonies team.

Amazingly one event changed my mind. I had a meeting with a photographer who was waiting for me in the middle of the Olympic Stadium in Atlanta. I couldn't get to him because a race was in progress and consequently I was short of time and found this race to be a major inconvenience to my daily planning. The race was the 800 metres wheelchair race. Louise Savage (an athlete who writes of her experience elsewhere in the beginning of the text) was battling it out with the American contenders. As they sped past me I saw the raw emotion on their faces and I instantly became hypnotised. I suddenly had a burst of patriotic pride overcame me and I found myself cheering for Louise. It was a really close race and the Australian won. I was elated. I suddenly realised that these athletes and this race had moved me in a way that the "normal" Olympians didn't. It was quite literally at that moment that I decided to focus on getting the job as the Paralympic Games Director of Ceremonies and to forget about the Sydney Olympic Games.

Whether Paralympic athletes are considered elite athletes or not there is little doubt that being selected as part of the Paralympic team is a major milestone in their lives. Once appointed as the Sydney 2000 Paralympic Games Director of Ceremonies I was determined that we would produce a memorable opening ceremony for the once in a lifetime Games.

THE TASK

In the modern era the Olympic Games Opening Ceremony is the first event sold out when tickets for the Games go on sale. When planning for the Paralympic Games Opening Ceremony began one of the first questions which I was asked was "how would we attract people to the Paralympic Games?" Part of the brief for the opening was that there must be a draw card as people were unlikely to come just for the event in its own right. The success of the Opening Ceremony would determine the success of the overall Games. We had to attract publicity through the planning and through the use of "big name" performers.

Unquestionably, it's an enormous task for a city to put on two such large international events in the space of just over a month. The Sydney Olympic Opening Ceremony was on the 15th September 2000, the Sydney Paralympic Opening Ceremony on the 18th October 2000. The budget for the Olympic Opening: in excess of $50m, the budget for the Paralympic Opening Ceremony: $5m. Yet both ceremonies really had the same goals - to launch their respective Games towards a successful outcome.

SOCOG AND SPOC

Lessons learnt from the organization of the two events in Atlanta and in previous cities meant that the SOCOG (Sydney Organising Committee of the Olympic Games) and SPOC (Sydney Paralympic Organising Committee) ceremonies teams formed some strong relationships. However, this was not always amicable. In a country the size of Australia there are only a few true international stars. Both ceremonies wanted the same names and this could have an adverse affect to ticket sales for the Paralympic Games. The Olympic Ceremonies didn't need names to sell tickets. Many artists eventually performed in both the Sydney Olympic Closing Ceremony and the Sydney Paralympic Opening Ceremony. Fortunately this didn't affect the Paralympic ticket sales.

In actuality it appeared that after the Olympics the people of Sydney wanted more entertainment and the Paralympic Games kept the Olympic euphoria going. The opening ceremony was a sell out – as was the closing ceremony. Numerous people commented that the Paralympic Games were friendly. Families who came to the Games could access the athletes and readily have their photos taken with medal winning athletes. As the athletes entered the stadium in the opening ceremony many were obviously overwhelmed by the reaction from the crowd. Many people also commented that during the athletes parade in the Olympic Games huge numbers of people left the stadium for refreshments. During the Paralympic's athlete parade most people stayed in their seats and enjoyed the reactions and interaction of the athletes.

Having approximately one tenth of the Olympic Ceremony budget yet having to produce an event suitable for the same size performance space meant the team had to be extremely creative and resourceful. Companies such as the lighting and audio suppliers for the Olympic Games agreed to leave most of the equipment in the stadium without hire fees for the time between the ceremonies. This saved large amounts of money, which would have been charged to set up the equipment. However, there were also problems with being so closely associated with the Olympic Games. Before the Olympic Games begun many SOCOG staff would only focus on their jobs for the Olympic Games. The fact that there was very little time between the two Games did not factor into their decisions to postpone work on the Paralympic Games until the Olympics concluded. Then when the Olympics were over, many of the necessary functional staff were exhausted and took sick leave. This lead to the Paralympic Production team having to work extremely long hours in the lead up to the Games completing planning that could have been finished months in advance. Both ceremonies teams were required to report to a Ceremonies Control group frequently before the ceremonies. This was to ensure all safety measures were under control and to ensure that planning was on track. It was amusing to see the Olympic presentations. They had models and drawings, which probably cost them the total amount of the Paralympic Ceremonies budget. We would go to these meetings which the essential diagrams and would frequently end up scribbling diagrams to explain certain concepts.

Working with the SOCOG ceremonies team also meant that we were privy to their most secret planning. Ric Birch shared with me, well in advance, his plans for lighting the cauldron. I remember him telling me all the details. The cost of this effect was literally more than our entire budget. There would be lots of water pumped up to create a waterfall effect down the grandstand and a ring of fire would be lit as the cauldron was revealed from within the stage. The cauldron would then rise up, tracking through the stands to come to rest high above the Stadium. I asked the question "so how does it come down again so we can reach it to reignite it". He replied, "It doesn't – all the equipment would be removed after the opening to allow maximum seating for the rest of the Games". There was no possible way we could have had someone personally light the Cauldron short of dropping them in by helicopter – and that wasn't possible because the helicopter would not have been allowed to fly that close to an audience. It was nice of Ric to share this though! Hence we had to develop a special effect way of lighting the cauldron. We spend many hours trying to come up with a spectacular means of lighting the cauldron.

Ironically both the Olympics team and our team had exactly the same idea of a way to extinguish the flame. We approached the Australian airforce first with our suggestion. We found out shortly after that the Olympic's team had approached them with the same idea. The air force was happy to do the effect for both ceremonies. However, once it had been done for the Olympics we felt it was necessary to come up with another idea for the Paralympics. The effect involved an air force plane flying over the cauldron, then starting the back burn effect. Simultaneous the gas would be turned off the Cauldron extinguishing the flame.

There were hundreds of people in the Olympic Ceremonies team. They occupied a huge amount of space in the stadium. We had a small office and a very dedicated, very small staff. We had to work extremely long hours and I often wanted to apologise to the team for making them have to work so hard. However they were all dedicated to the Paralympic Games and took on the task of creating a big show on a small budget.

THE MOST DISAPPOINTING MOMENTS

As part of the Ceremony we had erected a huge projection screen across one end of the stadium. Wonderful projection images had been developed for this screen. The weather had been extremely hot and many of the production crew working on the field were getting exhausted from working in the heat. A southerly change came through and relief was felt. However, as suddenly as the change had hit, the screen started to rip. I stood in the control room watching this expensive, important part of the ceremony self-destructing. The production director was near the screen and ran, towards it trying desperately to stop it ripping. This screen was approximately 50 metres long and once it started ripping there was no stopping it. This screen had taken several weeks to manufacture and we were now only days from the opening. However, once again the determination of the team to make this ceremony work came through and somehow another screen was made and in position in time for the ceremony. It wasn't as glamorous nor was it's quality as good as the original but we had another screen and were able to project the images.

Another problem we experienced was the weather. The Olympic preparations had experienced constant clear weather. Every time we had a rehearsal planned it seemed to rain. Our wonderful friends at the Olympics kindly offered us their wet weather ponchos. They hadn't needed them. We had a wet weather show plan however it wasn't as good as the fine weather plan and I felt we hadn't worked this hard and this long to put on a second rate show. On the morning of the opening I had returned home at about 6am. I was returning to the stadium at 9.00am when my mobile rang. It was the designer asking whether he should organise the pre-set for the fine weather or wet weather show. After agonising for a minute I boldly announced that we were going for the fine weather show. He pointed out all the clouds in the sky, and the forecast, which was for rain increasing during the day. I chose to ignore these comments. We were going to put on the best possible opening regardless of weather. The rain held off until about 5.00 p.m. The ceremony was to begin at 7.00 p.m. At 5.00 p.m. the rain became quite heavy. I felt extremely sick. A large part of the production involved children painting on "pixels" (essentially large tables) creating pictures. Half an hour before the show was to begin, the production director casually commented to me that the paint wouldn't work if it were painted onto water. In last minute desperation I asked everyone on our radio communication who was free, to find towels, rags or anything they could to get onto the field and try to dry the pixels. The rain had slightly eased and I hoped that it may be possible to salvage the show. Much to my surprise dozens of people entered the field, from the star performer's roadies to the special effect team, firework team, sound and lighting crew, police, stage managers. Everyone wanted to make the show work.

We cleared the field, started the show and as Jeff St. John sang the national anthem the rain started again. I stood in the control room feeling doomed. The production director again reminding me that paint wouldn't work on water. By this stage all I could do was hope. Amazing as the national anthem concluded with an air force flypast, the rain disappeared. However the pixels were still wet. As the children started painting their first image we realised that somehow the paint was working on the water and the image looked great. Ironically we had spent a lot of time trying to work out a way of getting a reflective surface on the pixels for the firework finale. The rain had created this effect.

THE CREATIVE CONCEPT

In planning the opening ceremony, the importance of this event to the athletes had a strong influence in the conceptual stages of the ceremony's direction. The creative concepts began with the production team's analysis of what motivates people with disabilities to physically push themselves and train to make the Paralympic Team. This was also necessary in creating a point of difference for the Paralympic Opening Ceremony.

Phrases such as "triumph over adversity" and "the fire within" and "the passion" were frequently discussed. This lead to the theme of "The Fire Within" being adopted by the production team. A story line centering on a child trying to understand what drives these athletes and people with disabilities to strive towards their goals was developed. Songs were commissioned for the opening ceremony including "The Challenge" sung by Jeff St John, The Fire Within and Being There. The lyrics of these songs asked questions and tried to explain the journey of the Paralympic athlete. Bryan Brown as the narrator of the Sydney 2000 Paralympic Opening Ceremony began by asking the question "What brings us all here tonight. What makes these Games different? The song titled "The Challenge" sung by Jeff St John followed this statement.

Some of the lyrics for this song are:

This may be the greatest challenge of all
To know the voice within and answer the call.
In every game
at every stage,

The bravest conquer pain with sacrifice
For every tiny game they pay the price
Just to compete
For victory is sweet
Just for the chance to bring the screaming crowd to its feet

What drives us on to reach the heights
Our weariness gone we stand up and fight
Why do we believe what is it we share
While we still breath we're willing to dare.

No matter the cost no matter how high
The battle not lost we'll never say die
It's out destiny to answer the call
For this may be the great challenge of all

For this may be the greatest challenge of all

To overcome a common misunderstanding that people with disabilities all have mental disabilities Professor Stephen Hawking (renowned for his intellectual abilities) was approached to have an input in the ceremony. His role was to answer the question of "Where is the Fire". The child in the ceremony asked this question and Professor Hawking reply was:

"The Fire is in our hearts, in our minds and in our spirits. The fire is within."

While the production team was aware many of these athletes had trained extremely hard to be selected for the games and were committed to winning, other athletes were happy to just be there. This lead to another song being written for the ceremony, "Being There", by Graeme Connors. The lyrics of this song:

Like winning isn't always being first across the line
As long as I do my best I'm winning every time
Reach up reach out being here what's its all about
This time this place to fight the good fight and run the good race

And then when it's all through I'll be proud to stand here beside you
Proud to remember being here

No-one else will ever know what it took to make us come this far

The music was an integral part of the ceremony and used to convey they story and create the mood for the performances.

THE INTERNATIONAL PARALYMPIC COMMITTEE INPUT INTO THE CEREMONY

The International Paralympic Committee showed great flexibility towards the protocol part of the ceremony. This is one of the reasons the Sydney 2000 Paralympic Ceremonies were able to develop in a more contemporary style than the Olympic Games Opening Ceremony. While the International Olympic Organising committee strictly controls various aspects of the opening ceremony, including the lighting levels which are set for television broadcast standards, strict limits regarding protocol, and restrictions forcing the athletes to march into the stadium in a very staid manner the IPC were much more flexible. This meant that it was possible to create much more of a fun, party atmosphere for the ceremony but in particular during the long athlete parade. This, in turn saw the hand walking demonstration by one athlete and numerous acts of spontaneous celebration in the form of dancing, singing, chanting and wheelchair dancing by many of the athletes present. As Opening Ceremonies for the Paralympic Games and indeed the Paralympic Games in total have a much less developed structure than the Olympic Games there are still ceremonial elements which the IPC were happy to relinquish control over to the local organising committee. These items included reworking the Paralympic Anthem to make it fit into the existing style of music for the ceremony, allowing flexibility with the torch entrance and with the lighting of the cauldron.

It was with great trepidation that I asked the IPC for their permission to change the arrangement of the Paralympic Anthem. It wasn't a small re-arrangement. We were changing an extremely droning anthem into an electric guitar solo. The new arrangement climaxed into a moving piece however I was worried that I wouldn't get past the first 30 seconds before they said "no". However, much to my relief they said something along the lines of "if you think that will work" and were happy with the changes. The Sydney Paralympic Games Opening Ceremony was a sell out. It most definitely drew attention to the event. The Games were extremely successful with huge attendances at all events. The Opening was televised nationally in Australia on ABC television and attracted 4.2 million viewers across the main five capital cities. This was the highest rating figure in Sydney for any ABC program ever.

The Sydney Paralympic Games ceremonies were memorable. Despite budget constraints, unfavourable weather conditions and its position following the world's biggest sporting event – the Olympics, we managed to create something special for the athletes, spectators and for everyone else involved in the Sydney 2000 Paralympic Games. I'm proud to say that at the end of the day, after working long hours and avoiding disaster we as a team can confidently state that we stirred the human 'fire within' to provide the Paralympic movement with a fitting spectacle for the athletes and public consumption.

3   ELITE WHEELCHAIR ATHLETES RELATE TO SPORT MEDIA

Marie Hardin & Brent Hardin

INTRODUCTION

During network coverage of the 1996 Paralympics in the United States, wheelchair tennis player Hope Lewellen was featured in a televised segment that focused on her life and athletic career. Schell & Rodriguez (2001), in an interrogation of this segment, found that the CBS network had reduced Lewellen's "complex and rich story to a single focus" (p. 130). She had been framed as a "supercrip." As such, explain the authors,

> "Lewellen becomes the exception to the rule of *pitiful brokenness*, keeping ableist stereotypes in place while allowing the viewer to applaud her escape, via hard work...from disability's perceived confinements and limitations". (p. 131, author's emphases)

Stress on individual (versus cultural) effort to address (misperceptions of) disability is precisely the reason scholars see "supercrip" framing of athletes with disabilities as ultimately belittling. The disabled-hero framework is seen as a hegemonic device to keep people with disabilities at the bottom of the social hierarchy and deflect the culture's responsibility for its albeit infrastructure. A "supercrip" is the presentation of a person, affected by a disability or illness, as "overcoming" to succeed as a meaningful member of society and to live a "normal" life; it is a common media frame for athletes with disabilities, who are, like women, generally excluded from mainstream sport media (Golden, 1992; Smart, 2001; Walsdorf, 2000).

Although, scholars have been critical of such an approach to coverage of athletes with disabilities, the athletes themselves may view such coverage differently and perhaps even facilitate it. To explore this issue, we interviewed 10 competitive American wheelchair basketball players about how they accepted, negotiated, or opposed their framing in U.S. sport media.

HEGEMONY AND THE MEDIA

To understand the role of the "supercrip," we must understand it in the context of cultural hegemony. Through cultural hegemony, a capitalist culture's most powerful economic groups obtain consent for their leadership through the use of ideological "norms." Social structures and relationships that help the powerful but disadvantage those on the margins are presented as "natural" (Altheide, 1984; Condit, 1994; Croteau & Hoynes, 2000; Holtzman, 2000). American scholars have adjusted their understanding of hegemony to reflect modern socio-political conditions in the United States (Artz & Murphy, 2000; Condit, 1994). Because of a ubiquitous system of competing media images, for instance, the hegemonic process is complicated (Croteau & Hoynes, 2000;

Lewis, 1992). Media content incorporates themes that speak to different publics (Condit, 1994; Crane, 1999; Croteau & Hoynes, 2000). Thus, the state of hegemony is fluid, allowing groups to seek better social conditions (Condit, 1994). Further, media messages do not exert absolute control over media audiences (Lewis, 1999; Morgan, 1997). Consumers are purposeful in their use of media; they are also capable of interpreting texts in ways that are individually meaningful (Duke, 2000; Lewis, 1999; Meenakshi, 1999). Although individuals may absorb the dominant ideology, others may negotiate such ideology or reject it (Duke, 2000; Holtzman, 2000).

The range of available texts and individuals' access to oppositional codes help determine their ability to resist dominant ideological messages (Meenakshi, 1999). If such factors are strong, members of disenfranchised groups may be more likely to resist and oppose dominant messages, opening the way to renegotiate their place in the social order (Morgan, 1997). However, the power of hegemonic messages is almost overwhelming, by virtue of their presentation as universally valid. As Duke (2000) argues, a text's polysemic qualities do not neutralize its ideological potential; alternative views are appropriated into the dominant frame, which is consumerism (Artz & Murphy, 2000; Condit, 1994).

THE IDEOLOGY OF SPORT MEDIA

The ideology embedded in U.S. sport media reinforces American cultural values as shaped by capitalism (Trujillo & Vande Berg, 1989). One major concept of success in American culture is "self-actualization"; success implies individual effort to overcome obstacles and better oneself (Trujillo & Vande Berg, 1989). American culture glorifies tales of the "rugged individualist" by rejecting interdependence as weak and undesirable (Barr, 2000). Autonomy and physical fitness are valued, and physical dependence is viewed with disdain (Ashton-Shaeffer, 2001). Thus, sport in its commercial form projects itself on the surveillance, modification and manipulation of the body. Through sport, the body has become a site of struggle over "symbolic and material rewards between dominant and subordinate groups" (Rowe, McKay, & Miller, 2000).

HEGEMONY, THE BODY, AND NEGOTIATION OF MEDIA FRAMING

The most examined subordinate group in relation to the body and sport has been female athletes. Sport media have overwhelmingly marginalized and stereotyped women, who are framed as subordinate to men, and, thus, less valuable (Bruce, 1998; Crane, 1999; Mason, 1992; Walsdorf, 2000). Researchers have examined how girls and women read, negotiate or oppose the messages in sport media (Bruce, 1998; Crane, 1999; Duke, 2000; Meenakshi, 1999). Although many females accept dominant ideology, they are not uniformly vulnerable to media messages. They also may read messages thought demeaning by scholars as empowering. Bruce (1998) found that female viewers of televised women's basketball games were aware of the dominant cultural meanings within media presentations of the sport (women as less able competitors); however, they negotiated the coverage they saw and often rejected the embedded hegemonic messages, turning their experience with sport media into one they saw as empowering.
Hegemony, disability and sport:

Indeed, sport media's male hegemony has been recognized through scholarship and advocacy, its able-bodied hegemony has gone virtually unnoticed. Disability is a socially constructed identity that has gone largely without criticism, as Davis (1999) writes:

"….one of the most egregious acts of omission committed in the 20th century by progressives and radicals has been the almost complete ignoring of issues surrounding people with disabilities …An ableist cultural hegemony is clearly the rule". (p. 1).

Scholars argue that the emergence of a consumer-driven, capitalist economy in the United States has rendered people with disabilities invisible. The ideal body fits an environment constructed for the majority; people with disabilities are a liability for their inability to navigate it (Davis, 1999).

DISABILITY AND SPORT

Despite images to the contrary, many individuals with disabilities do not view their bodies as entirely weak and frail, perhaps explaining the increase in their sports participation (DePauw, 1997; Hoffer, 1995; Schantz & Gilbert, 2001). Participation in sport "demonstrates that individuals with disabilities are more able and similar to their non-disabled peers than stereotypes suggest" (Taub, Blinde, & Greer, 1999, p. 1469). Over the past decade, coverage of disability sports has increased ever so slightly (Schantz & Gilbert, 2001). However, authors of the most recent studies acknowledge that the marginalized role of disabilities in media coverage has not improved. Reporters still focus primarily on the "disabled" instead of the "athlete" (Schantz & Gilbert, 2001). The Paralympics, the world's most elite sporting event for disabled athletes, receives scant coverage compared to the Olympics in the U.S. press. Coverage of the Salt Lake City Games in 2002 was virtually non-existent in U.S. media but received generous coverage in the foreign press (Golden, 2002). Golden, who interviewed sports reporters at the Paralympics, found that many U.S. sports reporters did not view disabled sports as valid or legitimate.

THE SUPERCRIP MODEL

When athletes with disabilities are covered, they are most often framed as supercrips (Schantz & Gilbert, 2001; Schell & Rodriguez, 2001). Scholars argue that this "disabled hero" model may be deeply moving for the able-bodied majority but is oppressive for individuals with disabilities (Barr, 2000; Golden, 1992; Iwakuma, 1997; Mitchell, 1989; Shapiro, 1993; Smart, 2001; Wolfe, 2001). The supercrip reinforces low societal expectations of people with disabilities (Golden, 1992; Iwakuma, 1997); it also reinforces the idea that people with disabilities should be able to accomplish at the level of disabled hero. Consequently, all people with disabilities are judged by the supercrip standard (Smart, 2001). What makes the supercrip stereotype most egregious, however, is the manner in which it emphasizes individual effort as a way to overcome barriers erected by an able-bodied culture (Clogston, 1991; Golden, 1992; Smart, 2001). The supercrip model promotes ableism, placing people with disabilities at the bottom of a hegemonically defined social hierarchy where a higher value is put on "normal" bodies that are part of the working majority (Smart, 2001).

Alternative models to the supercrip treat people with disabilities as an identifiable group with legitimate grievances and access issues, present disability as just one facet of a multi-dimensional, whole person, or frame disability as located in society's failure to accommodate (Auslander & Gold, 1999; Clogston, 1991; DePauw, 1997; Haller, 2000).

THE INTERVIEWS

We interviewed 10 active wheelchair athletes about their reading of the supercrip model in mainstream sport media, and we asked them about alternative models that might replace that framing. Most played on elite wheelchair basketball teams around the United States. Two had played on the 1996 Paralympic basketball team, and one player had been ranked as best in the world during the late 1990s. The participants' ages ranged from 16 to 45 years. To prompt conversation, we used the "auto driving" technique (McCracken, 1988) during the interviews. A *copy of Sports n Spokes* (an American disability sport magazine not available on newsstands but popular with disabled athletes) was used as a prompt during the interview. Participants were also asked to read two sports articles immediately before the interview: (1) an article about former Phoenix Suns player Neal Walk, published in the May 1, 2000 issue of the *East Valley* (Ariz.) *Tribune*, and, (b) an Associated Press article, also published in May, 2000, about accessibility of golf courses. The article about Neil Walk used ableist (supercrip) framing: It told the story of Walk's years in the NBA, before he began using a wheelchair after surgery for a spinal tumor, and of his "withstanding a challenge" by continuing his involvement with an NBA team from his wheelchair. Words such as "inspirational" and "phenomenal" were used to describe Walk.

The second article, about golf courses, used progressive framing to focus on people with disabilities in the United States as a minority group with accessibility rights that were not being met. Using the Casey Martin case, the writer described the concerns and discrimination faced by golfers and responses from golf clubs that refused accommodation. We began each interview with a "grand tour" question (Crabtree & Miller, 1992): "Tell me, and show me, how you use sport media." Participants were also handed a recent copy of *'Sports n Spokes'* and then copies of the articles. We asked a series of semi-structured questions about the athletes' perceptions of issues raised by framing used in each story.

HOW WHEELCHAIR ATHLETES VIEW THE 'SUPERCRIP'

The athletes described themselves as avid consumers of general-interest and specialty sport media, for several purposes: to learn more about their favorite sports, to seek able-bodied role models and to enhance their socialization with able-bodied peers. In other words, mainstream sport media are important tools to "fit in" the culture. Players mentioned the importance of consuming mainstream media so they could strike up conversations with others; several players mentioned their reputations as being knowledgeable about sports trivia and current events. They also sought role models among able-bodied athletes. They studied their favorite players in game situations, interviews and media features. One player said he liked to read about Dennis Rodman to get rebounding tips; another said he reads game stories to learn about player strategy. The athletes interviewed enjoyed paging through Sports n Spokes, but they articulated different reasons for consuming it (and other niche disability media): as a way to keep up on "insider news," to track other athletes in the disability community, and to affirm their own athletic status.

ACCEPTANCE OF THE SUPERCRIP MODEL

Most athletes talked at length about the supercrip model, although most were unaware of the term. Although they expressed misgivings, they were generally accepting of the model as perhaps helpful for disabled and non-disabled audiences. Several athletes talked about the Neil Walk story as one that inspired them. They saw the supercrip as valuable precisely because it highlighted the "rugged determination" of individuals with disabilities. John, 28, said he wanted to read something "inspirational."

> For somebody who just had a new injury, they'll want to hear what happened to Neil, and how he endured – I mean, he was an athlete – he had a great life as an NBA player, but then, gosh, his life made a turnaround, and he just has to deal with it.

Vic said he read supercrip stories "all the time, because I can relate to them."

He said about the Neil Walk story,

> Me and him can relate, because we both have the same mental attitude, because in the middle of the article he says that he uses a chair that someday he doesn't want to use anymore.... I've been using a chair all of my life, and someday I'm not going to use my chair. I know that one day I'm going to be out of it.

The athletes also believed that the supercrip model is good for the able-bodied public because it shows disabled individuals in a "positive" light. Stories with supercrip framing also show how "the human spirit can overcome." Ethan said:

> I think that there is a popular perception that people in wheelchairs are just hopelessly limited by their disability, and that people feel sorry for them – or people feel sorry for us because we're always in a wheelchair and they figure that we can't do much of anything anyway. And stories like this refute that – that people in wheelchairs can be just as creative and productive as anybody else. I mean, this guy is still working in sports! I mean, that's a real positive thing.

Joe, a 46-year-old player, defended the supercrip model as one not particular to people with disabilities.

> In all magazines you read articles about able-bodied people doing heroic things...Just because you're disabled doesn't mean we can't read about the good things they're doing...Do you read more about a disabled person doing something heroic or an able-bodied person doing something heroic? What's the difference?

NEGOTIATION OR REJECTION OF THE SUPERCRIP MODEL

Some athletes struggled with the supercrip model, using their own life experience as reason to question it. They said they fear that "hero" coverage of people with disabilities simultaneously lowers and raises societal expectations of the disabled. Alan, 21, said the supercrip model puts him in an awkward position.

I cannot count the number of times people have come up to me and said, 'I just think it's great you're out doing this and that' – like when I'm out at a bar. 'I just think it's awesome you're here,' and I'll say, 'Why?' Are they crazy? I'm at a bar!...People look at me like, 'Oh, that's so sad. You should be laying in bed everyday.'

Don, 42, who has been the subject of what he calls "supergimp" (supercrip) stories, said supercrip stories may be good "role-modeling." However, he echoed Alan's concerns. "The risk with some of the supergimp stories is this – not so much stereotyping, but narrowing of expectation".

PREFERENCE FOR PROGRESSIVE FRAMING

Most of the athletes interviewed expressed frustration with the supercrip emphasis on disability sport as a "human interest" story; more progressive models would illuminate their athleticism as valid. Joe talked about his frustration with being shut out by sports editors.

They put in pages of high school sports, and yet they refuse to put [us] in...That's so stupid! We're athletes...One thing people probably don't realize is that there's 53 million disabled people out there. We're probably the largest single group in the country.

Others talked about their desire to see sports coverage emphasize athletics over disability. "You don't have to focus on the fact that they play wheelchair basketball. Focus on the fact that they scored 21 points per game, 10 rebounds and the fact that he had a triple-double," said Alan. Ray said he did not want to see more coverage of sports such as the Paralympics if coverage is "going to make the general public say, 'Ah, wow, the poor pitiful soul:"

Talk about that person's athletic abilities or the team's athletic accomplishments.... The interest should not be that person's disability....Maybe the people in the media need to have an in-service or a memo that says, 'These guys would rather be treated as athletes when you're dealing with a sporting event, so let's put the emphasis there.'

The athletes expressed stronger support for the golf course accessibility story, which framed athletes with disabilities as a minority group with civil rights. They expressed a preference for that model because they believed it presented them as "real" to the able-bodied public and reminded the culture of a responsibility to accommodate the disabled community. Although some athletes said they had never played golf, they said the story about golf course accessibility reflected the reality of their lives more accurately. Ray, 36, said he preferred progressive framing of stories because it emphasizes the social and physical barriers people with disabilities still face. "You know, this is the year 2001, and these same old barriers were in place when the first black man tried to get into a golf clubhouse – the country club. And the disabled are running into those same old barriers," he said.

The athletes said progressive framing is also better for the able-bodied culture. Vic provided a list of examples.

Restaurant owners will say, 'Oh, we have ramps!' Yeah, but they're in the back of the building and the handicapped parking is up front, and the ramp should be up front so the person can just go straight up the ramp right into the restaurant.

FEARS ABOUT MEDIA IN AN ABLEIST SOCIETY

The athletes expressed an acute awareness of the hegemonic boundaries of U.S. mainstream media. Although they preferred increased use of progressive models for coverage, they believed that society would be less accepting of such changes. The athletes often spoke from a consumerist position; they expressed belief that supercrip stories "sell better" to an able- bodied population. Further, they worried that too many stories presenting disability as a social issue would make people uncomfortable. One athlete expressed concern that such coverage might make people resentful. Alan commented:

> It's going to make everybody scared about doing stuff. They're going to be so stressed out about looking for every little thing that a person in a wheelchair can complain about. They're not going to like somebody with a disability right when they come to their golf course because they'll think, 'Because of you, we had to do all this crud and spend all this money.'

Ethan contrasted what he thought are cultural sentiments about the two types of framing.

> I think that people don't like to be pushed…Businesses, corporations, agencies in general don't like to be told 'you must do this or else!' …You know, there's this initial inertia to not change, and dealing with issues of accessibility are, in essence, things that are demanding change…I think the other article – people can relate to that and people can say, 'Wow, he overcame. He's not limited. That's really good.'

CONCLUSIONS

Although, disability rights activists have long criticized the supercrip model as stigmatizing and patronizing, the disabled athletes interviewed do not see it as such, and some saw it as having value in their own lives. They did express concerns that ultimately, the model simultaneously lowers and raises cultural expectations of all people with disabilities; they are pitied, yet expected to become heroes. However, the athletes also saw the supercrip story as a way to increase the exposure of people with disabilities, and they believe that supercrip stories give people a favorable opinion of people with disabilities. There are perhaps several reasons for acceptance of the supercrip. One, mentioned by Meenakshi (1999), is the limited access disabled athletes have to "oppositional codes" and alternative texts. Athletes with disabilities have virtually no alternatives that would provide rejection of the supercrip model; the mainstream sport media they consume presents the supercrip as "normal," as these media are already embedded with 'hero' themes. Stories of personal triumph are common fare on the sports pages, reinforcing the capitalist premium on individualism. Thus, it would be reasonable to expect that they would be motivated and "inspired" by reading the disabled "hero" story as presented via the supercrip.

Another reason for acceptance of the supercrip may be what Artz & Murphy (2000) say is the dominant frame in U.S. media: consumerism. Athletes expressed an understanding of their non-value in relation to sport as a revenue-making industry; they internalize the value placed on them by the culture (Holtzman, 2000). These athletes also expressed a preference for alternative media models. However, they were also acutely aware that the kinds of more progressive coverage they seek may not sell (literally) to an ableist culture, and they expressed fear that the "overuse" of such models might result in a negative backlash. This, along with their rationalization about the supercrip stereotype, seems to be a reflection of an overall acceptance of the dominant hegemonic message about disability. Cultural body norms and social expectations shape their expectations, their motives and their fears. They reflect the force of great cultural pressure to accept the supercrip ideal and to reject ideas that might hold society more accountable.

Their preference for more progressive story models, however, is clear and valid. As competitive disability athletics (such as those found at the Paralympics) increase in prominence and these athletes become more visible, they might feel emboldened to demand more progressive coverage.

REFERENCES

Altheide, D.L. (1984). Media hegemony: A failure of perspective. *Public Opinion Quarterly, 48,* 476-490.

Artz, L., & Murphy, B.O. (2000). *Cultural Hegemony in the United States,* Thousand Oaks, Sage.

Ashton-Shaeffer, C., Gibson, H.J., Autry, C.E., & Hanson, C. (2001). Meaning of sport to adults with physical disabilities: a disability sports camp experience. *Sociology of Sport Journal, 18,* 95-114.

Auslander, G.K. & Gold, N. (1999). Media reports on disability: A binational comparison of types and causes of disability as reported in major newspapers. *Disability and Rehabilitation, 21* (9), 420-431.

Barr, G.W. (2000). Out of sight, out of mind. *America, 183* (19),15-16.

Bruce, T. (1998). Audience frustration and pleasure: Women viewers confront televised women's basketball. *Journal of Sport and Social Issues, 22* (4), 373-397.

Clogston, J.S. (1991). *Reporters' attitudes toward and newspaper coverage of persons with disabilities.* Ph.D. dissertation, Michigan State University.

Condit, C. (1994). Hegemony in a mass-mediated society: concordance about reproductive technologies. *Critical Studies in Media Communication, 11* (3), 205-223.

Crabtree, B.F. & Miller, W. (1992) *Doing qualitative research,* Newbury Park, Sage.

Crane, D. (1999). Gender and hegemony in fashion magazines: women's interpretations of fashion photographs. *The Sociological Quarterly, 40*(4), 541-563.

Croteau, D. & Hoynes, W. (2000). *Media/Society (2nd Ed.),* Thousand Oaks, Pine Forge Press.

Davis, L.J. (1999). J'Accuse! Cultural imperialism-ableist style. *Social Alternatives, 18*(1), 1-5.

DePauw, K. (1997). The (in)visibility of disability: Cultural contexts and 'sporting bodies.' *Quest, 49,* 416-430.

Duke, L. (2000). Black in a blonde world: Race and girls' interpretations of the feminine ideal in teen magazines. *Journalism and Mass Communication Quarterly, 77*(2), 367-392.

Golden, A. (2002). *An analysis of the dissimilar coverage of the 2002 Olympics and Paralympics: frenzied pack journalism versus the empty press room.* Paper presented at the Association for Education in Journalism and Mass Communication Annual Meeting, Miami.

Golden, M. (1992). Not on the front page. *Progressive, 56* (3), 43.

Haller, B. (2000). If they limp, they lead? News representations and the hierarchy of disability images. In D. Braithwaite & T. Thompson (Eds.), *Handbook of Communication and People with Disabilities,* (pp. 273-288). Lawrence Erlbaum Associates, Mahwah, N.J.

Hoffer, R. (1995, Aug. 14). Ready, willing and able. *Sports Illustrated, 83*(7), 64-74.

Holtzman, L. (2000). *Media Messages,* Armonk, M.E. Sharpe.

Iwakuma, M. (1997). *From pity to pride: People with disabilities, the media, and an emerging disability culture.* Paper presented at the Association for Education in Journalism and Mass Communication Annual Meeting, Chicago.

Lewis, C. (1992). Making sense of common sense: A framework for tracking hegemony. *Critical Studies in Media Communication, 9,* 277-292.

Lewis, J. (1999). Reproducing political hegemony in the United States. *Critical Studies in Media Communication, 16,* 251-267.

Mason, G. (1992). Looking into masculinity: Sport, media and the construction of the male body beautiful. *Social Alternatives, 11*(1), 27-32.

McCracken, G. (1988). *The Long Interview,* Newbury Park, Sage.

Meenakshi, G.D. (1999). Articulating adolescent girls' resistance to patriarchal discourse in popular media. *Women's Studies in Communication, 22,* 210-229.

Mitchell, L. (1989). Beyond the supercrip syndrome. *The Quill, 77*(10), 18-23.

Morgan, W.J. (1997). Yet another critical look at hegemony theory: A response to Ingham and Beamish. *Sociology of Sport Journal, 14,* 187-195.

Rowe, D., McKay, J., & Miller, T. (2000). Panic sport and the racialized masculine body. In J. McKay, M. Messner and D. Sabo (Eds.), *Masculinities, Gender Relations, and Sport,* (pp. 245-261). Thousand Oaks, CA: Sage.

Schantz, O. J. & Gilbert, K. (2001). An ideal misconstrued: Newspaper coverage of the Atlanta Paralympic Games in France and Germany. *Sociology of Sport Journal, 18,* 69-94.

Schell, B. & Rodriguez, S. (2001). Subverting bodies/ambivalent representations: media analysis of Paralympian, Hope Lewellen. *Sociology of Sport Journal, 18,* 127-135.

Shapiro, J. (1993). *No Pity: People with disabilities forging a new civil rights movement,* New York, Times Books.

Smart, J. (2001). *Disability, Society, and the Individual,* Gaithersburg, Aspen Publishers.

Taub, D., Blinde, E., & Greer, K. (1999). Stigma management through participation in sport and physical activity: experiences of male college students with physical disabilities. *Human Relations, 52*(11), 1469.

Trujillo, N. & Vande Berg, L.R. (1989). The rhetoric of winning and losing: The American dream and America's team. In L. Wenner (Ed.), *Media, Sports and Society,* (pp. 204-224). Newbury Park, Sage.

Walsdorf, K. (2000). *In Search of Post-Olympic 'Gender Equity': An examination of photographic images in Sports Illustrated for Kids.* Doctoral dissertation, Florida State University.

Wolfe, K. (2001, July 1). He's your inspiration, not mine. *The Washington Post,* B4.

This chapter was adapted from an article published in Sociology of Sport Online (SOSOL) in June 2004.

4   FRENCH AND GERMAN NEWSPAPER COVERAGE OF THE 1996 ATLANTA PARALYMPIC GAMES[1]

Otto J. Schantz & Keith Gilbert

INTRODUCTION

The purpose of this study was to analyze newspaper coverage of the 1996 Atlanta Paralympics by the French and German press. This was achieved by drawing on media theories and critical concepts of exclusion and disability and applying them to the journalistic construction of this event. In short, these Games were examined primarily because an analysis of the newspapers of that time period can be utilized to assist us in better understanding the social representation of sport for people with disabilities, as there is a clear need for this form of evaluation of the social context of sporting events.

Since the 1960 Games in Rome where 400 athletes from 23 nations competed (Guttmann 1979, 26) the program of the Paralympics has been extended and diversified involving more and more sports and further disability groupings. In 1996, two weeks after the centennial Olympic Games, the 10th Paralympic Games were organized in Atlanta, which included more than 3000 athletes representing 103 countries. The growing importance of the Paralympic Games seemed to be accompanied by an ever-increasing media presence and interest for this event. This fact begs the question, 'If the Paralympics are becoming equivalent to the Olympics does the media represent them as different or inferior Games?' With these thoughts in mind the following statement of the problem is discussed in relation to media representation of the event.

STATEMENT OF THE PROBLEM AND THEORETICAL BACKGROUND

Media representation is both: source and indicator of public opinion (Noelle-Neumann, 1994). Consequently, the media coverage of the Paralympics is an indicator of public representations of, and attitudes towards sports for persons with disabilities. This viewpoint is supported by transactional theories regarding media selection of events thus indicating the interdependence between news selection/construction by the journalists and consumers' attention. Indeed, the journalistic discourse reflects and influences the opinions and attitudes of the public (cf. Schönbach, 1992). Media thus, construct almost all of our knowledge beyond direct experience and they play a key role in shaping our representations of the world (cf. Früh, 1994; Luhmann, 1996; McCombs 1994)[2]. Their influence on our daily lives is so pervasive that often our thoughts, behaviors, styles and opinions are based on the mass media's actual

---

1 This chapter is a shorter and adapted version of Schantz, O. J., & Gilbert, K. (2001). An ideal misconstrued: Newspaper coverage of the Atlanta Paralympic Games in France and Germany. Sociology of Sport Journal, 18, 69-94.
2 Jean Baudrillard (1991) takes an extreme position and completely separates the real events and the reality constructed by the media. Paraphrasing the title of a novel from Jean Giraudoux he states in a provocative way: "La guerre du Golfe n'a pas eu lieu" (The Gulf War never happened).

construction of knowledge (cf. Kellner, 1995, pp. 151-152). Previous studies of the media effects on society have claimed that one of the major influences of the mass media is to reinforce existing norms and attitudes (Lazarsfeld & Merton, 1948). This underlines the importance of the way media represent Paralympic sport. Recent research also indicated that under certain conditions the media might serve to change public opinion (cf. Berelson, 1960; Kellner, 1995; Noelle-Neumann, 1994). Indeed, there is also substantial research stating that the family's and peer group's influence is more pertinent than the media's, but mass media have the power to inform or not to inform about an event or to construct reality from a particular perspective (Berghaus, 1999). They thus have power to influence our perspectives of the Paralympics. In this regard the agenda-setting approach of mass media (Dearing & Rogers, 1996; Erbring et al., 1980) suggests that media continually create subject matter which interests and influences people to talk about and discuss issues further. In fact, research shows that the public's knowledge about and attitudes toward individuals with disabilities are mostly constructed indirectly, often by the mass media (Hackforth, 1988; Stautner, 1989; cf. Farnall & Smith, 1999). This is significant because news and entertainment media seem to have played a significant role on the manner in which society stereotypes people with a disability (Farnall & Smith, 1999; Greenberg & Brand, 1994; Oakes et al. 1994).

Although, the most influential mass medium is television we chose to research the print media for the following reasons: While TV coverage focuses more and more on show and spectacle, the print media appear to offer marginal sports, sports for all and sport for people with disabilities a chance to become better known by the public (cf. Hackforth, 1994). Also influencing our opinion was a 1991 survey conducted by Oehmichen who found that 60% of German TV sport spectators older than 14 years regularly consulted newspapers to get further information about sport. This is interesting in particular to information regarding athletes and groups who are marginalized within society.

We wanted to discover if the coverage of the Atlanta Paralympic Games marginalized the Paralympic athletes as they did not meet the socially constructed ideals of physicality, masculinity and sexuality which according to Karin DePauw represent three key aspects of sport (cf. DePauw, 1997). Her concept defines physicality as the "socially accepted view of able bodied physical ability" (p. 421), masculinity includes "aggression, independence, strength, courage" (p. 421) and sexuality is defined as the "socially expected and accepted view of sexual behavior" (p. 421). Concerning the key aspects sexuality and physicality it is widely believed that, even more than the sexual behavior or the physical ability, appearance in form of stereotyped erotic attractiveness of the sporting body, especially the female body, plays an important role in the media coverage of sports (cf. e.g. Bette, 1999; Guttmann, 1996; Pfister, 1989; Rowe, 1999). A striking example is beach volleyball where the sexual attractiveness is emphasized by specific official rules and regulations limiting the covered surface of the female body. It could be argued therefore that, female athletes with a disability are exposed to a form of 'threefold discrimination', as in general they do not fit the social constructs of able-bodied athletes, including those of masculinity and sexual attractiveness.

We can draw conclusions about the consumers' attentions and attitudes towards the Atlanta Paralympics and the athletes by analyzing how the print media constructed the reality of these Games in order to interest the recipients. This was achieved principally by examining information that newspapers considered to be newsworthy.

According to the theoretical concept of news factors (Bell, 1991; Eilders, 1997; Galtung & Ruge, 1965), sport specific coverage of the Paralympic sport should focus on similar topics, which are considered to be newsworthy on the usual sports pages. When representing sports, the mass media in general emphasize action, records, elite performances, aggressions, heroic actions, drama, emotions and celebrities (sport stars). However, the newspapers also focus on performances, results, statistics, and behind the scene stories. Photos capture celebrities, actions and emotions (cf. e.g. Becker, 1983; Coakely, 1994; Hackfort, 1988; Krüger, 1993). Along with this, newspaper sport reporting emphasises a number of important general news values, for example the frequency criterion as a continuing activity, or simplicity due to the nature of winning or losing. Sports then are "consonant with expectations, their script follows a familiar pattern" (Bell, 1991, p. 160) and at the same time the unexpected outcome creates excitement (cf. Elias & Dunning, 1970). Another inherent condition of sport coverage involves play and competition between nations, which allows the newsworthy reporting of ethnocentric issues. Sport personalities are depicted as celebrities and as such are often cast to the forefront of public interest. Sport is organized conflict with losers and winners all of which can be highlighted in the press. Negativity, which is another important news value, can thus be represented by "bad guys" who take drugs or individuals who abuse the referee (cf. Becker, 1983; Bell, 1991; Hackfort 1988; Krueger, 1993).

Throughout the research we wanted to know if the coverage adhered to the guiding ideals of the Paralympics, which in general are considered as an extraordinary sports event, different from world championships. According to Landry (1992) the Paralympic movement has attempted to develop along the "course of the higher ideals of Olympism" (p. 13). Even if Olympism is a rather vague concept, claiming the legacy of Pierre de Coubertin, it is generally associated to values like peace and friendship between nations, fair-play, equal opportunity, a balanced whole between qualities of body and mind, strive for excellence, etc. (cf. e.g. Auberger, Brunet & Schantz 1994; International Olympic Committee 1996; Lenk, 1976; Segrave, 1988). It is often claimed that the ideals and the aims of the Paralympics are or should be in concordance to those of the Olympic movement. Issues of equality and integration would appear to form the basis of some form of philosophy and ideals for Paralympic sport but until recently such issues have been difficult to ascertain. Despite these thoughts the International Paralympic Committee gives us vagues visions of the organization and a rather superficial interpretation of the ideological or philosophical purposes (cf. International Paralympic Committee 2008) of Paralympic sports. Serious anthropological or philosophical debates on the Paralympic movement are rare. Many sections of the paralympic Charter are still under revision (ibd.). Some authors argue that there are parallels between the implicit aims and ideologies of both, the Paralympic and the Olympic movements (cf. Auberger, Brunet & Schantz 1994; Landry, 1995). Bob Price (1999) considers that the aims and the ambitions of the International Olympic Committee and those of the International Paralympic Committee are "virtually identical" (p. 144) even both organizations are not yet structured in the same way. Parallels between both movements are emphasized by similar organization of the Games (place, time, similar opening and closing ceremonies), similar symbols (Flagg, Olympic torch relay etc.).

Taking these thoughts seriously, Paralympic specific coverage should implicitly or explicitly refer, even in form of critical remarks, to some of those ideals of the Paralympic movement.

LITERATURE REVIEW

Studies in the 1990s indicated that the quality and quantity of print media coverage of people with disabilities were of a low standard and the media often portrayed these people unrealistically and stereotypically (e.g. Keller et al., 1990; Lachal, 1990a; 1990b; Nelson, 1994; Shapiro, 1993; Yoshida et al., 1990). Longmore (1985) explained these stereotypical media portrayals as a reflection of the public's fears and anxieties. He stated, "We harbor unspoken anxieties about the possibilities of disablement, to us or to someone close to us. What we fear we often stigmatize and shun and sometimes seek to destroy" (p. 32).

As early as 1985 Zola (p.8) observed that in films people with disabilities were most often portrayed as victims, relatively seldom as heroes or villains, and two of the most metaphorical traits that can be found are the marriage between media and disability sports coverage (cf. Hall, 1997). Nelson (1994) listed seven major stereotypes as they were shown in the American media: the person with disabilities as "pitiable and pathetic" (p. 5), as "supercrip" (p. 6), as "sinister, evil, and criminal" (p. 6), as "better-off dead" (p. 7), as "maladjusted" (p. 8), as "burden" (p. 8), and as "unable to live a successful life" (p. 9). From a semiological perspective Woodill (1994) distinguished different types of metaphors of disabilities in popular cultures, including newspaper presentations: The humanitarian ("disability as misfortune"), the medical ("disability as sickness"), the outsider ("disabled person as other"), the religious ("disability as divine plan"), the retribution ("disability as punishment"), the social control ("disability as threat"), and the zoological metaphor ("disability person as pet, disability as entertainment"), (p. 209). Of interest is the fact that Clogston (1994) divided newspaper coverage of people with disabilities in two distinct types: the traditional and the progressive models. The traditional model "views persons with disabilities as dysfunctions in a medical or economic way" (p. 46) and as such they must be cared for medically or economically by society. Another attitude of the traditional perspective is to regard them as "super crips" for the way they master their fates (Clogston, 1994, Shapiro, 1993; Zola, 1985, Hardin & Hardin, 2004). The progressive model views "the major limiting aspect of a person's disability as lying in society's inability to adapt its physical, social, or occupational environment as well as its attitudes, to accept those who are physically different" (Clogston, 1994, p. 47). A progressive coverage of people with disability would consider individuals as different, accepting their otherness as part of a cultural pluralism and thereby applying a pluralistic rationality (cf. Lyotard, 1983, p. 13), whereas the traditional discourse considers individuals with a disability as different and inferior to the hegemonic mainstream, thus exerting an excluding rationality (cf. Foucault, 1961).

Indeed, studies about print media coverage of sport activities of people with disabilities are rare (cf. Génolini, 1995; Kauer & Bös 1998; Schantz & Marty, 1995). Schimanski (1994) conducted one of the most important studies. When comparing German and North American journals for the period from 1984 to 1992 he found an increasing coverage of sport for persons with disabilities and observed that this coverage moved progressively from other headings to the sports pages. These findings were partly confirmed by the results of Schantz and Marty (1995) who analyzed the French daily sports journal *L'Équipe* and observed increasing frequencies of articles about sport for people with disabilities during a seven-year period from 1987 to 1993. But this evolution did not really improve the rather marginal role of sports for individuals with disabilities in this newspaper. The authors also observed that the articles often showed pity[3] for the athletes or focused on the way the people were coping with their fate instead of referring to the athletes and their performances in a sport specific manner. Paralympic athletes, as we know, would prefer to be reported for their physical feats and not their disability (Schantz & Alberto 1999).

Génolini (1995) analyzed newspaper clippings concerning physical activities for people with intellectual disabilities collected by French sports associations from 1979 to 1986. He found that these persons were portrayed as "gentle monsters" (p. 60), an image that is in-between the beast (mythical aspect) and the child (aspect of educability).

From another viewpoint, research on nationalism in the coverage of the Paralympics is unknown. However, there are different studies concerning nationalism and media coverage. Blain et al. (1993) for example indicated that mediated sport in Europe often serves nationalistic interests. Gebauer (1995) analyzed the TV coverage of the 1992 Olympic Games in Barcelona and concludes that in different European countries the new televisual technologies were used "to inject powerful doses of nationalism in the Olympic sport" (p. 105). Borcila (2000) analyzed the print media responses to the Atlanta Olympic Games and the women's gymnastics competition coverage and observed the nationalizing function of the narratives.

The print media coverage of sport for individuals with disabilities appears to privilege some specific types of disabilities: The main group of individuals with a physical disability, which was by far the most over-represented, is the wheelchair fraternity (cf. Schantz & Marty 1995; Schimanski 1994). This is perhaps because the public's perception of the athlete with disabilities is historically that of individuals in wheelchairs. Lachal (1990a; 1990b) who analyzed regional French newspapers from 1977 and 1988 found that in 1988 about half (49%) of the articles about disabilities concerned physical (motor) disabilities, 29% disability in general, 11.5 % sensorial disabilities, 7% intellectual deficiencies, and 3.5% "other" disabilities (Lachal, 1990a, p. 39). Topics concerning athletes with a mental disability figured rarely in the French L'Équipe, studied by Schantz & Marty (1995). In their content analysis of TV coverage of the Atlanta Games, Schell and Duncan (1999, p. 44) found that CBS featured less visible, war induced, or acquired disabilities more likely than others.

Gender bias reporting in the media is another important area which requires further research in the Paralympic arena. A great number of researchers have focused on gender biased media coverage (e.g. Duncan et al., 1991; Duncan, 1990; Eastmann & Billings 2000; Jones et al., 1999; Urquhart & Crossmann, 1999; Wann et al., 1998). In an analysis of German newspaper coverage of the Olympics from 1952 to 1980, Pfister (1989) found that for female Olympic participants appearance ("beauty") was of "central importance" (p. 11.29). Tuggle & Owen (1999) examined the amount of NBC's coverage

---

3 Persons with disabilities need respect, recognition and rights: Pity may be a first step for individuals and later lead to a form of regression if recognition, respect, and rights are lacking. Indeed, "Not its weakness, but its limits make pity questionable; pity is never enough" (Nicht die Weichheit, sondern das Beschränkende am Mitleid macht es fragwürdig, es ist immer zu wenig" Horkheimer, Adorno 1989 [1947], p. 121). Cf. Also Gill (1994), a disability activist, who asks for recognition and respect of difference.

given to females athletes at the 1996 Olympic Games and found that only women's individual events were covered extensively while the coverage of team competitions focused much more on men. Female athletes with a disability are in fact subjected to multiple discrimination concerning gender, disability severity and race (cf. DePauw, 1994; DePauw & Gavron, 1995; Sherill 1993). Analyses undertaken of the 1996 Paralympics by Sherill (1997) and Schell & Duncan (1999) confirmed greater discrimination against female Paralympians than their male counterparts.

Researchers clearly indicated the influence of culture on the attitudes towards people with disabilities even though there was no consensus concerning the explanation of these differences (cf. Cloerkes, 1997; Ingstad & Whyte, 1995). No research could be found about differences in coverage of sport for people with a disability in France and Germany, but interviews with French athletes living at the German-French border and with a coach of the Swiss Paralympic team suggested that the awareness of Paralympic sports is higher in the German speaking press than in the French.

Studies relating to print media coverage of Paralympic Games are almost nonexistent. However, Enting (1997) compared the Atlanta Paralympics coverage in a nationwide, a regional and a tabloid German newspaper (*Frankfurter Allgemeine Zeitung, Rhein-Zeitung Koblenz and Bildzeitung*). These newspapers offered respectively 10%, 7.5% and 0.3% of their sports pages to this event. Schell and Duncan (1999) made a content analysis of American television coverage of the Atlanta Paralympics and found that beside some empowering comments, athletes were portrayed as "victims of misfortune, as different, as Other" (p. 27). They observed an absence of sport specific commentaries, like information about rules, comments on strategies or physical abilities. Contrary, to Olympic coverage, where defeats were considered as catastrophes (Duncan, 1986), the defeat of Paralympic athletes were described from patronizing perspectives (Shell & Duncan 1999). Extraordinary performances were portrayed as heroic achievements by using the "super crip" stereotype (Shell & Duncan 1999). According to Shapiro (1993) this "super crip" myth harms the average people with disabilities because it suggests that only heroic performances of persons with disabilities should be respected. It is interesting, when referring to the Paralympic ideals, that Schell and Duncan (1999) found, that "war and the hope for peace among people of different nationalities was a recurrent theme" and that "spectators were shown the debilitating results of war and the political barriers that may be dissolved through friendly sport competition" (p. 43).

RESEARCH QUESTIONS

There were six important research questions, which after careful consideration of the literature and theoretical considerations underpinned this research. These were:
1) How far did the leading French and German newspapers relate to the Atlanta Paralympic Games?
2) Which were the themes and facts considered to be newsworthy by the French and German press?
3) Were athletes with disabilities depicted as sportswomen or - men or rather as persons with disabilities and was the discourse sports specific or did it consider the athletes as victims of their fate?

4) Was there a difference in the coverage between male and female athletes and was there a difference concerning depiction of the disabilities?[4] Were there cross-cultural differences concerning the coverage of these issues?

5) How were the ideals of the Paralympic Games (e.g. mutual understanding, international friendship, and fair play) reflected in the press coverage in both countries?

6) What was the frequency of photographs and more importantly how did the photographs portray the athletes in French and German newspapers?

These questions were the driving force behind the research and served as guides to the better understanding of the print media coverage of the Atlanta Paralympic games in Germany and France.

METHODS

Our corpus included 104 articles on the Atlanta Paralympic Games from the following 4 French and 4 German newspapers:

Le Monde	Frankfurter Allgemeine Zeitung
Libération	Frankfurter Rundschau
Le Figaro	Die Welt
L'Équipe	Süddeutsche Zeitung

We wanted to compare the press coverage in two different countries in order to detect cross-cultural differences in the way print journalists construct the reality of the Paralympics and to give us more information about the representation and position of the Paralympic sport in the two countries. We chose the most important daily newspapers of each country. Influence, quality and nation-wide circulation were the criteria for our choice. Regional and tabloid press were not taken into consideration. The selected newspapers are part of the so-called "quality press" and covered for each nation the political spectrum from right (conservative) to left (social-democrat; cf. Wilke, 1994). These newspapers can be categorized as elite media and as such they are opinion leaders and affect the decisions made in other media (cf. Jamieson & Campbell 1997; Wilke 1994). Le Monde is an independent newspaper that provides in-depth articles on national and international politics, social and cultural issues, including sports. "Ideologically the paper is committed to socially progressive and political left-of-centre goals, described by his founder Hubert Beuve-Méry as 'social liberalism or liberal socialism' (Kuhn 1995, p. 73), but in the 1980 it became more conservative. The Süddeutsche Zeitung and the Frankfurter Allgemeine could be considered as the equivalent papers in Germany, even though the Frankfurter Allgemeine is more conservative and aims at political center or right-of-center goals. Differences between Libération and Le Monde are more due to the style and its tone than

---

4 Racial discrimination can be considered as a minor topic in German and the French Paralympic media sports coverage, as both teams are almost exclusively composed of white Europeans.

to political tendencies. *Libération* is more iconoclastic, and for example is more concerned with environmental or minority issues (cf. Kuhn, 1995). *The Frankfurter Rundschau* is probably its equivalent in Germany when concerning the political orientation. *Le Figaro* as well as the German *Die Welt* have a liberal conservative tradition and represent right-of-center goals. *L'Équipe* is a French daily uniquely covering sports events. There is no equivalent German sports newspaper.

The 8 newspapers were monitored during a period of one and a half months (1st August through 10th September), beginning two weeks before and ending two weeks after the Games. The articles, systematically collected in the course of this period, were submitted to a quantitative and qualitative content analysis and a qualitative interpretation. We considered 62 variables for the content analysis. In order to code the data we developed a standardized worksheet (Eidlers, 1997). The variables taken into consideration concerned news factors (frequency, size, presentation, drama and conflict, negativity, ethnocentrism etc.) and rhetorical aspects (cf. Donsbach, 1991; Eilders, 1997; Galtung & Ruge 1965; Peltu, 1985). The portrayals of the athletes were coded according to the metaphors recorded by Woodwill (1994) and Longmore (1985). An important part of the variables related to disability and gender specific topics. Gender balanced coverage was rated as "very important", "important" and "not important" in function of the importance given to adequate women's coverage.

One part of the worksheet was constructed to record variables (size, focus, content, gender, disability, visibility of disability) concerning the illustrations. These data served as a base for a detailed semiotic analysis of the illustrations recorded as free comments on an annexed sheet (cf. Holicki, 1993; Kepplinger, 1987).

In order to evaluate the intercoder consistency of our criteria of analysis, two trained experts analyzed 20 randomly chosen articles. The coefficient for the intercoder reliability π was equal to or higher than .85 for all analyzed items (cf. Merten, 1995). This coefficient was measured for all items, except those, which consisted in metrical measures like size of the headlines or space of the articles. Data processing was based on descriptive and nonparametric statistics (Chi-Square). Descriptive statistics (frequencies, means, standard deviations, percentages) were calculated to describe frequencies, sizes and spaces from articles, photos and headlines. The frequencies of different disabilities mentioned in the articles were examined as well as the frequency of special terms and expressions (e.g. "handicapped", "valid"; "disabled swimmer"; "blind runner"). Differences between newspapers and countries concerning nonparametric data were tested by Chi-Square procedures. We computed ANOVA to compare parametric data between nations and newspapers. For a posteriori comparisons (differences between the journals) the Scheffé-Test was used. The probability of a Type I error was maintained at .05 for all subsequent analyses.

Interpretations of the media coverage by the individual recipient and the direct effects of the recipients were not evaluated. Research indicates that they can be different according to the personal experiences and socializations of the individual recipient (Berghaus, 1999; Fiske, 1993; Kellner, 1995). Our results cannot be interpreted as direct media effects, despite the power of the mass media.

The authors of this article are not officially considered to be part of the people with disabilities, which means that we are probably lacking a certain perspective, despite our efforts to discuss our results and our interpretations with Paralympic athletes.

RESULTS

Approximately, 2200 male (64%) and 800 female (36%) athletes from 103 countries participated in the 1996 Atlanta Paralympic Games. They competed in 17 different sports (Sherill 1997). The German team consisted of 227 athletes (*Frankfurter Rundschau* 14-8-96, p. 15), and the French 146 athletes (*L'Équipe* 15-9-96, p. 8).

More than two thirds (68%) of the selected articles were published in Germany. The frequency of articles is presented in the following table 1:

Table 1
Frequency of articles per newspaper

Newspapers (France)	articles	Newspapers (Germany)	articles
Le Monde	7	Frankfurter Allgemeine Zeitung	20
Libération	10	Frankfurter Rundschau	25
Le Figaro	8	Die Welt	10
L'Équipe	11	Süddeutsche Zeitung	13
total	36	total	68

Five days before the opening ceremony, most newspapers began to publish articles relating to the Paralympics. Only one article was published two weeks before the starting of the Games. Nearly 80% of the articles concerning the Paralympics appeared the day after the opening ceremony through the games period to the day following the closing ceremony. Only two articles were published two days after the end of the Paralympics, whereas the centennial Olympic Games were objects of comments up until two weeks after they're closing.

30.8% of the German and 38.9% of the French articles were provided by the general news agencies DPA (*Deutsche Presseagentur*) and AFP (*Agence France Presse*); only 5.9% of the German articles by the sport specific information service SID (*Sport-Informations-Dienst*).

About 73 % of the articles comprised more than 100 cm2, and the surface of half of the articles covered more than 176 cm^2 (cf. table 2). The French and German right-of-center newspapers (Le Figaro, Die Welt) offered the smallest space to the Paralympics, F (3, 32; 3,64) $\geq$ 3.5; p $\leq$ .021. The average surface of German articles (255 cm^2 $\pm$ 167 cm^2) was significantly, F(1, 102) = 18.9, p = .000, greater than that of the French ones (122 cm^2 $\pm$ 101 cm^2).

Table 2
Average article size per newspaper

Newspapers (France)	size (cm²) ± s	Newspapers (Germany)	size (cm²) ± s
Le Monde	161 ± 96	Frankfurter Allgemeine Zeitung	335 ± 161
Libération	143 ± 109	Frankfurter Rundschau	255 ± 153
Le Figaro	23 ± 15	Die Welt	146 ± 93
L'Équipe	151 ± 95	Süddeutsche Zeitung	220 ± 200

Subaverage size headlines could be found for 51.9% of the articles, average size headlines for 36.5 % and big headlines for 7.7% (3.8 % had no headline).

Topics
Competitions (26%), problems and scandals (15.4 %), opinions and reflections about the Paralympics (18.3 %) were the main subject of the articles (40,4 % deal with other topics like portraits of athletes, opening and closing ceremonies, etc.). Only 11 articles (10.6 %) gave us some results in the form of tables. Ten of these articles were published in L'Équipe, but in contrast with the usual tables of sports newspapers these tables were entitled "selected results". They presented only rankings without performances and this almost exclusively in those events where French athletes reached the finals. Performances, deemed as essentials in ordinary sports-journalism, are totally neglected in French newspapers.

German articles focused on scandals and organizational problems. Six out of thirteen headlines of the Süddeutsche Zeitung were negative. For example, "It's not as nice as in Barcelona"[5], "Untenable Conditions"[6], or "Switzerland provokes scandal"[7]. The Frankfurter Allgemeine complained in a headline: "The Olympic stadium in Atlanta looks like a pigsty".[8]

The French underlined the technical progress of high-tech prostheses and wheelchairs. In an article of almost one page length Libération (1996, August 22) portrayed the sprinter Volpentest and his "miraculous prostheses" (p. 21). Volpentest was called "the man who is at least worth 100 000 million francs" (p. 21) in comparison with the bionic hero of the TV series "The man who is worth 3 billion". As the article focused nearly exclusively on Volpentest's high tech prosthesis, the reader got the impression that the performance of this athlete was only due to technological progress. The physical capacities and the hard training indispensable in order to establish such a record were completely neglected. L'Équipe (1996, August 21) published a similar article entitled "Volpentest 'Bionic Man'" (p. 9) and stated that it is "thanks to his prostheses" (p. 9) that Volpentest had broken the 100m world record in his category.

---

5 "So schön wie in Barcelona ist es doch nicht", Süddeutsche, 20/8/96, p. 31.
6 "Unhaltbarer Zustand", Süddeutsche, 23/8/96, p. 39.
7 "Schweiz verursacht Eklat", Süddeutsche, 27/8/96, p. 19.
8 "Das Olympiastadion von Atlanta sieht aus wie ein Saustall", Frankfurter Allgemeine (FAZ), 15/8/96, p. 24.

German newspapers accorded significantly, x^2 (2, N= 88) = 16.06, p = .001, more importance to the gender issue than the French did, and in certain articles focused equally or even more on female athletes than on male athletes. Six out of 55 German articles concerning athletes emphasized a great importance to gender balanced coverage (French: N = 0 of 33). In 27 of 55 articles this issue was treated as to be important (French: N = 6 of 33). Some of the German articles were concerned exclusively with women and portrayed them as athletes first (cf. Frankfurter Rundschau, 1996, August 19). In one article an athlete with paraplegia was characterized as an "attractive young lady"[9], a common comment on sports pages to characterize sportswomen without disabilities, but rare for Paralympic athletes (cf. Schell & Duncan, 1999).

Considering the whole corpus, 72.8 % of the articles discussed general matters and did not privilege any type of disability. 16.3 % of the articles concerned exclusively wheelchair athletes, 8.7 % athletes with an amputation and only 1.9 % dealt exclusively with people having a visual impairment. Cerebral palsy was never mentioned, even when journalists wrote about athletes having CP and only two articles, which reported on the opening ceremony, mentioned that there would be demonstration sports for people with an intellectual disability.

Rather than respect for athletes' performances, 4.1 % of the articles indicated traces of pity for individuals with disabilities. Stories like the following attempted to evoke pity amongst the readership:

> He was born as somebody obstinate, as a fighter, wild and indestructible. However, his terrible destiny didn't even wait until he could make his first steps before it stopped him. He was just nine months old, when the poliomyelitis invaded his body. He will not be able to walk. Ever.[10]

More often, the portrayals of athletes show admiration (27.6 %) for the way 'these people' have beaten all odds to 'overcome their disability'. Often the athletes were depicted as victims, like the following German swimmer who was portrayed as somebody who established a world record after "never ending bad luck"[11]. But there was a happy end: "Kay Espenhain's streak of bad luck ends with a gold medal "[12]. Some athletes were portrayed as "super crips" like the horse rider who despite his paralyzed legs due to a horse riding accident showed such a physical and mental power that he "enjoys riding the animals that caused his accident"[13].

It appeared patronizing when the Frankfurter Allgemeine stated "the medals from Atlanta accompanied by a bit of Mozart produced some moments of happiness for the athletes. But now that it's over, everyday life will bring other challenges."[14]

---

9 "Attraktive junge Frau"; Frankfurter Rundschau, 19/8/96, p. 26.

10 Il serait né tel quel, obstiné et bagarreur, féroce et indestructible. Mais le destin mauvais n'attend même pas ses premiers pas pour lui barrer la route. Il a seulement neuf mois le jour ou la polio s'incruste dans son corps. Il ne marchera pas. Jamais". Le Monde, 24/8/96, p. 12.

11 "nach schier endlosem Pech", Die Welt, 19/8/96, p. 20.

12 "Pechsträhne von Kay Espenhayn endet mit Goldmedaille", FAZ, 19/08/96, 24.

13 "[...] trouve toujours plaisir à chevaucher ceux par qui son accident est arrivé." L'Équipe, 23/8/96, p. 4.

14 "Die Medaillen von Atlanta und ein bisschen Mozart dazu, haben Glücksmomente für die Beteiligten erzeugt. Der Alltag hält für sie nun wieder andere Herausforderungen bereit.", FAZ, 25/08/96, p. 4.

In 12 French articles (33.3%) nondisabled persons were called "valide", a term used by athletes themselves. Journalists and athletes did not seem to be aware of the discriminating connotation of this term. German articles sometimes used the expression "normal" people but they always put the term *normal* in quotation marks to signal their dissociation from this term. In 46.2 % of the articles we found the newspapers highlighted *handicapped* or other disability-specific attributes (*paraplegic, blind*, etc.) associated with the athletes. Most of the time athletes were just referred to as *swimmers, players, athletes*, etc. without specifying their disabilities. Very often the style was similar to the general style of sports journalism, however, with relatively poor commentary on strategies, rules or performances compared to articles about the Olympic Games, where performances, techniques and tactics were described in length. One rare exception was an article in *Le Monde* where Tony Volpentest's running style was described as followed:

> You only notice the incredible impression of power in his style. You notice nothing else than the velocity of his movements. You look at him from the starting blocks to the finish line, before watching the time appearing in form of luminous numbers on the electronic display and you almost can't believe your eyes." [15]

Greatest attention was given to national success. About 93% of the articles related to the competitions had a very strong ethnocentric and sometimes even nationalistic tenor. Le Figaro informs exclusively about national medal ranking. Its 7 minuscule articles highlighting the following headlines: "Paralympic Games: French medals", "Paralympic Games: France second", "Paralympic Games: France third", Paralympic Games: France fourth". "Paralympic Games: France third". "Paralympic Games: France second". As France finally finished at sixth place in the medal tally *Le Figaro* stopped its article series and only at the end of the Games its title: "Paralympic Games: The Americans masters at home" regretted that "France, fourth in Barcelona, could only finish in sixth place". The whole coverage of this newspaper focused exclusively on the French medal tally. Some similar headlines could be read in *Libération*: "The French started to bring in their harvest of medals. The *Tricolores* have already put sixteen in their pocket and are at the second place, just behind Australia".[16] Some German newspapers were no less nationalistic as the example of the *Frankfurter Allgemeine* indicated. This paper claimed without modesty: "You can relay on German Athletes".[17]

In the French newspapers analyzed we found only 2 photos (5.5% of the articles), while the German newspapers published 23 (33.8%). Even the abundantly illustrated daily French sports journal presented only one photo of the Paralympics (cf. table 3). More than half of the photos showed athletes with wheelchairs, 32% athletes with visual disabilities and 16% athletes with amputations. Often the athlete's handicap remains hidden in the photos. Only in a single photo is an amputation clearly shown. This photograph is of a swimmer on the starting block. Interestingly, depicting athletes in wheelchairs seems to be acceptable by most newspapers as wheelchairs represent the stereotype of the person and athlete with a disability.

---

15 "On ne retient alors de lui que l'incroyable impression de puissance que dégage son style. On ne remarque plus rien d'autre que la vélocité de ses mouvements. On le suit du regard du départ à l'arrivée, avant de s'arrêter sur le temps inscrit en chiffres lumineux sur le panneau de chronométrage, pour en croire à peine ses yeux." Le Monde, 21/8/96, p. 16.
16 "Les Français entament leur moisson de médailles. Les Tricolores en ont déjà empoché seize et se classent deuxième derrière l'Australie." Libération, 20/08/96, p. 27
17 "Auch auf die deutschen Leichtathleten ist weiterhin Verlaß." FAZ 20/08/96, p. 23.

Table 3
Number of photographs per newspaper

Newspapers (France)	n	Newspapers (Germany)	n
Le Monde	0	FrankfurterAllgemeine Zeitung	12
Libération	1	Frankfurter Rundschau	7
Le Figaro	0	Die Welt	1
L'Équipe	1	Süddeutsche Zeitung	3
Total	**2**	**Total**	**23**

Almost half of the photos (44%) focussed on the face or on the upper body from the chest upwards, often in a static position, while sport photos in general focus on the whole body in action. Three photos of men showed the upper body, 11 the whole body, and only one just the face, while 3 photos of women focused on their face. Throughout, there were three times as many photos showing men (n = 15; 60%) as women (n = 5; 20%); in the remaining pictures (n = 5; 20%) both genders are represented. Both French photos included in our study are of men only.

DISCUSSION

Despite the selective public consumption of mass media and according to convictions and interests observed by Lazarsfeld and others (cf. Lazarsfeld, Berelseon & Gaudet 1968; Klapper, 1960), formal aspects of presentation have an important influence on the reader of newspaper articles. Big headlines and photos exert attraction on newspaper readers. This has been proven even if the tenor of the article is in opposition to the reader's attitude (cf. Donsbach, 1991:1992). In other words the decision to read an article depends more on the presentation of the article than on the reader's opinion. The presentation of the analyzed articles are, however, in most of the cases, not very eye-catching; thus readers are likely to skip them unless they are particularly interested in the topic.

Of major consequence is the fact that disability is generally associated with a wheelchair. For example, to identify its heading concerning Paralympic sports the French newspaper L'Equipe uses a pictograph showing an athlete in a wheelchair and employs the term handisport, the official denomination of the French Federation for Athletes with Physical Disabilities (Fédération Française Handisport). This example illustrates how the press reinforces stereotypical representations regarding individuals with disabilities.

Interestingly, the condition of cerebral palsy was neither mentioned nor shown, which equated to the CBS coverage analyzed by Schell and Duncan (1999, 33). In the only photograph showing an athlete with cerebral palsy the disability was hidden and not mentioned. The photo showed a female athlete standing behind a row of javelins, which partly covered her face hiding its distortions caused by the cerebral palsy. According to our findings, and those of several other studies there is more attention given to persons with a physical handicap who can communicate efficiently, than to individual athletes with a mental or a sensorial handicap (Chambre des Communes, 1988; Lachal 1990a; 1990b; Schell & Duncan, 1999).

The rarity of illustrated articles on the Paralympics is confirmed by the study of Schantz and Marty (1995). One could argue that the smaller number of photos with female athletes is due to the smaller number of women participating in the Paralympic Games. However, statistics demonstrate that it is just a fact that women are underrepresented in the photos: while about 37% of the Paralympic participants were women[18], only 20% of the photos in which just one gender is represented highlighted female athletes. These results confirm the findings that female athletes in general are underrepresented in the media (e.g. Eastman & Billing, 2000; Luebke, 1989) and especially in sports related print media (Duncan et al. 1991; Duncan 1990; Jones et al., 1999; Pfister 1989; Urquhart & Crossmann, 1999; Wann et al. 1998). The lack of photos with female athletes is accompanied by a poor coverage of the female perspective in the narrative, especially in the French newspapers.

Due to the poor number of photos depicting women it is difficult to draw valid conclusions, but it is worth noting that 3 out of 5 photos only showed the face of the female athletes, while some researchers seem to suggested that there is a tendency to show the whole body of women athletes more often compared to male athletes (cf. Wanta & Leggett 1989). In general media appeared to pay more interest to physical attractiveness of women than to their sports performances (cf. Krüger, 1993) as Pfister (1987) also showed for German newspaper coverage of female Olympic athletes. However, the presentation of a "disabled" body, specially a "disabled" female body, does not correspond with the common criteria of beauty and public acceptability (cf. Shapiro, 1993; Waxman, 1994). There does seem to be a kind of 'moral turn' in some fields like dance and cinema where the staging of "disabled" bodies has an ethical implication like art which is becoming more frequent (cf. Schantz, 1999), but in western societies we still associate sport with fitness, health, dynamics, youth and sex appeal. This is indeed a direct contrast to the image of sport for individuals with disabilities, as showing "ill", "lame", "crippled", "mutilated" athletes does not fit the stereotyped fitness image put forward by the lifestyle magazines and advertisings. According to Ann C. Albright (1997), "disability signifies the antithesis of the fit and healthy body" (p. 57). Postmodern commercial culture celebrates "the possibilities of pleasure derived from cultivated and enhanced embodiment" (Turner, 1998, p. vi). "The principal challenge to this comes from aging, death and disability" (ibid.). The youth cult, which dominates in high-level sports, represses topics like illness, disability and death, and topics that remind us of the fragility and the transitoriness or ephemerality of human beings (cf. Bette, 1999). Not too long ago many newspapers presented articles about sports for people with disabilities under the headings reserved for health, medical or social topics[19].

---

18 This percentage was computed on the base of the official results edited by the Atlanta Paralympic Organizing Committee.

19 Reviewing the TV coverage of the Barcelona Paralympic Games in 1992, Kauer and Bös (1998) reported that journalists who specialized in medical topics often covered these Games. That is why, for example, spectators of a documentary transmitted by one of the most important German federal network stations were more informed about the qualities of athletes' prostheses than about their sports performances (cf. also Schimanski, 1994).

Nationalism in Paralympic sport is even more evident than in general media coverage of sport. While reading the Paralympic coverage in French and German newspapers, the reader gets the impression that two different Games are described. This is not specific to the Paralympic Games, as nationalism is also evident in the media coverage of the Olympic Games (cf. Bourdieu, 1994; Gebauer, 1994). However, whereas during the Olympics readers and spectators are informed about all the records and a great number of foreign star athletes, the analyzed newspapers reported almost exclusively on national athletes and performances. Tony Volpentest was the only foreign athlete in French newspapers who was considered to be newsworthy because of his high tech prosthesis, which transformed him into a bionic "super crip". Indeed, one of the French newspapers, Le Figaro, exclusively focused on French success. Most of the time it neither gave the names of the athletes nor stated their performances. The only center of interest was the number of French medals and the medal ranking compared to other nations.

Results clearly indicated that there was not really sport specific coverage, which confirmed findings for the TV coverage of Schell and Duncan (1999). Contrary to these authors we could not find a patronizing attitude concerning the defeat of athletes, simply because the newspapers did only talk about medal winners. This non-reporting of defeat is another indicator that the coverage was not really sport specific, as the drama of victory and defeat is a part of the general sport coverage. Probably there was a practical reason for this. We think that it was simply that the newspapers limited the space for Paralympic coverage and as there were many medal winners, they focused on the winners only. The portrayal of a female swimmer who overcame a multitude of obstacles is another example of non-sport specific coverage. After having mentioned the world record of this athlete, a long list of incidents, accidents and illness is given to the reader, who finally gets the impression that after all this bad luck, the world record was due to luck and not to the inherent capacities or training efforts of the athlete. Another interpretation would be to consider this swimmer a "super grip" who, despite all these obstacles, established a world record.

The French *L'Équipe*, a sports newspaper in which results, comments of results and photos are of major importance, published only a single photo. It was taken during the centennial Olympic Games, showing the male winner of the 1500m-wheelchair demonstration event, Claude Issorat. The tables of results displayed only individual rankings (mostly French) without any indication of performances. During the Olympic Games this journal related all the different events on several pages with abundant illustrations and informed us about all the results, including the performances, in form of tables.

Instead of sport-specific news values (e.g. records, results, tactics, etc.), scandals, problems, high-tech, and ethnocentrism were the main criteria of the news selection, which was essentially based on commercial considerations. In other words news had to be sold to the public (cf. Bourdieu, 1996). During the selection process of events, gatekeepers (cf. White, 1950), often general news agencies like DPA (*Deutsche Presseagentur*), and AFP (*Agence France Press*) pass over sport-specific aspects when taking into consideration and prioritizing the news factors. In emphasizing these general news values, the journalists neglect information concerning performances and records that would seem necessary, as most of the recipients do not know the value of Paralympic performances. Thus, a vicious circle begins: good results or records cannot be news because there is no old information (cf. Luhmann, 1996). If there is no redundant information, i.e. no knowledge about the value of performances of Paralympic athletes, a new record will not be newsworthy information, because as readers we have no comparison (cf. Luhmann, 1996). Based on this viewpoint, journalists focus on redundant news factors such as scandals and particularly their own national athletes, medal-ranking and its patriotic logic (Riggs, Eastman & Golobic, 1993).

The main differences between the French and German press concerned the amount of coverage, the discrimination of women, and the use of discriminating terminology for people with a disability. Feminist concerns do not seem to be very popular in France, where the percentage of women in politics until 1999 appeared as one of the lowest in Europe, and where women still fight without great success against sexist language (cf. Internenettes, 2000). However, one could argue that there is a greater sensibility towards female athletes in Germany. This can be partly explained by the fact that most of the articles which indicated a high consideration for female concerns were written by a female correspondent of the *Frankfurter Rundschau*, Iris Hilbert.

An older tradition of sport for individuals with disabilities, and a larger and more successful German team could be some reasons for the greater amount of coverage in Germany. Is the greater awareness of disability rights due to religious influences, a catholic France versus a more protestant-influenced Germany? Latin versus Scandinavian influences, individualism in France versus civism in Germany, could be other reasons for these disparities and the inappropriate use of terminology (cf. Duhamel, 1985; Münch, 1993). We have to be careful not to be caught in the pitfall of national stereotyping when we interpret these differences as cultural induced. Indeed, there were probably a multitude of factors responsible for these differences which were not exclusively culturally determined.

CONCLUSIONS AND IMPLICATIONS FOR FUTURE RESEARCH

The media coverage of sport has undergone a process of spectacularization. Sport has become a commodity; its media value is "determined by the size and composition of audience it can deliver to potential advertisers and sponsors" (Maguire, 1993, pp. 38-39). Most of the analyzed newspapers (especially the conservatives ones) seem to have a rather low opinion regarding the media value of sport for persons with disabilities. Indeed, sport for such people is still marginalized and trivialized in most newspapers.

In many articles the Paralympic Games are not taken seriously as a sporting event. There were some articles that treated these Games adequately as a worldwide sport competition parallel to the Olympic Games, but most of the time newspapers seem to give some space to the coverage of the Paralympics only for image reasons. Further investigations should be completed in order to explain the fact that the quantity and the quality of the coverage of the Atlanta Paralympics is more important in the newspapers from the left-to-center political spectrum than in those which can be considered to be on the political right-to-center wing.

The coverage of the Atlanta Paralympic Games by the French and German print journalists reminds us of the headlines of a Scottish newspaper in 1912: "Aberdeen Man Lost at Sea".[20] The reason for this headline was the shipwreck of the Titanic. When 1513 people lost their lives, only the death of the local person was newsworthy. In Atlanta 3500 world-class athletes competed together and broke about 200 world-records, but the German and French press focused almost exclusively on the national medal-winners and their own ranking of medals.

The Paralympics, much more so than the Olympics, has become a mere instrument of nationalist and parochial logic. The idea of a worldwide competition without discrimination of any kind, promoting willpower, ambition, fair-play, mutual respect and peace (cf. Auberger, Brunet & Schantz, 1994; Landry, 1995) was perverted in order to serve national pride and evoke feelings of national identity.

Having to choose between depicting the aims and values of the Paralympic Games and thereby considering the Games as a means of empowering athletes with disabilities on the one hand and following the commercial logic of news values on the other, the print media in general chose the latter option. The small space accorded to this event – especially in France – the lack of sports specific information, and the focus on general news factors confirm the conclusion drawn by Schell and Duncan (1999) based on a content analysis of CBS's coverage of the Atlanta Paralympic Games that: "[...] the Paralympic Games are less than, not parallel to, the Olympics" (p. 27). Indeed, not only are the Paralympics considered to be less important than the Olympics, they are also considered to be different. However, not different in the sense of pluralist rationality (cf. Lyotard, 1983), but of an excluding rationality (cf. Foucault, 1961). Consequently, by imposing its own logic, the media discourse is changing the Games, misconstruing the Paralympic ideals and the individual intentions of the sportswomen and men with disability. It instrumentalizes the Games for its own commercial finalities and keeps the athletes, who just want to be athletes, excluded from the mainstream sports movement. Similar to the CBS's TV coverage in the USA (Schell & Duncan, 1999) it can thus be fairly stated that much of the print media coverage of the Atlanta Paralympics Games in France and Germany reinforced the consumers' prejudice that the Paralympics were not "real" sport competitions" (p. 33). This was highlighted by a German newspaper which labeled the Olympic Games the "real Games"[21].

From a practical point of view Paralympic athletes and organizers should have a clear understanding about the way media cover the Paralympic Games in order to react and to contribute to an improvement of the media coverage. It should guarantee that the sport activities of the members of our society with disabilities who are more or less excluded from most sport competitions are accepted and respected.

Other aspects include the important commercial interest at stake. The Paralympic movement is undergoing a similar evolution as the sports movement for able-bodied

---

20 Quoted in R. Robertson (1992, 174).
21 "richtigen Spielen", FAZ, 14/08/96, p. 22.

individuals: It must improve its economic value in terms of audience in order to continue to evolve (cf. Cole, 1999; Hiestand, 2000; Levine, 2000; Sutton, 1998). However, there is the danger that this search for media and commercial success might degrade the athletes with disabilities to 'receivers of alms' or 'prostitute them in a media scrum' by degrading the Paralympic Games to a 'mere freak show' where events are run for media promotion and commercial success only. This cannot be in the interest of the athletes who consider themselves just as much athletes as the able bodied sporting community and moreover they want to be seen as such (cf. Schantz & Alberto 1999). Therefore it is important to be aware of these impending dangers and to follow and scrutinize attentively and diagnose critically the media coverage of Paralympic events as their effects have become complex and very powerful (cf. Kellner, 1995, p. 151).

In order to improve the media coverage, both the Paralympic movement and the media have to make some efforts. Even for insiders it is difficult to understand all the Paralympic sports with all their rules and differing classifications. Important changes towards a greater visibility and easier comprehension seem to be necessary to improve the acceptance by the public at large. Therefore, the rules should be simplified and the great number of categories, which are the cause of real medal inflation, should be reduced.

Parallel to this, the persons responsible for the sport for people with disabilities have to strengthen the contacts with the media, in order to train and to inform journalists (cf. Dummer, 1998; Levine, 2000). Universities and schools of journalism and mass communication should integrate coverage of people with disabilities in their curriculum. Journalists should be encouraged to accept offers of information and education and should remember their own educational mission and responsibility (cf. Eco, 1997). Organizations like DMedia, a project founded in 1999 by Suzanne Levine, which aims to provide a bridge between media and disability communities, should to be encouraged, supported, and include sport journalists (Levine 2000). Balanced and accurate reporting is indeed possible as shown in our corpus by Iris Hilbert, a female correspondent of the Frankfurter Rundschau. She took into consideration women and athletes' perspectives as she treated women and men equally and accorded much space to comments of the athletes. We need more of the same type of balanced reporting if we are to ensure Paralympic sport receives future equality in the mass media.

REFERENCES

Albright, A. C. (1997). *Choreographing difference. The body and identity contemporary dance.* Hanover, NH: Wesleyan University Press.

Auberger, A. Brunet, F., & Schantz, O. J. , (1994). Sport, Olympism and disability. In Research Group of the CNOSF (Ed.), *For a humanism of sport* (pp. 163-177). Paris: CNOSF, Editions Revue E.P.S.

Baudrillard, J. (1991, March 29). La guerre du Golfe n'a pas eu lieu. *Libération.*

Becker, p. (1983). Sport in den Massenmedien. *Sportwissenschaft 13* (1), 24-45.

Bell, A. (1991). *The language of news media.* Oxford, UK, Cambridge MA: Blackwell.

Berelson, B. (1960). Communication and public opinion. In W. Schramm (Ed.), *Mass communications* (pp. 527-543). Urbana: University of Illinois Press.

Berghaus, M. (1999). Wie Massenmedien wirken. *Rundfunk und Fernsehen 47* (2), 181-199.

Bette, K.-H. (1999). *Systemtheorie und Sport*. Frankfurt a. M.: Suhrkamp.

Borcila, A. (2000). Nationalizing the Olympics around and away from "vulnerable" bodies of women: The NBC coverage of the 1996 Olympics and some moments after. *Journal of Sport and Social Issues, 24* (2), 118-147.

Bourdieu, P. (1994). Les Jeux Olympiques. Programme pour une analyse. Actes de la *Recherche en Sciences Sociales, 103*, 102-103.

Bourdieu, P. (1996). *Sur la télévision*. Paris: Liber.

Chambre des Communes (1988). *Pas de nouvelles, mauvaises nouvelles*. Premier rapport du Comité permanent de la condition des personnes handicapées. Ottawa: Chambre des Communes.

Cloerkes, G. (1997). *Soziologie der Behinderten*. Heidelberg: Schindle.

Clogston, J. S. (1994). Disability coverage in American newspapers. In J. A. Nelson (Ed.), *The disabled, the media, and the information age* (pp. 45-53).Westport, CN: Greenwood Press.

Coakley, Jay J. (1994) *Sport in society. Issues and controversies*. St. Louis: Mosby

Cole, C. (1999 August, 27). *Faster, higher, poorer*. National Post, Canada.

Dearing, J. W., Rogers, E. M. (1996). *Agenda setting*. London: Sage.

DePauw, K. P. (1997). The (In)Visibility of DisAbility: Cultural contexts and "sporting bodies". *Quest, 49*, 416-430.

Donsbach, W. (1991). *Medienwirkung trotz Selektion. Einflußfaktoren auf die Zuwendung zu Zeitungsinhalten*. Köln: Böhlauer.

Donsbach, W. (1992). Die Selektivität der Rezipienten. Faktoren, die die Zuwendung zu Zeitungsinhalten beeinflussen. In W. Schulz (Ed.), *Medienwirkungen. Einflüsse von Presse Radio und Fernsehen auf Individuen und Gesellschaft* (pp. 25-71). Weinheim: VCH.

Duhamel, A. (1985). *Le complexe d'Astérix*. Paris: Gallimard.

Dummer, G. M. (1998). Media coverage of disability sport. *Palaestra, 14* (4), 56.

Duncan, M. C. (1990). Sports photographs and sexual difference. The images of women and men in the 1984 and 1988 Olympic Games. *Sociology of Sport Journal, 7*, 22-43.

Duncan, M. C. (1986). A hermeneutic of spectator sport: The 1976 and 1984 Olympic Games. *Quest, 38*, 50-77.

Duncan, M. C.; Messner, M., & Williams, L. (1991). *Coverage of women's sports in four daily newspapers*. Edited by W. Wayne. Los Angeles: AAF publications. Retrieved January 27, 2000 from the World Wide Web: http://www.AAFLA.org/Publications/-ResearchReports/ResearchReport1_.htm.

Eastman, S. T. & Billings, A. (2000). Sportcasting and sports reporting. The power of the gender bias. *Journal of Sport & Social Issues, 24* (2), 192-213.

Eco, U. (1997). Cinque scritti morali. Milano: Bompiani.

Eilders, C. (1997). *Nachrichtenfaktoren und Rezeption. Eine empirische Analyse zur Auswahl und Verarbeitung politischer Information*. Opladen: Westdeutscher Verlag.

Elias, N. & Dunning E. (1970). The quest of excitement in unexciting societies. In G. Lüschen (ed.). *The cross-cultural analysis of sport and games* (pp. 31-51). Champaign, IL: Stipes.

Enting, B. (1997). *Die Berichterstattung über die Paralympics 1996 in Atlanta - dargestellt in ausgewählten Printmedien*. Unpublished master's thesis, Sport University Cologne, Köln, Germany.

Erbring, L., Goldenberg, E., & Miller, A. (1980). Front pages news and real world cues: A New Look at Agenda-Setting by the Media. *American Journal of Political Science, 24* (1), pp- 19-49.

Farnall, O. & K.A. Smith (1999). Reactions to people with disabilities: Personal contact versus viewing of specific media portrayals. *Journalism and Mass Communication Quarterly, 76* (4), 659-672.

Fiske, J. (1993). *Power plays, power works.* London: Verso.

Foucault, M. (1961). *Histoire de la folie à l'âge classique.* Paris: Gallimard.

Früh, W. (1994). *Realitätsvermittlung durch Massenmedien. Die permanente Transformation der Wirklichkeit.* Opladen: Westdeutscher Verlag.

Galtung, J., & Ruge, H. (1965). The structure of foreign news. *Journal of Peace Research, 2,* 64-91.

Gebauer, G. (1994). Le nouveau nationalisme sportif. *Actes de la Recherche en Sciences Sociales, 103,* 104-107.

Génolini, J.P. (1995). L'expression euphémique du handicap mental dans les messages de presse sur le sport. *Revue Européenne du Handicap Mental, 2* (8), 54-63.

Gill, C.J. (1994), Questioning continuum. In B. Shaw (Ed.), *The ragged edge: The disability experience from the pages of the first fifteen years of The Disability Rag* (pp. 42-49). Louisville, KY: Avocado Press.

Greenberg, B.S. & J. S. Brand (1994). Minorities and the mass media: 1970 to 1990. In J. Bryant & D. Zillmann (Eds.), *Media Effects: Advances in Theory and Research* (pp. 273-314). Hillsdale NJ: L. Erlbaum.

Guttmann, A. (1996). *The erotics in sport.* New York: Columbia University Press.

Guttmann, L. (1979). *Sport für Körperbehinderte* [Textbook of Sport for the Disabled]. München: Urban & Schwarzenberg.

Hackforth, J. (1988). Publizistische Wirkungsforschung: Ansätze, Analysen und Analogien. In J. Hackforth (Ed.), *Sportmedien und Mediensport* (pp. 15-33). Berlin: Vistas.

Hackforth, J. (1994). Behindertensport in den Medien. In: Behinderten-Sportverband Nordrhein-Westfalen (Hrsg.). *Behindertensport: Sein Stellenwert in der Arbeitswelt und Gesellschaft.* Duisburg: BSVNW, pp. 46-48.

Hall, S. (1997). The spectacle of the 'other'. In S. Hall (Ed.). Representation. *Cultural representations and signifying practices* (pp. 223- 290). London: Sage

Hardin, M. M. & B. Hardin (2004). The 'Supercrip' in sport media: Wheelchair athletes discuss hegemony's disabled hero. sosol 7/ 1 (http://physed.otago.ac.nz/sosol/v7i1/v7i1_1.html)

Hiestand, M. (July 25, 2000). Paralympics online to test live market. *US Today,* C.9.

Holicki, S. (1993). *Pressefoto und Pressetext im Wirkungsvergleich. Eine experimentelle Untersuchung am Beispiel von Politikerdarstellungen.* München: Fischer.

Horkheimer, M., & Adorno, Th. W. (1989). *Dialektik der Aufklärung. Philosophische Fragmente.* Leipzig: Reclam. (Original work published 1947)

Ingstad, B. & Whyte, S. R. (1995). *Disability and culture.* Berkley: University of California Press.

International Olympic Committee (1996). *Olympic charter.* Lausanne: I.O.C.

International Paralympic Committee (2008). *IPC Handbook.* Retrieved February 1st, 2008 from the World Wide Web: http://www.paralympic.org

Internenettes (Eds.) (2000). *Représentations des femmes dans la vie politique française.* Retrieved April 2nd, 2000 from the World Wide Web: http://www.internenettes.fr /femmes/politique.html

Jamieson, K. H., Campbell, K. K. (1997). *The interplay of influence. News, advertising, politics, and the mass media.* Belmont, 4th edition. CA: Wadsworth.

Jones, R., Murell, A. J. & Jackson J. (1999). Pretty versus powerful in the sports pages. *Journal of Sport & Social Issues, 23* (2), 183-192.

Kauer, O., & Bös, K. (1998). *Behindertensport in den Medien.* Aachen: Meyer & Meyer:

Keller, C. E., Hallahan, D. P., McShane, E. A., Crowley, E. P., & Blandford, B.J. (1990). The coverage of persons with disabilities in American newspapers. *The Journal of Special Education, 24* (3), 271-282.

Kellner, D. (1995). *Media culture- Cultural studies, identity and politics between the modern and the postmodern.* London: Routledge.

Kepplinger, M. H. (1986). Begriffe und Modelle langfristiger Medienwirkung. In W.A. Mahle (Ed.), *Langfristige Medienwirkung* (pp. 27-38). Berlin: Wissenschaftsverlag Volker Spiess.

Klapper, J.T. (1960). *The effects of mass Communication.* Glencoe, Ill.: Free Press.

Krüger, A. (1993). Cui bono? Die Rolle des Sports in den Massenmedien. In A. Krüger, & A., Scharenberg (Eds.), *Wie die Medien den Sport aufbereiten - Ausgewählte Aspekte der Sportpublizistik* (pp. 24-63). Berlin: Tischler.

Kuhn, R. (1995). *The media in France.* London: Routledge.

Lachal, R.-C. (1990a). La presse française et les personnes handicapées de 1977 à 1988. In Institut de l'Enfance et de la Famille (Ed.), *Handicap, famille et société* (pp. 39-44). Paris: IDEF.

Lachal, R.-C. (1990b). Les personnes handicapées vues par la presse régionale française. Constantes et évolutions de 1977 à 1988. *Handicaps et Inadaptations - Les Cahiers du CTNERHI, 51/52,* 1-29.

Landry, F. (1995); The Paralympic Games of Barcelona '92. In M. de Moragas, & M. Botello (Eds.). *The keys to success* (pp. 124-138). Barcelona: Universitat Autònoma de Barcelona.

Lazarsfeld, P.F., & Merton, R. K. (1948). Mass communication, popular taste and organized social action. In L. Bryson (Ed.), *Communication of ideas* (pp. 95-118). New York: Harper & Bros.

Lazarsfeld, P.F., Berelseon, B., & Gaudet, H. (1968). *The people's choice* (3rd ed.). New York: Columbia University Press.

Lenk, H. (1976): Toward a social philosophy of the Olympics: Values, aims, reality of the modern Olympic movement. In P. Graham & H. Ueberhorst (Eds.), *The modern Olympics* (pp. 107-167). Cornwall, NY: Leisure Press.

Levine, S. (2000). Narrowing the perception gap. *The Quill, 88* (3), 35.

Longmore, P. K. (1985). Screening stereotypes: Images of disabled people. *Social Policy, 16* (1), 31-37.

Luebke, B. (1989). Out of focus. Images of women and men in the newspaper photographs. *Sex Roles, 20* (3-4), 121-133.

Luhmann, N. (1996). *Die Realität der Massenmedien* (2nd ed.). Opladen: Westdeutscher Verlag.

Lyotard, J.-F. (1983). *Le différend.* Paris: Editions de Minuit.

Maguire, J. (1993). Globalization, sport development and the media/sport production complex. *Sport Science Review, 2* (1), 29-47.

McCombs, M. (1994). News influence on our pictures of the world. In J. Bryant, & D.

Zillmann (Eds.), Media effects. *Advances in theory and research* (pp. 1- 16). Hillsdale, NJ: Lawrence Erlbaum.

Merten, K. (1995). *Inhaltsanalyse.* Opladen: Westdeutscher Verlag.

Münch, R. (1993). *Die Kultur der Moderne. Band2: Ihre Entwicklung in Frankreich und Deutschland.* Frankfurt a. M.: Suhrkamp.

Nelson, J. A. (1994). Broken Images: Portrayals of those with disabilities in American media. In J. A. Nelson (Ed.), *The disabled, the media, and the information age* (pp. 1- 17).Westport, CN: Greenwood Press.

Noelle-Neumann, E. (1994). Wirkung der Massenmedien auf die Meinungsbildung. In E. Noelle-Neumann, W. Schulz, & J. Wilke (Eds.), *Publizistik, Massenkommunikation* (pp. 518-571). Frankfurt a. M.: Fischer.

Oakes, P. J., Haslam, A., & J. C. Turner (1994). *Stereotyping and social reality.* Cambridge, MA: Blackwell.

Oehmichen, E. (1991). Sport im Alltag - Sport im Fernsehen. *Media Perspektiven, 11,* 744- 758.

Peltu, M. (1985). The role of communication media. In H. Ottway, & M. Peltu (Eds.), *Regulating industrial risks: Science, hazards and public protection* (pp. 128-148). London.

Pfister, G. (1987). Women in the Olympics (1952-1980): An analysis of German newspapers (beauty vs. gold medals). In *The Olympic movement and the mass media* (pp. 11.27–11.37). Calgary: Hurford.

Price, B. (1999). Paralympic compatibility with the Olympic movement. In International Olympic Committee /International Olympic Academy (Eds.). *Report of the thirty-eighth session 15th July- 30th July 1998* (pp. 140-148). Lausanne: IOC.

Riggs, K. E., Eastman, S.T., & Golobic, T. S. (1993). Manufactured conflict in the 1992 Olympics: the discourse of television and politics. *Critical Studies in Mass Communication, 10* (3), 253-272.

Robertson, R. (1992). *Globalization: social theory and global culture.* London: Sage.

Rowe, D. (1999). *Sport, culture and the media. The untruly trinity.* Buckingham, PH: Open University Press.

Schantz, O. J. (1999). La mise en scène du corps extraordinaire - Freak show ou implication éthique de l'esthétique. In Centre de Recherche en Education Corporelle (Ed.). *La danse, une culture en mouvement* (pp. 67-74). Strasbourg : UMB.

Schantz, O. J., & Alberto, C. (1999). Coping strategies of Paralympic athletes." In *12° Congreso Mundial de Actividad Fisica Adaptada - COMAFA '99, 4-8 de Mayo de 1999 Barcelona - Lleida. Resumenes.* Barcelona: Institut Nacional d'educació Física de Catalunya, pp. 95-96.

Schantz, O. J., & Gilbert, K. (2001). An ideal misconstrued: Newspaper coverage of the Atlanta Paralympic Games in France and Germany. *Sociology of Sport Journal, 18.* 69- 94.

Schantz, O. J., & Marty, C. (1995). The French press and sport for people with handicapping conditions. In I. Morisbak, P. E. Jørgensen (Eds.) *Quality of live through adapted physical activity* (pp. 72-79). Oslo: Hamtrykk.

Schell, L.A., & Duncan, M. C. (1999). A content analysis of CBS's coverage of the 1996 Paralympic Games. *Adapted Physical Activity Quarterly, 16* (1), pp. 27-47.

Schimanski, M. (1994). *Behindertensport in der deutschen und amerikanischen Iagespresse*

1984-1992. Unter besonderer Berücksichtigung der Paralympics. Eine Analyse anhand ausgewählter Printmedien. Unpublished master's thesis, Sport University Cologne, Köln, Germany.

Schönbach, K. (1992). Transaktionale Modelle der Medienwirkung: Stand der Forschung. In W. Schulz (Ed.), *Medienwirkungen. Einflüsse von Presse Radio und Fernsehen auf Individuen und Gesellschaft* (pp. 109-120).Weinheim: VCH.

Segrave, J. O. (1988). Toward a definition of Olympism. In J. O. Segrave & D. Chu (Eds.). *The Olympic Games in transition* (pp. 149-161). Champaign, IL: Human Kinetics.

Shapiro, J. P. (1993). *No pity: People with disabilities forging a new civil rights movement.* New York: Times Books.

Sherill, C. (1997). Paralympic Games 1996: Feminist and other concerns: What's your excuse? *Palestra, 13,* 32-38.

Sherill, C. (1993). Women with disabilities. In G. Cohen (Ed.), *Women in sport: Issues and controversies* (pp. 238-248). Newbury Park, CA: Sage.

Stautner, B. K. (1989). *Abweichung - Behinderung - Sport in der modernen Gesellschaft. Eine Bestandsaufnahme und systemtheoretische Neuformulierung.* Unpublished doctoral dissertation. Julius-Maximilians University, Würzburg.

Sutton, J. (Jan 5, 1998). Sponsors shy away from Paralympic Games. *Marketing News, 32* (1), 21-22.

Tuggle, C. A. & A. Owen (1999). A descriptive analysis of the centennial Olympics: the 'Games of the Women'? *Journal of Sport and Social Issues, 23* (2), 171-182.

Turner, B. S. (1998). Foreword. In W. Seymour, *Remaking the Body. Rehabilitation and Change* (v-viii). St Leonards: Allen & Unwin.

Urquhart, J. & Crossman, J. (1999). The Globe and Mail coverage of the winter Olympic Games. *Journal of Sport & Social Issues, 23* (2), 193-202.

Wann, D. L., Schrader, M. P., Allison, J. A. & McGeorge K.K. (1998). The inequitable newspaper coverage of men's and women's athletics at small, medium, and large universities. *Journal of Sport & Social Issues, 22* (1), 79-87.

Waxman, B. F. (1994). It's time to politicize our sexual oppression. In B. Shaw (Ed.), *The ragged edge: The disability experience from the pages of the first fifteen years of The Disability Rag* (pp. 82-87). Louisville, KY: Avocado Press.

White, D., M. (1950). The »Gatekeeper«: A case study in the selection of news. *Journalism Quarterly, 27,* 383-390.

Wilke, J. (1994). Presse. In E. Noelle-Neumann, W. Schulz, & J. Wilke (Eds.), *Publizistik, Massenkommunikation* (pp. 382-417). Frankfurt a. M.: Fischer.

Woodill, G. (1994). The social semiotics of disability. In M. H. Rioux & M. Bach (Eds.). *Disability is not measles. New research paradigms in disability* (pp. 201-226). North York, Ontario: Roeher.

Yoshida, R. K., Wasilewski, L., & Friedman, D. L. (1990). Recent newspaper coverage about persons with disabilities. *Exceptional children, 56,* 418-423.

Zola, I.K. (1985). Depictions of disability – Metaphor, message, and medium in the media: A research and political agenda. *The Social Science Journal, 22* (4), 5-17.

5   SPECTATING AT THE PARALYMPIC GAMES: ATHENS 2004

Frédéric Reichhart, Anne Dinel & Otto J. Schantz

"A top Paralympics official [IPC-president Phil Craven] said [...] that filling the Athens stadiums at the 2004 Paralympics and changing public attitudes toward the disabled were his priorities."

Kathimerini, April 7, 2003

(The Greek International English Language Newspaper)

INTRODUCTION

The Paralympic Games such as we know them today remain the result, and the inheritance of a loaded history by bringing together, not only, the history of sport and sports practices, but also the evolution of the treatment and the representations of people with disabilities. It is with this last aspect that we site our approach in this chapter which views the Paralympic Games as "a shop window", a prism through which the relationship that society maintains with people with disabilities reveals itself. Drawing from the 2004 Athens Paralympic Games, we examine the spectators who participated in the Games and check their motivations. We will describe the public's perceptions, and propose a taxonomy (cf. Giulianotti 2002), in order to explain the function, the representation and the use of these Games through the eyes of the flaneurs, primary and secondary school pupils, athletes' friends and close relations rather than spectators coming specifically to admire and contemplate the sports events.

FROM SEOUL (1988) TO ATHENS (2004)

At the 1988 Seoul Summer Paralympic Games, a determining change had been noted and since that moment, the Olympic and Paralympic Games are celebrated in identical places of competition. This point was made official in June 19, 20011, by an agreement signed between the International Olympic committee and the International Paralympic Committee. This agreement stipulates that, from 2008, the Paralympic Games will be held after the Olympic Games, and will use the same sites and infrastructure. From the procedure of candidature for 2012, the city chosen to welcome the Olympic Games will also be obligated to organize the Paralympic Games. The fate of the Paralympic Games is now sealed to that of the Olympic Games. Nevertheless, it is necessary to note that since the 2002 Salt Lake City Winter Olympic Games, the same steering committee is responsible for the organisation of the Olympic and the Paralympic Games. The network set up for ticketing, technology and transport for the Olympic Games is also the same used for the Paralympic Games.

Forty four years after the first Paralympic Games were held in Rome in 1960; more than 3,806 athletes from approximately 136 countries came to Athens in 2004 to compete in the Paralympic Games. Indeed, with regard to the attendance figures, the Paralympic Games remain the 2nd largest world multisport celebration, with the Olympic Games retaining first position. So, the best athletes with disabilities in the world compete in 19 sports disciplines. This event was covered by 3,000 media representatives, through images, by radio and the print media. It seems that a large number of spectators rushed to the competition sites. According to the organizing committee of the games (ATHOC) and the International Paralympic Committee (IPC), about 850,000 tickets were sold for the Athens Paralympic Games competitions (IPC 2005, 5).

The purpose of our research was to examine the motivations and to establish a taxonomy of this public support for the Games. To do this, several variables were defined in order to work out the profile of the spectators that watched the Paralympic Games. Were they mainly Greek, and more precisely (local) Athenians? Athletes' close relations (friends or family)? Passing tourists? Simply curious people who happened to have arrived there? Spectators not having been able to attend the Olympic Games? etc. Finally, the study aimed to understand the multiple motivations and the representations of the spectators who came to watch the Paralympic Games.

METHODS

To tackle these questions, we set up a research protocol inspired by the Grounded Theory (cf. Strauss, Corbin 1991, Glaser, Strauss 1967), ethnography and visual sociology (cf. Faccioli, Losacco 2003; Harper 2000) and adopted multiple methods of data collection that combine informal conversations, participatory and non-participatory observations and an analysis of photos and other documents (cf. Denzin, Lincoln 2005; Laplantine 1996). The interviews and observations were conducted by a team of three researchers during the Paralympic Games, from September 17th through 28th, 2004. The interviews, which were mainly informal, were conducted in English, French and German. Some of them were recorded and all were later transcribed in the written form. Observations were formalized by photos taken with digital cameras.

Although the activities took place at over 10 sites, the bulk of them were performed on the main site OAKA (Central Site of the Athens Olympics) for a number of reasons. First of all, the main site housed 5 different sports disciplines - athletics, wheelchair basketball, wheelchair tennis, cycling and swimming. It therefore included five infrastructure entities - the Olympic stadium, the Olympic Aquatic Centre, the Olympic Tennis Centre, the Olympic Cycle Stadium and the Olympic Indoor Hall. Secondly, this complex represented in a sense the symbol of the Paralympic Games, as it is at the Olympic Stadium that the Paralympic flame burned. Furthermore, this site marks the beginning and end of the Games with the opening and closing ceremonies. Finally, next to this sports infrastructure, spectacular and expensive architectural realizations indicated a particular organization of the site. A long path in metal structures crossing the site from the East to the West led to the Olympic stadium; "the waves of the nation", a real mobile and flexible structure, giving the impression of being an undulating wave, also attracted the crowds, while multiple ponds of water decorated and cooled the area.

The events which were organized outside of this main Olympic site, like sailing or boccia, attracted often less than a dozen spectators. We observed sailing competitions without any spectator and a boccia competition where the spectators were composed only of relatives and three children playing games and eating ice-cream while waiting to be picked up by her mother who has been shopping in a nearby commercial centre.

Sampling of the informants varied according to the spectators and the place of action. Regarding spectators, we chose supporters, who could be identified thanks to their outfit (make-up, hat, jersey, T-shirt, tattoo), their behaviour (shouting, singing, whistling) as well as some accessories (flag, pennant, whistle, horn). On the other hand, we also interviewed people drawn from a more discrete and less visible fraction of the public: isolated individuals, couples, families, small and large groups of people. As for the places of action, interviews were conducted in the terraces of the structure, and still within the complex, in restaurants and alleys. The difficulties we encountered were mainly linguistic. Numerous spectators did not know English or had a low proficiency in it, which affected the quality and the appropriateness of the information gathered. However, interviews with Anglophones were highly precise. In all, over 140 informal and formal interviews and more than 1200 photographs' were collected.

RESULTS

The first observation made was that some informants interviewed in the Olympic complex proper did not go there to watch the sports events. This was due to the fact that entrance into the complex was free, while entrance into the places of competition cost money. Tickets could be obtained in three ways: first via the internet, secondly, the buyer assisted by sponsors, had to report to a specific point of sale and thirdly he/she could go to the ticket box offices set up within the OAKA complex. The price of the ticket was fairly low, 5 Euros for half rate (children, students, elderly) and 10 Euros for full rate. In any case, access to the site was independent of access to the terraces, which explains why many people found in the complex were not necessarily there for the Paralympic competitions. These people without tickets were mainly flaneurs who had come simply to admire the site. During the Olympic Games, such strolling was not possible. As one Athenian aged around 30 noted, access to the Olympic site was conditioned by the possession of a ticket, he noted "During the Olympic Games, you had to pay if you wanted to come here". Also during the Olympic Games period the high number of visitors does not give one the desire to go to the site for a stroll. A young couple interviewed compared the high attendance in the Olympics Games events and the relatively low attendance in the Paralympic Games commenting, "It was busy, it was crowded during the Olympics, there were people everywhere; I prefer now, it's more quiet".

In short, The Paralympics allowed people to stroll and experience the culture, sounds and smells associated with a large sporting event. Individuals just strolled and walked throughout this time period. Actually, some people were seen having their rest in the shade on a nice lawn while others did not hesitate to take off their shoes and quietly smoke a cigarette, still in the shade. A few others, like one particular family, benefited from the coolness brought by the water from the ponds. It may seem surprising that nobody had lunch on the grass. In fact visitors were warned against taking food into the complex; food was provided only by authorised services. It is to be noted these flaneurs were more numerous during weekends and more precisely on Sundays as well as in the evenings during weekdays. Two factors can account for this: first, because of people's professional activities, they can come to the site only after work, that is in the evenings and weekends. Visiting the site is tantamount to an outing in the evening or a stroll on a Sunday. There is another parameter which influences the visits of these flaneurs – the weather. People in Greece prefer the coolness of the evenings to the scorching heat of daytime. This parameter is more important for older people. Lastly, there was a high proportion of Athenians among the flaneurs, and very few foreign tourists. Comments on the limited number of foreign tourists on the scene are provided in the section labelled "regular customers" below.

Besides being a space for stroll, relaxation and walk, the OAKA site has became the meeting and exchange point for certain groups of young people. Indeed, in the evenings and during weekends, teenagers liked to meet and while away time within the complex. We interviewed many of these teenagers who happened to be found within the complex in the evenings and they reported that they had come to either stroll or watch a sports event. In the latter case, they had come to encourage either a team, or an athlete but exclusively a local one. Most of these teenagers knew the places and the schedules, having been brought to the site by their schools or having personally visited it in the evenings. Thus, on Friday September 24th, at around 9:30 pm., a score of teenagers gathered in the middle of the complex and, to the rhythm of drums, sang and danced. Having come to encourage the Greek team of wheelchair Basketball, they decided to party there: "We want to have fun, we want to dance and to sing Greek songs, even if we have lost at the basketball." they declared.

This example shows that the teenagers viewed the OAKA space as their territory, as a place of demonstration, of exhibition of the self and of the group, most importantly, they considered this space as a place full of life, a place of animation, a social place in the sense that it brings people together. To some extent, it is a place where something is happening. It was there space.

We also noticed another grouping which was more visible and audible, namely school groups. Essentially in the mornings, between 9:00 am and 1:00 pm, from Monday to Saturday, very numerous school groups moved along the paths of the site as well as the terraces of the sports fields. Parking, although often very congested, allowed the buses to drop these pupils in front of the West entrance, and the number were testament to the importance of school attendance. Interestingly, pupils' ages and classes varied, ranging from 5 year old primary school kids to 17 or 18 year old high school children.

In fact, it was obvious that the teachers used the Paralympic Games as a real educational tool and an instrument of sensitisation of disabilities to the students. Two points need to be underscored here. First of all, as the teachers interviewed reported, the pupils had been prepared for this Day. Using various pedagogic tools (Paralympic Education Kit) adapted to the ages of the learners including drawings, readings, stories, subject of writings, teachers had discussed disability issues with their pupils. We did not check the precise contents of this preparation, but we observed that for a given class, the views of the pupils were very similar to those of their teachers. This preparation seemed to have gone a little beyond the normal curricular set-up, as some informal features were observed in some cases. Flags, pennants, blue and white make-up on the children's faces in the colours of Greece, carefully painted on the face of some pupils, but also placards with encouragements illustrated an informal rather than institutional preparation. Some initiatives seemed to be individual while others were institutional. For example, there was a peculiar group of pupils from the French School of Athens who watched a wheelchair Basketball match where Great Britain and France opposed each other. Most of these pupils had flags bearing the Blue, White and Red colours of France. Besides, this fact the pupils of the class prepared a special poster for that Day. The second point and important point about school children's attendance at the Paralympics is that the visits took place under the framework of a school excursion, in fact the first of the year, given the period of the Games. This finding was confirmed by a French teacher of the Franco-Greek Institute of Athens, who explained that every year, excursions in gardens, museums and zoos were organised. The following comments were indicative of the sort of responses we received from the teachers.

- "Visiting the Paralympic Games site is the first outing for this year", she revealed.
- "Do you organise many in a year?" - "Yes, we go to many places. We visit parks sometimes, museums and zoos", she added.

From the pupils' responses to our questions, it is evident that these pupils were highly satisfied with this particular excursion. The satisfaction and euphoria results not from the appeal of the sports events, but from the splendour of the site they were visiting. They liked the outing simply because they were together, in groups, with their mates (their peers) : "I like (it) because I'm here with my friends, it's great because we are all together" on boy commented.

However, the pupils' being together was not the only explanation for this euphoria... The mere fact of not being in class contributed to the joy. A 14-year-old girl admitted, screaming with laughter: "I like to be here, I prefer to be here than to be in the school" and she continues: "Here, it's like a party." This clearly indicates that the complex was appreciated for its festive atmosphere: a massive crowd, numerous school groups, the possibility of making friends, of benefiting among friends relaxing and eating good food. A group of 15-16-year-old pupils reported that it was for these other reasons that they so highly appreciated these places: "It is nice to be here, I like this place ... It's a nice place, because there are a lot of facilities and it's a beautiful stadium." Inside the complex and in the terraces, the behaviour of the pupils as the competitions were in progress corroborated our initial findings. In fact, these pupils were distant and indifferent to the sports spectacle going on. This observation was illustrated by the scene at a wheelchair Basketball match opposing France and Britain at the Olympic Indoor Hall on 21 September 2004. Numerous groups of pupils were seated in the terraces of the south wing. Many children, aged between 6 and 10, did not watch the match; they rather enjoyed themselves, discussed among themselves and quarrelled. Some moved to the refreshment point, and returned with something to eat and drink. While eating, they did not bother to look at the match that was taking place in front of them. The next match, which opposed Canada and Australia that same day in the afternoon, confirmed the observations made in the morning. The school group on the scene, made up of children aged 7 to 10 years, proved to be aloof and turbulent: the children did not remain seated, they ran across the terraces, got hold of one another, played all types of games screaming and moving noisily. As the match was going on, they ignored it altogether, failing to notice even the starts of applause from the public during spectacular action.

Besides the school groups, the 'strollers' in the evenings and Sundays, there was a third category of spectators, namely the regular customers. These regular people did not constitute a homogenous group, but they shared the fact that they were not attending the Games for the first time. Their presence was justified by the fact that they came to encourage a relative or a friend. This is for example the case of a group of people seated at the foot of the stands of the Olympic Aquatic Centre, all wearing a T-shirt bearing the inscription "Sacha". They were parents and friends who came to encourage a swimmer. During the wheelchair Basketball encounter between Greece and the Netherlands, we met a group of happy Dutch supporters in front of the Olympic Indoor Hall. They came to support a brother and a friend. Hoisting a flag, they confirmed the closeness of their relation with an athlete.

- "We are going to win, Roos is the best"
- "I don't know who's Roos?"
- "He's my brother." And another to add: "He is our friend; we are here to encourage him."

A similar example confirms the closeness of the relation between some spectators and the athletes. On our way to the Olympic stadium on Friday 24th September, we met a group of Irish supporters. Among them, there was a father who had come specifically to encourage his daughter - who was participating in the Paralympic Games for the first time. From the interviews conducted, two types of perceptions of these Games can be identified. The first is people's representations of the Paralympic Games which, unlike the Olympic Games, do not witness cases of doping and cheating. A teenager disclosed his preference for the Paralympic Games by stating that: "I prefer Paralympic Games because there is no doping, they should be called super games..." (Interview conducted at noon, Thursday 23rd September). Secondly, the Paralympic Games project an image of amateurism, as opposed to the Olympic Games. A forty year old woman made the following remark: "These are the real Games; there is no big money, no corruption".

The present analysis of the type of spectators at the Paralympic Games reveals a diversity of motivations and diversity of representations of the Games and the Paralympic athletes. It discloses the diverse nature of the spectators and their diverse motivations to come to the Games. From the interviews of spectators and the observations in the field, we can group these spectators into five broad categories: strollers (Flaneurs), teenagers, pupils on excursion, regular customers made up of relatives (family members and friends) and admirers.

To begin with, strollers found within the OAKA complex tended to have little interest in the actual sports competitions. What seems to interest them was the attractiveness resulting from the media coverage of the magnificent architectural construction and the beauty of the prestigious site. Consequently, the Paralympic Games are viewed as a type of park, garden, space for strolling and Sunday walks, an alibi for an evening outing rather than a space for sports competitions.

Next are school groups, who view the Paralympic Games as a possibility, a support and a means to discover and explore a new field, unknown, underestimated, badly known, that of the disability? Even if the pupils present on the OAKA site had prepared the day with their teachers, the question of the choice and the relevance of visiting the Paralympic Games was not clearly expressed by the teachers. In short, it can be asserted that the Paralympic Games constitute an educational tool which the teachers used to sensitise their pupils to the persons with disabilities. In this sense, the Games remain not only a space to discover but also a shop window, an organised "show". This show takes the shape of a sort of short-lived bridge between the world of the disabled and that of the ablebodied. It is, in a sense, an opera glass enabling the pupils to cast a fast blow of eye on the world of disability. On the other hand, we notice a certain dynamism and enthusiasm of the pupils, but which seem to result more from their satisfaction of meeting among female and male friends, far from their school premises, of being able to amuse themselves at the expense of the interest and motivation to watch the Paralympic Games encounters.

Teenagers not in school groups fall in the latter category. They like to meet in the OAKA complex in the evenings or during weekends. Some of them do watch the sports activities while others just stroll within the complex. So teenagers consider the OAKA space as a social space, a place where something is going on.

Unlike the preceding categories, the fourth referred to as "regular customers", exhibit a very pronounced interest for the athletes. The reason is that they are closely related to the athletes, as they are friends, parents and relatives who come specifically to encourage the handicapped people, whom they know very well. In some cases, it is their first participation in the Games. In others, they had participated in the previous Games. This explains why some people assert a certain allegiance in the Paralympic Games by evoking the 2002 Sydney Games and the 1998 Atlanta

Finally, a last category of spectators completes this typology. These are admirers who are highly interested in the Games and the athletes who take part in them. They tend to idealize the Paralympic Games, giving them specific values and representations. In their opinion, the games are associated with sports ethics, with clean and honest practice, without deceit nor doping, and they remain neither motivated nor slanted by economic and financial factors. Courage and honesty are the athletes' master word. In this sense, the Paralympic Games remain the receptacle of a set of values which are lacking to modern sport. To some extent, they crystallize the lost values of sport, becoming the anteroom of the drift of modern sporting events.

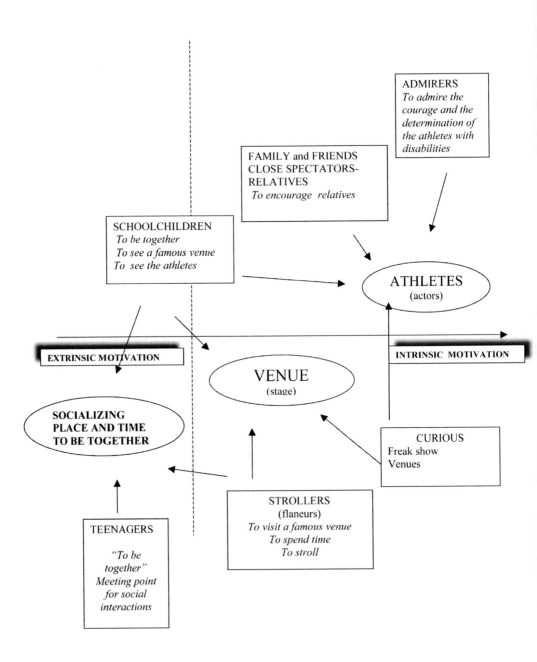

Fig. 3: Framework of spectator typology

CONCLUSION

To conclude, we can assert that the 2004 Paralympic Games have attracted many people. Nevertheless, the great majority of them cannot be classified in the typical sport spectator categories as described in established spectator research (Elias, Dunning 1970; Loy 1981; Opaschowski et al. 1987; Messing, Lames 1996; Schantz 1996; Wann et al. 2001). The Paralympic spectacle is viewed in various ways and for various reasons. Some attend it to admire the prestigious new spaces and facilities in which the spectacle takes place. Others attend it because they personally know the actors on the scene. Others seem indifferent to the performance of the actors and the prestige of the site, simply taking advantage of this occasion to be together. Some spectators did come to admire a sports performance, to specifically encourage an athlete or a team. The motivations vary according to a continuum ranging from "external" motivations to "internal" motivations to the Paralympic Games. These motivations show an interest more or less distant from the sports spectacle of the Paralympic Games. The external motivations define the Paralympic Games as a support independent from sporting events of persons with disabilities: this is the case with teenagers who meet at the complex to spend the evening together. But certain pupils, who come with their classmates within the framework of a school excursion, show the same interest: what is important for them is the fact of being together with their classmates, away from the classroom environment. Contrary to this external logic, we distinguished an internal logic. This logic remains characterized by an interest directed towards the facilities and the contents of the Games. These interests are manifested either towards the athletes or towards the places of practices, the complex of OAKA in particular, sometimes both. But this logic remains slanted by the prestige and the media reports on the beauty of the places, which attracts a crowd of curious, admiring walkers and flaneurs. It is also slanted by the relatives of the participating athletes who come to encourage a brother, sister, son, daughter or friend.

Finally, some admirers idealize the athletes' strength and courage, not with regards to performances but with regard to the representations of the Paralympic Games and the persons overcoming their fates. Indeed, this idealistic speech of "clean games", without deceit nor doping, under the image of the 'Games of the heart', reveals perhaps the true image of the Paralympic Games and the participants.

The absence of deceit and doping seems to signal the absence of stakes: For example questions need asking as to why on earth should one cheat in a game which is not worth the trouble? Only major sports competitions are valuable and prestigious enough for a participant to be tempted to cheat or be dishonest. Besides the value of the Games, the representation of the person with disabilities can also explain this idealized vision. The individual with disabilities in its misfortune, cannot cheat or take drugs, he/she remains intrinsically and naturally honest. Some spectators seemed to consider the Paralympic Games as a freak show. Especially during the swimming events where the almost nude bodies display disabilities overtly, in this case we observed a high fluctuation of spectators and behaviours close to that in side shows. Schantz (2003) made similar observation at the boccia event during the 2000 Sydney Paralympic Games.

The wheelchair Basketball final took place in front of many empty seats. Compared to Sydney where a huge crowed rooted for the Australian team and where wheelchair basketball seemed to become an exciting game, displaying physical prowess and tactical finesse, it means that it is a spectator sport (Schantz 2003).

The motivations and the perceptions of the 2004 Paralympic spectators ranged from that of an engineer who travelled 2000 miles to visit the Games, and who just wanted to take photos of the facilities and who refused to watch any Paralympic competition, which is for him "no great sport", to a 22 year old art student, whom we interviewed in the subway on her way back home from a classical dance lesson, who told us, that she went as much as possible to the Paralympic Games, as she considered these Games much more pure and emotionally charged than the over commercialised Olympics.

The wish of the IPC-president to fill the stadium was at least fulfilled for the main Olympic Sports Centre. However, most of them didn't come for the sport and the athletic prowess. There seems to still be a long way to go before Paralympic sport will exert the same attraction to spectators as sport of able bodied athletes. Concerning the second part of the IPC-presidents wish, which aimed to change public attitudes toward the disabled, this allows a more optimistic perspective as an important part of the spectators were school children. Even they have in general not been much concerned with the sporting outcome of the Games; they probably have been sensitized for the concerns of people with disabilities especially as this issue was, thanks to the Paralympic Games, part of the curriculum for all Greek schools.

REFERENCES

Denzin, N.K. & Lincoln Y S. (2005). *The Sage Handbook of Qualitative Research*. Thousand Oaks: Sage.

Elias, N. & Dunning, E. (1970). *The Quest of Excitement in Unexciting Societies*, pp. 31-51. In Lüschen, G. (Ed.). The Cross-Cultural Analysis of Sport and Games. Champaign, Ill.: Human Kinetics.

Faccioli,, P. & Losacco, G. (2003). *Manuale di Sociologia visuale*. Milano: Angeli

Glaser, B. & Strauss, A. (1967). *The Discovery of Grounded Theory*. Chicago: Aldine.

Giulianotti, R. (2002). Supporters, Followers, and Flaneurs: A Taxonomy of Spectator Identities in Football. *Journal of Sport and Social Issues* 26/1, 25-46.

Harper, D. (2000). *Fotografien als sozialwissenschaftliche Daten*, pp. 402-416. In Flick, U., Kardoff von E. & Steinke, I. (eds.). Qualitative Forschung. Reinbek bei Hamburg: Rowohlt.

International Paralympic Committee (2005). *Annual Report 2004*. Bonn: IPC.

Loy, J.W. (1981). *An Emerging Theory of Sportspectatorship - Implications fort he Olympic Games*, pp. 262-294. In Segrave, J. & Chu, D. (Eds.). Olympism. Champaign, Ill.: Human Kinetics.

Laplantine, F. (1996). *La description ethnographique*. Paris: Nathan.

Messing, M. & Lames, M. (Eds.) (1996). *Zur Sozialfigur des Sportzuschauers*. Niedernhausen: Schors.

Opaschowski, H.W., Neubauer, U., Stubenvoll, R., Wernitz, R. (1987). *Sport in der Freizeit. Mehr Lust als Leistung. Auf dem Weg zu einem neuen Sportverständnis.* Hamburg: BAT Freizeit-Forschungsinstitut.

Schantz, O. J. (1996). *Fußball: deutsche und französische Zuschauer - Probleme eines interkulturellen Vergleichs*, pp. 68-81. In Messing, M.; Lames, M. (Eds.) Zur Sozialfigur des Sportzuschauers. Niedernhausen: Schors.

Schantz, O. J. (2003). *Spectators at the Sydney 2000 Paralympics: A Field Study*, pp. 84-85. In KOSAPE/IFAPA (Eds.) 14th International Symposium of Adapted Physical Education. August 4-7, 2003, Seoul: KOSAPE/IFAPA.

Strauss, A. & Corbin J. (1991). *Basics of Qualitative Research*. Thousand Oaks: Sage.

Wann, D. L. , Melnick, M.J., Russell, G.W. & Pease, D.G. (2001). *Sport Fans. The psychology and social impact of spectators*. New York, London: Routledge.

6   MEDIA AND THE PARALYMPIC GAMES

Margie MacDonald

INTRODUCTION

The following chapter is broken into three basic parts. The first deals with what reporters found covering their first Paralympic Games. The second looks at the evolution of media services, ie. what is provided for the media in terms of information at a Games. The third discusses what future Games organising committees and the International Paralympic Committee (IPC) need to keep providing and improving on as far as the media is concerned.

JOURNALISTS PERCEPTIONS AND IMPRESSIONS OF THE PARALYMPIC GAMES

The old adage, 'seeing is believing' could be an alternate motto for the Paralympic Games if the IPC ever decided to have a change from 'Mind, Body, Spirit'. Back in 1996, the then Olympic reporter with leading Sydney radio station 2UE, Murray Olds, was asked to cover the Atlanta Olympic Games in July and then the Atlanta Paralympic Games two weeks later.

He had this to say, when asked to sum up what it was like to cover an event as big as an Olympic Games, fly home to see family and friends and have some brief 'down time' and then to return to the US state of Georgia and its summer humidity to cover his first ever Paralympic Games.

"I was exhausted after the Olympics, but I was exhilarated after the Paralympics," Olds said.

Why? The reasons are simple – it is a product that is worth watching and reporting on; it is a big event in its own right; it has sports and athletes who have their own unique flavour even though they are most similar to the Olympic sports and Olympians. At the Sydney 2000 Paralympic Games, 14 of the 18 sports on the 11-day program were Olympic sports. There are subtle differences – in judo the same weight divisions apply, in basketball or tennis the rules and point scoring is the same and the net is the same height.

But then in comes the unique flavour – in judo all athletes are blind, in basketball and tennis the players are in wheelchairs, which you would think would make it impossible to give spectators quality sport. In reality, seeing is believing and the first sport in Sydney to have its reserved seating sold out for the finals was wheelchair basketball.

> The greatest catch for the media to come and report on the Games in the first instance is that it will not be completely strange and alien to them.

From their Olympic experiences, they know the sports, the rules, all they have to learn is the names of new athletes, and new ways of playing that sport – shooting from the free throw line in a chair; hitting a volley or cross-court backhand from a chair; running a track race or marathon on the road with a guide tethered to your wrist the whole way; leaping over the high jump with one leg; getting close to 10 seconds in the 100m with only one arm; being able to lift four times your body weight without the use of your legs; or skiing down a slope at around 100km/h with only one leg or with just the voice of your guide for direction.

These characteristics provide the colour, the great descriptive copy, the action caught in a newspaper photograph, or the sequence of shots and the action story for a television report.

The athletes, and access to them, provide the quotes which people see on TV, read in a newspaper, magazine or website, or hear on the radio. Host organising committees must continue to provide easy access to the athletes because these athletes and their individual stories are the real "currency" of the Games that will get reporters back time and again. The same elements – human triumph after four long years of hard work – are what has made the Olympics so special from 1896 and it is doing the same for the Paralympics.

The value of athletes in being able to tell their stories really began to be recognised in the Paralympics from 1996, although the Games had been going since 1960 for Summer and 1976 for Winter.

Once these "moments" of history begin to be recorded and remain accessible via newspaper and television station files and libraries, website archives, then word continues to be spread about the Paralympic Games. Journalists are the true 'word of mouth' vessels by which the message is passed not only to the public, but back to other journalists, to sports editors and news directors so that the next time a Summer or Winter Paralympics comes around, the pool of knowledgable reporters and media has grown.

This is supported by the facts from organising committee post-Games reports:

1996 Atlanta Paralympics – 1,600 media accredited (800 broadcasters, 100 photographers, 700 written press, which includes newspapers, magazines, journals, and websites)

2000 Sydney Paralympics – 2,400 media accredited (1,100 broadcasters, 300 crew for the Host Broadcaster separate from TV/radio rights holders, 1,000 written press and photographers)

2004 Athens Paralympics – 3,100 media accredited (the breakdown not available yet from the IPC)

So what are the impressions from some journalists? The first wave of media was felt at the 1996 Atlanta Paralympics. Previous Games in Seoul in 1988 and Barcelona in 1992 had very limited numbers of media – usually a media spokesman attached to an NPC (National Paralympic Committee) who fed stories or results of his/her country's athletes to local media back home – or media back home rang the media contact and did reports but they were not eye-witness, the journalists were not on the ground at the Games. They were covering it from thousands of kilometres away. Why? Apart from the official results service, there were few other services for media – no historical information, background on sports and events, no biographies of athletes, no-one to approach at a VPC (Venue Press Centre) who might be able to explain more about the sport or an athlete. This made it hard for journalists to cover the Games. The Olympic Games is a huge undertaking for media organisations at very significant costs to transport personnel and equipment to a foreign country, then pay the rental fees at the Main Press Centres (Print and Photographers) and International Broadcast Centres (TV and Radio), the accommodation costs for your staff, wages and expenses for your staff.

The costs can be quite prohibitive with foreign exchange values. So often the Paralympics was an added expense few organisations were willing to commit to, even if they were going to send just a small compliment of staff compared with their Olympic numbers. If the level of service journalists expect and receive at an Olympic Games, is not provided at a Paralympic Games, it will be even harder to convince news organisations to send staff – either fresh or 'recycled' Olympic writers – back to the Paralympics. The progression of services to the media is covered later, but again the famous line from the Kevin Costner baseball movie 'Field of Dreams' can be applied here: "If you build it, they will come."

One of the biggest coups for the IPC was to sign a memorandum of understanding at the 2000 Games in Sydney with the IOC. The then IPC President, Dr Robert Stedward, and the then IOC President, Juan Antonio Samaranch, agreed that from then onwards, each city bidding to host an Olympic Games would include the Paralympic Games in its bidding documents. Previously, prospective host cities had two different bidding committees and two different sets of bidding documents – one for each Games. Although since 1988 in Seoul both Games have been held in the same city, previous they had not – sometimes not even in the same country - apart from Rome in 1960 and Tokyo in 1964. This meant completely different sets of venues in operation, different transport services, Athletes Villages, and two different sets of staff. And it meant two different standards in the provision of services for the media.

Stephen Dettre, general news and sports reporter for the domestic wire serive, AAP (Australian Associated Press), whose subscribers include major metropolitan and regional newspapers, commercial radio stations and TV stations (excluding the government-funded ABC, Australian Broadcasting Corporation). Stephen had covered the 1988 Seoul and 1992 Barcelona Olympics and was back for AAP on its team for the 1996 Atlanta Olympics. He was then asked to stay on in the USA and report on the Paralympic Games, since Sydney was the next host city in 2000.

"I was extremely reluctant to go. The APC did the hard sell several times on me and I finally agreed to do it," he said. The APC combined with the Sydney Paralympic Organising Committee (SPOC) to help cover some of the expenses of a group of journalists - from print, TV and radio – who covered the Atlanta Olympics to remain for the Paralympics.

"The Paras had some parts which were extremely exciting, and I'm talking here about a spectator, but there are still some sports that aren't good for TV, not good for spectators and hard to write about.

"There is absolutely no question that it was one of the highlights of my professional career as a journalist because there were just so many unusual stories and so many great stories – not just the emotional stories, there were plenty of those – but all the technology stories in the equipment, chairs, legs etc.

"It was never an issue 'what am I going to write about today?'. It was more an issue of 'what am I going to leave out?' "

Louise Evans, was a reporter for 'The Sydney Morning Herald' at the 2000 Sydney Olympics and the flagship paper from the Fairfax group asked journalists covering the major sports at the Olympics – Louise was head athletics writer - to stay on for the Paralympics 18 days later.

"Now while that was a very admirable decision it didn't actually work as well as it should, in my opinion, because the time we got to the Paralympics, which was fast on the heels of the Olympics, we were exhausted," she said.

"The Olympics is as big as sport gets in the world - bigger than the World Cup, any world championships, the Commonwealth Games - and the hardest sporting event to cover. The Paralympics were very much secondary to reporters.

"I personally thought it would be better to get someone not tainted by the Olympics, not exhausted by the Olympics, to come in fresh because I think they would have brought more enthusiasm to the coverage."

Did her feelings change after the Paralympics were all over?

"After the first two days at athletics at the Paralympics, I was pretty impressed. I'd never watched Paralympic sport of any description. I'd just seen (Australian wheelchair athlete) Louise Sauvage do exhibition events at the Olympics," Evans said.

"I was amazed by what these people were doing. There were people with one leg, one arm.... doing what I considered to be really quite world class performances.

"There was one guy who was a sprinter but born with a congenital defect where half his side wasn't there including a couple of ribs, and he was running the 100m and 200m. And he was running times that would have made him a relay reserve in the main Olympic team".

"The 'wow' factor definitely kicked in when you got to see for yourself and write about what these people were doing."

Stuart Honeysett, was one of the rugby league writers for the other broadsheet metropolitan newspaper in Sydney 'The Australian', flagship of the News Ltd group. As the league season was adjusted so it finished before the Olympics started on September 15,

2000, Stuart did not get to cover the Olympics. He was offered two sports – wheelchair rugby and power lifting – at the Paralympics.

"Not at all," Honeysett said when asked if he felt like he'd been given second prize.

"I was looking forward to it because I was given wheelchair rugby and it was a contact sport and the Australian team had a good world ranking. So I thought it would be good to watch a team on the rise as well as being a medal chance.

"I obviously don't watch a lot of Paralympic sport but I had a feeling before it all began that I'd enjoying watching it. They got good crowds because it had that degree of contact about it that was probably rare in the Paralympics, apart from wheelchair basketball.

"I wasn't surprised by the crowds because it was good, physical sport. I thought they dressed it up really well – it's a good spectator sport."

The power lifting did not get as much coverage in his newspaper as Australians were not among the top-ranked lifters. But again the 'surprise' factor in how good the sport is to watch, kicks in.

"These athletes were people who basically had no use of their lower body and were able to lift incredibly heavy weights with just their chest, shoulders and arms. It was amazing to watch what some of them could lift, especially when they get towards world record weights," Honeysett said.

If asked to cover a Paralympics again, would they do it?

Honeysett: "I wouldn't have a problem with it. I'd love to do the wheelchair rugby again – without hesitation."

Evans: "Absolutely... it's a big sporting event."

Gerry O'Leary was a TV producer with the ABC, which held the Australian domestic rights for the Atlanta Paralympics, although Gerry was not in Atlanta. At the Sydney 2000 Paralympic Games, Gerry was SPOC's (Sydney Paralympic Organising Committee) Broadcast Media Manager, looking after rights holders and non-rights holders from television and radio and the host broadcaster crew. At the 2004 Athens Paralympics, Gerry was asked by the IPC to help co-ordinate the production of the daily highlights package, which all TV rights holders receive as part of their rights fee.

The experience she gained from the Sydney Paralympics, about which sports gave some of the best pictures for TV and where to place cameras at these sports to get the best pictures, she put into use at Athens.

"The reason I was brought over there (to Greece) was because these people hadn't worked in Paralympic sport before – they hadn't seen it; hadn't done it. You had top TV production people but they had no idea of how big the event was, the scale of the event," O'Leary said.

"Then they saw these athletes doing what they do and they were just blown away. Because they had just done the Olympics it was a real hard slog but not much planning had been done from a host broadcast point of view about the Paralympics.

"In Sydney, we had a fresh crew come in.

"But in Athens they were still as impressed with the athletes – same as the crews in Sydney. The people, who worked on the Paralympic Games in 2004, loved it. They just had no idea how big an event it was.''

The disadvantage in Sydney was that while SOBO – Sydney Olympic Broadcasting Organisation – has been set up to be the Host Broadcaster and provide the pictures and graphics material that each TV rights holder could then pick and choose or 'package', for their respective audiences, SPOC had to find a host broadcaster from scratch. This leads us into the next section to be discussed.

MEDIA SERVICES PROVIDED AT A PARALYMPIC GAMES

The company Global Television, which is contracted by the major commercial TV stations – Nine, Seven and Ten – to do the majority of their outside broadcasting for events like NRL (National Rugby League) and AFL (Australian Football League), the Melbourne Cup etc, became SPOC's host broadcaster providing television pictures for the rights holders, who then add their own flavour and colour and commentators and package it for their audiences. The host broadcaster did not come on line until late 1999 – less than 12 months before the Games Opening Ceremony on October 18, 2000. The IPC learnt from the experience and the company ISB (International Sports Broadcasting) which was the host broadcaster for the 2002 Salt Lake City Winter Olympics and 2004 Athens Summer Olympics was also made the host broadcaster for the 2002 Paralympics and 2004 Paralympics. This gives a smooth transition from Games to Games and it gives rights holders coming in for the Paralympics – who may not have been rights holders at the Olympics – the confidence that service to be provided will be of a high standard. At the time of writing, ISB had been appointed the Paralympics host broadcaster for the 2006 Turin Winter Games. The same expertise will begin moving from Games to Games even though the crews in each country might change due to language and technical requirements.

The first Paralympic Games to have a host broadcaster was the 1996 Atlanta Summer Games. But it was a combined effort of two broadcasters, the cable TV station 'Sports South' and one of the main national commercial networks, CBS. And it was only very limited coverage for audiences – highlights shown over two weekends in the USA.

Only three sports – athletics, swimming and basketball – had multi-camera coverage. Single camera coverage was for the remaining 15 sports, which did not provide good action TV footage because of the very limited angles shots could be taken from. Sydney had multi-camera for all 18 sports and covered every medal event – all 580 of them. Athens and beyond will have the same multi-camera feeds and as each Games comes, the sophistication of graphics presentation and highlights packages production grows. The print media – newspapers, magazines, websites – had very limited material to work from at the Atlanta Paralympics. There were no flash quotes from athletes to help those newspapers on deadline – just the very basic official results sheets, daily competition schedule, but no historical background or records for each sport or country, no information on the sports or previous Games.

Stephen Dettre, after covering three Olympics and one Paralympics as a reporter, joined SOCOG (Sydney Organising Committee for the Olympic Games) to set up and run the Olympic News Services (ONS) and Paralympic News Service (PNS) in conjunction with SOCOG's technical service and results providers.

This was a vital link in the communication of stories and information for all forms of media. It provided flash quotes from athletes immediately after an event for those news organisations on deadline – deadlines varied greatly with reporters from all over the globe in a multitude of time zones. It also provided short and sharp Event Previews (telling you which athletes or events were on the next day including if defending Olympic champions or current world record holders were in action) and Event Reviews (looking back at the event or sport once it had finished for that day telling you how the favourites fared and any significant news that happened apart from the obvious, the three medal winners).

The ONS and PNS also provided historical information from previous Games about each sport, previous medal winners, a country's medal tally, multi-medal athletes etc.

Due to the smaller budget and different technical support at the Sydney Paralympics, the PNS was not as extensive or detailed as the ONS.

> "There was never a question that we wouldn't do it, provide a PNS for the first time. It was just at what level. We wanted a good service but budget kicked in and we couldn't do this or that and then we found the computer system could not deliver all we wanted."

The Spanish company MSL was sub-contracted by IBM to do the Sydney Paralympics. It was a different company for the Olympics, who had a bigger budget and more historical data and information at their fingertips. The IPC had only formed in 1989 and the keeping of historical records had fallen into disarray for some sports.

But the PNS' debut in Sydney meant a much better service than journalists had ever received before at a Paralympics.

> "Everyone got what they wanted in terms of news items, event previews and reviews, quotes, athlete biographies, results and some historical information but still would have liked to have done more. The Olympic system had more," Dettre said.

The journalists covering the Paralympics in Sydney for the first time – which was the vast majority – did not notice too much difference between the ONS and PNS.

They knew the Paralympics was "a newer" Games, still experiencing some teething problems in terms of services to the media, but they expected something similar to the information they received at the Olympics and they got it.

"Because it comes off the back of the Olympics, it's already set up, well-oiled and is brilliant," Evans said of the PNS and of the other services provided to media in terms of transport, accommodation etc etc. Again SOCOG and SPOC combined to ensure the same venue managers stayed on for each Games, the same competition managers, the same transport system provided by the government-run ORTA (Olympic Roads and Transport Authority), and the other seamless delivery of services in between games by the OCA (Olympic Co-ordination Authority).

"Any problems they had in the first couple of days at the Olympics were non existent in the first couple of days of the Paralympics - they'd been ironed out,'" Evans said.

Thus, once the 2002 Salt Lake City Games and 2004 Athens Games came around, there was the expectation – and the necessity – that the PNS would continue.

"Once you've let the genie out of the bottle, you can't get it back in. So every Games has got to at least match what was delivered before – journalists would just expect it. You can't go backwards."

Which brings us to the final section.

WHERE TO FROM HERE IN TERMS OF MEDIA SERVICES

Delivering the Paralympic Games to the public is best done by media exposure. And the greatest way to get your message out is by mass media – television, radio and newspapers – which the vast majority of the public, no matter what language they speak, consume daily.

The Atlanta Olympics and Paralympics showed that you can have magnificent venues, marvellous athletes, competition and results, but unless you "look after" the media, the Games will not be successful. Basic media services like transport, accommodation, fast and accurate results service, proper press tribunes – the media working benches at venues – were not provided, were slow or were useless. Reporters began writing stories slamming the organisation of the Games and the mud stuck. The public might think the press if pampered, but at an Olympics or Paralympics, you can never do too much pampering. Photographers, cameramen and reporters have "an instant" to get the picture, receive and process the result, speak to an athlete, file the story. If you make their job easier in doing all that, they will keep coming back to report on your Games.

Television and radio reach the largest audiences. From less than 20 television or radio networks who were at the Atlanta Paralympic Games in 1996, the number grew to 35 broadcast rights holders at the Sydney Paralympic Games in 2000 and a new record of 50 broadcaster rights holders at the Athens Paralympic Games in 2004. The list of countries which signed up to screen the Paralympics via their broadcasters buying the rights even before the Games began was impressive in 2004: Austria, Australia, Belarus, Belgium, Brazil, Canada, China, Czech Republic, Denmark, Egypt, Finland, France, Germany, Greece, Hungary, Ireland, Israel, Italy, Iran, Japan, Korea, Mexico, New Zealand, the Netherlands, Norway, Russia, Slovakia, Spain, Sweden, Switzerland, Tunisia, Pakistan, Portugal, South Africa, Urakine, United Kingdom, the pan-European broadcaster 'Eurosport' with a footprint right across Europe even if countries had no rightsholder. As the Games came on line, Bulgaria, Colombia, Iceland, India, Turkey, the United States and Venezuela took up rights.

The IPC, via the host broadcaster secured by each host organising committee, must continue to strive to keep the list of broadcasters growing; to make sure previous broadcasters are signed up again for the next Games.

TV rights generate revenue for a host organising committee and the IPC but the Games must be careful not to price itself out of the market and continue to deliver value for the dollars asked for to secure broadcast rights. As the list of NPCs (National Paralympic Committees) competing at a Games grows each four years, so too should the broadcasters and written press from those countries be encouraged to come.

The growth of the Summer Games is below:
1992 Barcelona Paralympic Games – 83 countries

1996 Atlanta Paralympic Games – 103 countries

2000 Sydney Paralympic Games – 121 countries

2004 Athens Paralympic Games – 136 countries

As each Games brings a continued level of service for the media, it will be easier to convince them to come back in four years time. But in the intervening four years, there needs to be information provided regularly on the IPC and Host City websites in the main followed up by each individual NPC. Here journalists can track how their national team in each Paralympic sport is doing in the years between Games where usually a national titles is held annually, a world championships is held and other major competitions and tournaments. This lack of information on the movement of athletes, and the progress of a Host City in preparing for the next Paralympics was a constant them in interviews with journalists.

Stuart Honeysett: "I suppose one of the sad things is it was an event for two weeks and then disappeared off the face of the planet. I haven't heard anything about how the guys are going, whether they're all still together as a team, what they've been doing at tournaments."

Stephen Dettre continues this theme of while journalists chase progress stories on athletes, host cities must keep progressing the level and standard of their PNS.

"The future is what Athens did where the Olympic system and the Paralympic system were one in the same – they just dumped in new content into the system, new branding, sports logos, so the look was a bit different," he said.

"Eventually, the two should be running in conjunction with each other so you just select which one you want to look at. That would make more sense."

ATOS was the technology provider for the 2004 Olympics and Paralympics. They had an involvement in the 2002 Salt Lake City Paralympics, but Athens was their first Summer Games – ATOS will be in Turin, now the worldwide partner with results service provider, IBM.

"The advantage they've got is a lot of people from Salt Lake and Sydney who've got Olympic and Paralympic experience. They're not stupid – they went and hired some really good people who understand what is needed and what should be improved on," Dettre said.

This expertise and technology has helped make Paralympics a serious, respected and viable international sporting event.

"But the challenge is that there are many multi-sport events, that the Paralympics are endangered of being over-run not so much by the Olympics but by things like the Pan American Games, the Asian Games, Pan Arab Games," Dettre said.

"And 10 or 15 years ago single sport events like the world athletics and world swimming championships were not as big as they are now. They have become huge events in their own right. So suddenly there's a massive amount of events out there that are all trying to attract media attention.

"The one thing the Paralympics has if that is the premium and only recognisable event for disabled sportsmen and women so that is what will help keep its allure.

"So if they want to be in that pantheon of stars, then they've got to provide good quality facilities and services for media to ensure they still get coverage."

The reality is that at each Paralympics, media organisations will send a smaller team than for the Olympics – in some cases just one reporter where they might have had a team or 10 to 15 for the Olympics.

"This means the organising committee has even more responsibility to help the media cover the event by providing lots of good and useful information and background that is easy to access and easy to understand," Dettre said.

"You just can't say 'here are the results, go for it'. That's not enough any more. You've got to provide summaries of what happened and point people to the best stories".

"Journalists don't want pre-written stories by someone else. They just need quality information and results so they can pull out what is most interesting to them and their audiences and do their own pieces."

PERSONAL FOOTNOTE FROM THE AUTHOR – MARGIE MCDONALD

As a sports reporter, I covered the 1992 and 1996 Olympic Games, the 1982, 1986 and 2002 Commonwealth Games. At the 2000 Sydney Olympics I worked for SOCOG in the ONS and during the 2000 Sydney Paralympics I worked with the PNS. I was also a media officer helping journalists with their stories and athlete information at the 1998 Nagano, 2002 Salt Lake City Winter Paralympics and at the 2004 Athens Paralympics. The most pleasing aspect of being from both sides of the fence – firstly as a reporter at a Games and then secondly as someone to help reporters at a Games – is the way journalists come to look past any pre-conceived ideas and straight at the athletes and the sport. They approached it the same as the Olympics and by doing that, they gave the greatest respect to the Paralympians. Journalists want to tell the athletes stories, why they succeeded, why they failed. Through the words and pictures spun around the world, it gives Paralympic sport and Paralympic athlete's recognition – not patronisation or tokenism. But because they want to be judged as elite athletes, the harshest critics in the world – the media – will be there to do just that. Giving journalists the best environment and platform to do their jobs, is the best way to keep the Paralympics Games – both Winter and Summer – up there with Olympics. As I constantly repeated the IPC message to the media coming to the Sydney 2000 Paralympics, "these will be the parallel Games to the Olympics". Reporters would ask me why I worked for SPOC and the Paralympics and not SOCOG and the Olympics – the bigger, fancier sister in the Sydney 2000 family.

"Because it's like working for the Northern Ireland Tourism Board," I would tell them. "Everyone wants to go to Ireland; they are scared of Northern Ireland because they don't know what's gone on there. But Northern Ireland has the same countryside, same people, same pubs, same music but you will STILL notice some differences – my job is to get you to come and see for yourself."

They came, they loved it, they will come back for more.

7   INNOVATIVE MARKETING FOR THE PARALYMPICS

Barbara J. Emener

"When I saw Marlon Shirley on a McDonald's cup with Vancouver and Paris marketing the Games as a 60 day event, I knew corporate marketers were finally paying attention to the value of the Paralympic marks."

Barbara Emener, August 2004

"Some of the best advice I received while writing this chapter came from Charlie Huebner, current Chief of Staff with the US Olympic Committee, former CEO of the U.S. Paralympics and former Executive Director of the US Association of Blind Athletes. After explaining the premise of this chapter and a lengthy discussion about the past, present and future of Paralympic Marketing, he broke it down so simply. "Use the term Paralympic instead of the word disabled," he said understatedly. "If you avoid using the word Paralympic, no one will know what it is."

Barbara Emener, June 2006

INTRODUCTION

Paralympic. Paraplegia. Stargardt's Disease. Tetraplegia. T4, B2 or S10 Classification. Arthrogryposis. Below the knee amputee. These are not typical terms that appear on the desks of corporate sports marketers every day. Marla Runyon, Tony Volpentest, Tricia Zorn, Cheri Blauwet, Chris Waddell, John Register, Scot Hollonbeck. These are not typical names of elite athletes that appear on the desks of corporate sports marketers every day. Boccia, Powerlifting, Quad Rugby, Sledge Hockey, Sitting Volleyball. These are not typical types of elite sports that appear on the desks of corporate sports marketers every day. Yet each is highly relevant and extremely important for the corporate sponsors of the Paralympic Games.

Steadily, since the beginning of the Paralympic Movement, corporate and individual support has continued to grow, and in particular, funding has nearly tripled for United States Paralympians since 2001. This is perhaps due in part to the 54 million Americans classified with some type of disability with $1.2 trillion in total income.[1]

In turn, sports marketing executives engaged in sponsoring the Games are leveraging the Paralympic 'marks' and athletes in more traditional ways, much like that of the Olympic counterparts with integrated advertising, cross promotions and local activation. If VISA, McDonald's, The Home Depot or any other sponsor for that matter, spends millions of dollars and put internal resources behind Paralympic sponsorship, the marketing executives are held to a return on the investment. There are tremendous differences between the Paralympics and their Olympic counterparts and this chapter is not meant to dissect or analyze the differences. However, what follows is intended to create a better understanding of the 'Marketing of the Paralympic Games' to consumers, and in particular the fundamentals of building successful programs, a review of some previous success stories and a discussion on what the future may hold.

At what point does a CMO (Chief Marketing Officer) find the Paralympics an appealing platform for sponsor activation either globally or locally? The successful ones will identify the opportunities to utilize the Paralympic marks, the athletes, images, etc. of the Games to increase awareness and they will do it well enough to find a solid return on their investment. For example, a sports marketing executive of a nutritional supplement or a healthy consumer package good should be salivating when U.S. bilateral amputee Grady "Matt" Aldridge creates a new national record for 445 lbs in Powerlifting. Inherently, this scenario provides a unique visual, the undeniable human element and built-in "wow factor" ready to be capitalized upon.

Corporate sponsors need to stretch their consumer marketing ideas and minds and develop strategic visions to new heights. In the United States, The Home Depot has done this well with their US Paralympic Team sponsorship. A natural fit for sponsorship and corporate support of elite athletes, The Home Depot's corporate ideals of "perseverance, hard work and a commitment to excellence" are the same and equate intrinsically to the success of top level athletes[2]. Former GE executive and as I write current President and CEO for The Home Depot, Robert L. Nardelli explains:

> "Stretch means to really challenging yourself and believing there is an infinite capacity to improve upon everything you do. Once you get through the denial period, then you embrace stretch as something you want to do, not as something management tells you to do. It is far better to challenge yourself and then experience the satisfaction of winning, than to be driven to the same point anyway. With this mindset, the term stretch becomes secondary to the way you run business. You expect to get top-line growth regardless of the industry environment because it's ingrained in your attitude."[3]

It is precisely that vision which proves The Home Depot was fully engaged to maximize its sponsorship of the Paralympic teams. To promote the 2002 Winter Paralympic Games in Salt Lake City, the Home Depot showcased Paralympic athlete, Monte Meier, in a television spot promoting the Games and its participation in the OJOP program (Olympic Job Opportunities Program). They supported this with a comprehensive print campaign and Public Relations plan, with every employee's Home Depot apron adorned with an acknowledgement of the sponsorship. The Home Depot recently renewed its sponsorship of the U.S. Olympic and Paralympic Teams.

FUNDAMENTAL RESOURCES

A fundamental component for a successful marketing program is overriding financial and resource support. For example in 2000, the IOC and the IPC signed a Treaty stating "the IOC and the IPC share equal faith in the right of all human beings to achieve their physical and intellectual progress.[4]" Critical to the success of the Paralympics in terms of this agreement are IOC and IPC co-existing responsibilities for marketing, media, licensing and sponsorship. At the worldwide level, the marketing of the Paralympic Games relies somewhat on the financial structure set forth by the IOC and IPC. Even more critical to the success of the Paralympic Games is the relationship between and among the IPC, IOC, National Paralympic Committees and Local Organizing Committees in order for the marketing plans to be developed, supported and implemented through smart, consistent strategies. The slightest disconnection – in any part of the marketing communication chain – will yield less than optimum marketing results. The Beijing Organizing Committee for the Olympic Games (BOCOG) officially released the Beijing 2008 Sponsor Program components, engaging activation opportunities in non-Paralympic years and further proving that enhancing brand awareness occurs for years before and after the Games officially occurred. At the highest level, BOCOG executives have set forth plans in alignment with the IOC and the IPC which ensure sponsors are "rewarded with significant investment returns," inclusive of both worldwide, national and local Olympic and Paralympic Games sponsors. If we assume the previous statement to be true then how does a successful marketing strategy work for individual Paralympic Committees and the IPC?

SITUATION ANALYSIS

There are important points to consider here. For example, the USOC does more for Paralympic athletes "than any other nation"[5] having increased funding for the Paralympic programs from previous quadrennial budgets: $7.7 million (1997-2000), $18.3 million (2001-2004) with a $23 million projected budget for 2005-2008[6]. Current U.S. Paralympic sponsors include VISA, The Home Depot, Adidas, Roots, Oroweat, Bank of America, Gateway, All State, McDonald's, Chevron Texaco, Jet Set Sports, Herman Miller, The Hartford and Freightliner Sprinter vans[7]. As with all sports programs, the financial resources are split between many U.S. Paralympic business units such as athlete and coaching development, research and sports science, competition, equipment and travel, overhead and administration and, of course, marketing.

ESTABLISHMENT OF GOALS AND OBJECTIVES

Like any sports marketing program, goals and objectives must be clearly defined, measurable and scalable. Indeed, what are the objectives of the Paralympic Games marketing strategies in its current state? Are they to increase general awareness? To increase Games attendance figures? To increase TV viewership? To increase media coverage? To attract new athletes or coaches? To increase support and raise new funds? Or all of the above? In other words, do the goals and objectives change when the Games are in your own country? With major international sports leagues – with known global coverage like and Olympics, Super Bowl or World Cup Soccer – a primary goal of the marketing platform is tune-in, or television viewership. For the Paralympic Games, very few countries have the opportunity to watch the events on television, much less watch live coverage. A tune-in call to action would not be a relevant message point in the marketing communications, whereas perhaps driving consumers to a central web site for more information would be relevant. In the United States, the 1996 Paralympic Summer Games in Atlanta had very little media coverage. Four years later, we were fortunate enough to have increased coverage of the

Paralympic Summer and Winter Games from Sydney (2000), Salt Lake City (2002) and Athens (2004), including a live-to-tape two-hour highlight titled U.S. Paralympics Show, presented by VISA, which aired well after the Games concluded (November 2004) on the Outdoor Life Network, an NBC cable affiliate. Perhaps the best plan is to develop consistent messaging throughout the marketing opportunities and institute an aggressive overlay of Public Relations to maximize audience penetration and reach.

IDENTIFY THE TARGET AUDIENCE

One primary focus for Paralympic marketers is the defining of the target audience. Comparatively, the Paralympic Games are still in their infancy and, marketing should build baseline awareness for its audiences. Defining the target audience for each marketing strategy – globally, nationally or locally – is paramount. The hard-core Paralympic Games fan is the primary audience. This category includes Paralympians, their families, coaches, media, volunteers or industry members. Another target audience is the Olympic fan, consumers who already have an affinity for world-class elite athletics and the Olympic Games, and who may have already heard of the Paralympic Games. Attracting the attention of casual sports fans is important, yet a tertiary target audience. Lastly, capturing new fans is another opportunity, but further down on the list than the other consumer groups.

DEVELOP SCALABLE PLANS

Consistency in the marketing and communications of the Paralympic Games is important for many reasons, more especially for the development of scalable plans and programs. One critical component to market the Paralympics on a global level as well as a grass roots level, is to understand the big marketing picture for opportunities first, then apply the strategy to the local level on a smaller scale. There is one critical acronym on every marketer's mind and possibly the most important component to every integrated marketing campaign: OPM (Other People's Money).

For example, VISA holds an exclusive partnership deal directly with the IPC ("the official payment services for the Games") and a sponsorship with the U.S. Paralympic Team. Obviously, VISA place high importance for this sponsorship on activating as many credit card transactions as possible through merchants and consumers, and new card holder activation (albeit business or individual consumer card holder). On the global level, VISA is the payment service for tickets and merchandise, with logo and tag on all advertising, in ticket marketing communications, at venues, etc., which allows for incredible ways to activate at both the business-to-business and business-to-consumer levels. The Paralympic Games represents approximately 161 participating countries and VISA is accepted at more than 22 million places worldwide and in approximately 150 countries. The Paralympic Games – the awareness for the name and marks – reaped tremendous benefit by capitalizing on the VISA sponsorship through the immediate and natural penetration in these 150 countries. Following the 2000 Sydney Olympic Games, VISA enjoyed an unprecedented 72 percent unaided consumer awareness of its sponsorship, and consistently rated the highest or among the highest awareness of any Olympic sponsor[8].

RELEVANCE

The greatest strategy for Paralympic marketers today is to create meaningful, relevant marketing programs. As shown earlier with the 2004 Paralympic Games highlight program on OLN (Outdoor Life Network) presented by VISA, the timing of the program (6 weeks after the Games concluded) was every bit of a challenge for the marketing executives because the content was not timely or relevant, and yielded only a low rating[9]. If we are targeting the hard core Paralympic fan, the Olympic fan and the casual sports fan, with a small goal of attracting new fans, without major marketing support, the program is just not relevant anymore for our core audience. What is relevant for most of the target consumer groups, for example, in November 2004 was catching up on the professional and college football seasons, the end of the NASCAR season and the beginning of professional and college basketball season. Instead, another thought might be that OLN break down the two hour special broadcast into four 30-minute shows, all presented by VISA. Supported by an aggressive public relations campaign to drive awareness and tune-in for the Paralympic Games, two of the segments would air prior to the beginning of the Games. To build upon the Games momentum, one segment would air in the middle of the Games, with highlights of the Opening Ceremony, recent medal ceremonies, competitions, athlete interviews and a preview of upcoming competitions and Closing Ceremony. Closely following the Games, the fourth and final segment would run with second half highlights and a snapshot of the upcoming 2006 Paralympic Winter Games. With increased frequency and greater relevancy, the exposure for VISA and the U.S. Paralympics may have yielded larger results.

PLANNING AND MEDIA

The IPC currently does have a worldwide broadcasting rights partner for the Paralympic Games and in 2004, the United States was one of the largest countries at the 2004 Paralympic Summer Games in Athens 'WITHOUT' a national broadcast partner to provide daily coverage. For marketers, guaranteed (licensed or Value in Kind) media inventory at minimum provides a starting point for developing an overall marketing plan. One benefit of solidifying media partners on a worldwide or local level (broadcast, print, radio, outdoor) provides a concrete way to contractually bind sponsors to purchase a particular media allocation. Another benefit is to construct a media plan (with your partners) that reflects a "media recency" theory, providing constant, relevant exposure over long periods of time versus media advertising and coverage that spikes quickly for short periods of time and then disappears. As the sanctioning national governing body, you have influence on messaging, branding and placement. Sponsors may recognize that in order to truly maximize their exposure in terms of the Paralympic Games marks and association, strategic media buys (and local converted buys) in and out of Games periods will increase awareness and market penetration. Many sponsors will take advantage of the U.S. Paralympic '501c3 non-profit status' with pass through savings on advertising placements, production costs or media commissions.

Referencing the OLN Paralympic Show once again, VISA may have had an opportunity to convert national and local media over four flight periods (promoting all four shows) versus one flight (the one, two hour special which aired.) To hit upon our earlier point of relevance and scalability, the national spots for VISA could have had the opportunity to provide local "tags" to accommodate local merchant special offers or promotional opportunities. Additionally, each of the spots across the four flights may have had an opportunity to reflect various brand image campaigns and pay off certain marketing functions. To showcase different athletes in each spot would have increased awareness for the numerous disciplines in the Paralympics (athletes from each DSO to be showcased – wheelchair, amputee, cerebral palsy, dwarf and blind.) To tailor calls to action in each spot would have allowed the organizations to pay-off various measurements, meaning each spot would have the overriding tune-in message about the 30 minute special and possibly a limited edition licensed product to raise revenues, but other messages could have been intertwined: flight one encourages "getting involved and support the team" (translation: donate or support the sponsors who support the team); flights two and three during the games showcase a message for consumers to follow the team on usparalympicteam.com during the Games (translation: we want to measure web site hits); and flight four highlights the holiday merchandise as well as the upcoming 2006 Paralympic Winter Games athletes (translation: buy some holiday gear and here's a plug for the upcoming OLN shows.) Unfortunately, OLN only signed a broadcast agreement with the U.S. Paralympics to air one, nationwide two-hour highlight show in November 2004.

Under the Ted Stevens Olympic and Amateur Sports Act, the USOC must authorize any marketing and television rights for the Paralympic Games in the United States[10]. In stark contrast for the United States, the 2002 Paralympic Winter Games had daily highlight coverage (more than 16 hours in total) which was hosted by Harry Smith and Joan Lunden on the A&E Network, produced by Bud Sports Productions, a division of Anheuser-Busch, Inc. This historical television partnership was negotiated with the help of U.S. Paralympics, a division of the United States Olympic Committee, the USOC's Entertainment Properties Division and the Copley Entertainment Group.

In the 2000 Paralympic Summer Games in Sydney, Australia reflected daily live highlight updates on PAX-TV with daily live event coverage via Web Casts on wemedia.com, a first in Paralympic Games history.

PUBLIC RELATIONS

Paralympic marketers rely heavily on public relations in order for the marketing programs to be successful. With sights set to capture the widest, most positive, accurate and informative local, national and international media coverage prior to and during the Games, most Public Relations professionals will tell you there are a few mandatory rules to follow when introducing new coverage opportunities. First, provide relevant, meaningful content. We should not expect national coverage with major features every time story is pitched or footage is placed in a VNR or on the weekly feed. While national coverage is always optimal, tailored regional or local pitches can yield just as positive of results. For a local network affiliate or O&O who has yet to run Paralympic stories, a local piece will lay the foundation for future editorial opportunities. Second, make it easy to cover, by providing turn-key communication pieces and images that are easy to customize. Third, separate the coverage opportunities into subject categories, such as results by individual or sport, corporate news, lifestyle segments, regional competitions or trials, current marketing programs or promotional coverage, or any other niche segment category.

PLAN AHEAD

As with the Olympic counterparts, the inherent challenge (or opportunity) is identifying and securing editorial and programming coverage during non-Games years. Developing strategic public relations plans years in advance that overlay the marketing programs of both the media partners, sanctioning body, sports organizations, athlete representatives, and sponsors will increase year-round coverage for two main reasons. First, over time, the journalists will gain a greater respect for the "big picture" while being pitched relevant stories. Importantly, the journalist will not feel unreasonably held to an expectation of running full-page, above the fold stories or airing long segments every time. Second, the editorial opportunities will arrive on the assignment desks from more than one source. Lets imagine that in the course of a year, a journalist will entertain editorial pitches on a variety of Paralympic stories from the sanctioning body, a DSO, a sponsor or the athlete public relations representative. In all, it is a positive step in the right direction that the "asks" come from varied sources and the end result – and hopefully a result of increased exposure – benefits the Paralympic brand and reflects its core communications messages every time. For example, The Home Depot leveraged an existing relationship with a show of its supports on The Learning Channel (TLC) to create a new public relations angle for its Olympic and Paralympic sponsorship during a non-games year. Partnering with the Lakeshore Foundation, The Home Depot chose to renovate and upgrade the athlete housing at Lakeshore's USOC Olympic and Paralympic Training Site. Home Depot associates from the 10 stores in the greater Birmingham district donated over 1,300 hours of labor and more than $30,000 to the "While You Were Working Out" project, a benefit for the company as the foundation is a non-profit[11]. The amount of public relations exposure garnered by this episode for The Home Depot and the U.S. Olympic and Paralympic teams was invaluable, especially during a non-games year.

BRAND IDENTITY

Establishing clear, consistent messages across all communication channels is an important key to a successful marketing strategic plan. For example, the U.S. Paralympic mission statement is as follows: "To be the world leader in the Paralympic movement and to promote excellence in the lives of persons with physical disabilities.[12]" However, for the scalable, macro view of Paralympic Games, the brand messaging for each NPC should reflect the overall brand messaging by the IPC, the LOCs and OCOGs. Each U.S. Paralympic marketing component will reflect the mission statement, as will the sponsors, teams and athletes' marketing efforts and with this clear consistent content and messaging, there leave no room for error or misinterpretation.

On February 4th 2003, the communications campaign phase for the Athens 2004 Volunteer Program began with a television advertising spot entitled "Remember". Through a series of images of expectation, enthusiasm and joy there is a "back to the future" type of review of the announcement with the basic feelings of the Games: joy, celebration, pride and willingness to pursue a collective effort. The message that is conveyed through the television spot is that the Olympic and Paralympic Games have the image and soul of the volunteers who help in the staging of the Games and that consequently the 2004 Games, which will promote the human dimension, will be unique "because they will reflect our own image". The slogan of the promotion campaign "we will all be there", reminds us how valuable the participation at the Athens 2004 Olympic and Paralympic Games is for all[13]. Reflecting an 18-month lead time, the Athens 2004 Olympic and Paralympic Games organizers set the tone and temperament of the brand messaging that NPC, sponsors and athletes should follow for all marketing communications in reference of the Games.

The good news is that as Paralympic Games marks and licensing programs are now launched well in advance (five to six years) in advance of the Games (BOCOG announced the marks, licensing guidelines and sponsor program for the 2008 Summer Olympic and Paralympic Games five years in advance). With the trend of bundling Olympic and Paralympic sponsorships renewal agreements into multi year sponsorship deals, encourages advance planning. With aggressive planning and long lead times (as with any project – not just marketing), the opportunity for greater results increases. Such is the case with an example of U.S. Olympic and Paralympic Sponsor, Hilton Hotels, signed in January 2005 and will continue its sponsorship through 2008. The contract with the United States Olympic Committee (USOC) entitles the Hilton Family of Hotels Hilton, Conrad, Doubletree, Embassy Suites Hotels, Hampton Hotels, Hilton Garden Inn, Hilton Grand Vacations Club and Homewood Suites by Hilton — to use the official hotel sponsor designation, and the U.S. Olympic Team and U.S. Paralympic Team logos in all advertising and marketing materials[14]. Coupled with a strategic media plan, leveraged media, local activation, and great creative (imagine athletes getting good nights rest during training), this partnership is poised to increase brand association and awareness and hopefully, for Hilton Hotels, a way to generate additional 'bed night' revenues.

PARTNERSHIP AND CONSUMER MARKETING

The word relevance has popped up many times in this chapter, and in this section it could not be a more important word. At every customer touch point – from leveraged media, advertising, and public relations, to branding, licensing and promotions – relevant imagery and messaging will allow the consumer to recognize the Paralympic Games mark with greater understanding and open the mind for consideration, resulting in an overall increase in market penetration.

As an industry, awareness traditionally drives awareness through its core subjects, the athletes or teams. Similar to the world of NASCAR (a driver driven sport), sports fans typically follow and support individual athletes or teams. To tap into the minds of consumers to promote ideas, products or marketing initiatives, a smart tactic is the use of creative talent and relevant images (athletes) in advertising and marketing campaigns (broadcast, print, radio, outdoor, online, etc.) and public relations campaigns (brand ambassadors and spokespersons). As the years progress, corporate sponsors increase the use of athletes in campaigns more and more. Recent years proved successful for

McDonald's, who used the Paralympic Games mark and track and field athlete Marlon Shirley on the beverage cups, and The Home Depot, who uses the Olympic and Paralympic marks on staff aprons year round and also showcased Monte Meier in their Paralympic advertising campaign.

The first step in creating the programs is to understand the value of the Paralympic "marks." Clearly, one of the newest US Olympic Committee sponsors, Nike[15], probably understands the value of the marks more than any other sponsors at this time. At the grass roots level, Nike, could be poised to raise the bar for Paralympic sports marketers. Historically, Nike's grass roots efforts have been seen as a driving force in building awareness for their brands, creating the demand among consumers one community at a time. Marketing at the grass roots level is critical to the overall groundswell for the Paralympic movement and Nike will no doubt take full advantage of the marks, imagery and joint marketing to increase awareness for its own brands as well as the Paralympic brand.

As the sanctioning and governing body, the U.S. Paralympics has a fiduciary responsibility to provide partnership marketing guidance and sales integration support for the corporate sponsors. Leveraging resources bilaterally and partnering on marketing programs increases the opportunity for success.

MEASUREMENT AND RESULTS

Before compiling or analyzing results, I typically try to regain my focus on the objectives and goals set forth from the beginning of the project, reviewing the same questions asked at the beginning. Was the objective to increase awareness and media coverage? Increase participation? Increase Games attendance? Increase viewership? Increase corporate and individual support? Over the years, I found tremendous benefit from utilizing outside resources and support (agencies, consultants, researchers) for planning, executing and analyzing marketing programs. One important note and piece of advice for marketers is to perform ongoing "audits" of the marketing programs. You may realize that you need outside resources to gain an objective opinion to determine how a program is working. Marketers must also keep in mind that it is all right to change directions mid-stream. If you have done the homework, analyzed the mid-project results and need to modify the program, and then do so. A former client gave me great advice that still stays with me today. "It is perfectly fine to give recommendations or make decisions, but be sure they are backed up with facts." Marketing relies on numbers as a point of reference for planning, through execution, and ending with drawing meaningful conclusions. Marketing creates numbers – ratings, sales, fans, attendance, etc. It is our job to understand, and know intimately, the numbers:

LOOKING TOWARDS TOMORROW

Set higher goals. Know the numbers, it's what we live and die by as marketers. Forecast and plan ahead. Identify new marketing partners. Spend wisely and remember, it's not how much you spend, it's where you spend it and with whom you spend it. Conduct annual marketing summits and planning strategy sessions. Monitor your competition and understand what your competition does at every marketing level. Build the brand from within – ask yourself, is every employee of each U.S. Paralympic sponsor aware of the Paralympics or a fan? On a final note have fun and do fewer things really, really, well.

REFERENCES

1   United States Census, (2000).

2   Solutions Marketing Group, (2005),
     www.disability-marketing.com/profiles/homedepot.

3   Slater, R. (1999) Jack Welch and the GE Way, Management Insights and Leadership Secrets of the Legendary CEO, The McGraw-Hill Companies.

4   IOC/IPC Treaty, January 15, (2000).

5   Seibel, D., USOC Spokesperson, CBS News Interview (2003).

6   US Olympic Committee/US Paralympics (2005).

7   US Olympic Committee/US Paralympics, (2005).

8   VISA (November 31, 2001), www.visa.com.

9   Outdoor Life Network, (2004), www.olntv.com

10   US Olympic Committee/US Paralympics (2005).

11   The Home Depot (2005), www.homedepot.com.

12   US Olympic Committee/US Paralympics (2005).

13   International Paralympic Committee (2002), Advertising Spot Launched,
     www.paralympic.org.

14   Hilton Hotels (2005), Hilton Hotels Corporation Announces Sponsorship of U.S. Olympic Team Through 2008: Hilton Family Named Official Hotel Sponsor.

15   US Olympic Committee/US Paralympics (2005).

SECTION 2

INSIDE THE PARALYMPICS

This section takes a closer look at the some of the important aspects which are in constant flux within the Games structures. These include the often contentious area of classification and the meaning of classification in the Games context as it stacks up for athletes and administrators alike. It also takes a reflective look at the divide between administrators and coaching staff and the benefits of utilising sports science information to develop better athlete awareness and to support the coaching process. This chapter is followed by a further reflective piece into the world of intellectual disability as viewed by a leading basketball coach and also breaks new ground by viewing aspects of the Otto Bock operations at the Games and the increasing interest being shown to the disabled riders groups.

8   CLASSIFICATION AND THE GAMES

Jane Buckley

INTRODUCTION

All competitors at a Paralympic Games have gone through a process known as classification. Classification attempts to place individuals with disabilities into groups of comparable ability and function. The individual is then allocated a class or classification. It is designed to provide the structure for competition at the Paralympic level. Without classification the Games simply would not exist. It is also probably one of the more contentious and controversial areas of the Games. This is largely due to its evolving nature in response to a rapidly growing Paralympic movement and also a misunderstanding of its basis and purpose.

The ultimate purpose is to provide the opportunity for most of the vast array of physical disabilities to have competition at the highest level of sport. It is designed with elite competition in mind, not to simply allow an individual to participate. Even with the best intentions, not all physical disabilities can be classified. It is quite possible to have a physical disability and not be allocated a class. Classification in sport is not unique to the Paralympics. Many sports are conducted by separating competitors into two basic groups – male and female. Olympic Sports such as judo, boxing, weightlifting and wrestling categorize athletes by weight to provide a more matched contest. This in turn provides opportunities to a greater range of competitors and increases the numbers involved. At other levels of sport, competitors are classified into groupings of age.

Each Paralympic sport has its own system or approach to classification. While there are sports that have evolved with the movement, some sports and disability groups persist with old systems that do not consider the requirements of the sport. The Paralympics is currently perceived as a serious sporting endeavor. The challenge for classification is while providing the structure for competition, it should never be the focus of attention. As classification forms part of the rules of each sport, decisions can be challenged or protested. Competitors seek legal advice and on occasions have taken classification disputes to the Court of Arbitration for Sport (CAS). The classifiers can get it wrong and the athlete has the right to protest. However, it now "pays" to be a disabled athlete and classification decisions can mean the difference between winning and losing, so there is much at stake.

Many competitors approach classification in a similar way to doping in sport. Some will try to misrepresent their true ability in an attempt to get a class advantage (Shephard, 1988). There have been cases of competitors who have claimed to be significantly visually impaired who have been later found to have current driver's licenses. On occasions other similarly impaired competitors have been observed reading printed material or negotiating obstacles without difficulty. Most sports now insist on a signed form of consent to classification agreeing to abide by the sport requirements. Competitors are removed from a sport if their ability has been misrepresented and some have also been known to go to desperate and seemingly bizarre and dangerous lengths to be eligible for a class. Amputations have been performed and restorative surgery and medication refused in order to qualify for a class. To understand why classification is such a hot topic, it is best first to review its origins within the Paralympic Movement.

HISTORY OF CLASSIFICATION

Ludwig Guttman has long been acknowledged as the originator of the international sports movement which is now known as the Paralympic Games (Legg, Emes, Stewart, & Steadward, 2004; Strohkendl, 1996). Guttman revolutionized the care of individuals with spinal cord injuries and introduced sport as a means of rehabilitation. The Paralympic movement began as a rehabilitation endeavour not as an arena for elite sport. The classification system that first came into place was based on a medical examination that grouped competitors on the level of their spinal cord lesion. At the first major games in Rome, 1960, the classification involved a medical examination determining if the individual was a complete or incomplete paraplegic or tetraplegic. The only disability group present at these Games was competitors in wheelchairs with either spinal cord injury or poliomyelitis. This seemingly straightforward approach was then further redefined due to the difference between poliomyelitis and spinal cord injury. Quite often competitors with poliomyelitis were incomplete and in addition had sensation in the paralyzed trunk or limbs. This was perceived as an advantage and points were then allocated differently for this group (Strohkendl, 1996). Controversy in classification was only just beginning.

The games rolled on with few changes until 1976 when two disability groups representing the amputees and the visually impaired (blind) became part of the movement. The wheelchair group of the spinal cord injured and the polios had evolved into organizing competition by eight classes. The amputees eventually added nine classes to the competitive mix. The visually impaired started with two classes and then expanded this to three classes which have remained unchanged to the present day. The winter Paralympics also were held for the first time in 1976. The movement was fast gaining momentum. Competitors with cerebral palsy joined the fray in 1980 adding an additional eight classes. The term cerebral palsy is misleading as the group also included competitors with a non progressive acquired brain lesion. During this time yet another group emerged representing athletes that did not fit into the neat categorization of wheelchair (either spinal cord or polio), amputee, blind or cerebral palsy. A further six classes was added by this group known as "les autres" (french for "the others").

The Paralympics were faced with a situation where they were providing 34 different classes of disability with competition in some individual sports. In 1988 in Seoul, two pools had to be used to get through the number of events – it would be almost like multiplying some events of an Olympic Games by 34. In many situations, the sport, although considerably changed since 1960, still could not be considered an elite or high level of competition. Moving on from the rehabilitation origins which focused more on inclusive participation was to prove difficult for some sports. Wheelchair Basketball, possibly one of the oldest organized sports in the movement, embraced a new system in 1982 which was developed by Horst Strohkendl (1996). Acceptance had been slow as the system had been ready for implementation since 1974. The approach involved a functional evaluation of the player's ability and combined individuals with spinal cord injury and polio with lower limb amputees by awarding points predominantly for trunk function. Strohkendl (1996) laid the foundation for "functional" or sports based classification systems.

Currently, the International Paralympic Committee (IPC) refers to the Paralympics as "elite sport events for athletes from six different disability groups … with the emphasis on athletic achievement rather than their disability" (International Paralympic Committee, 2005). These six groups have their own international organizations and are member groups of the IPC. They include Wheelchair, Amputees, Cerebral Palsy, Les Autres, Blind and Intellectual Disability. Although these six groups exist, in many sports the disabilities are combined and the classes are based on the ability or sports function of the competitor. The Paralympic movement has evolved from being a disability based organization to one with a sport focus (Legg et al., 2004). The traditional medical testing has been modified in most cases and is usually applied to determine eligibility. Combining four of these groups (Wheelchair, Amputees, Cerebral Palsy, Les Autres) for the purpose of competition, has met with harsh criticism in some quarters (Richter, Adams-Mushett, Ferrara, & McCann, 1992; Williamson, 2004). This was predominantly seen in swimming which substantially changed the number of classes from 31 to 10 at the Paralympics Games in 1992. Lack of a strong scientific basis for changing the system was the major criticism. Additionally there was a concern that the visible differences between the physical disabilities would mean that the differences in function would not be appreciated (Richter et al., 1992). However, the swimming system, like most Paralympic Sport classification systems has attempted to evolve with the movement, and has since significantly refined class criteria. Swimming currently enjoys support from performance based research literature (Daly & Vanlandewijck, 1999; Wu & Williams, 1999).

Credibility of the classification system is reliant on the approach being sports based (Williamson, 2004). Currently the Paralympics has a mixture of sports specific and disability specific classification systems which will now be outlined.

THE CLASSIFICATION PROCESS

Classification for most sports involves a three part process, a bench test (physical examination), a sports based test, and observation during competition. Most sports begin the process with a form of physical or medical examination to establish that the competitor has a disability. This is also important as each sport has its own definition of minimal disability or eligibility. Some competitors, although disabled, do not meet the requirements for a given sport. However, although ineligible for some sports they may meet the criteria for others, as each sport requires different functions. Some disability groups require no further examination of function – this occurs with the visually impaired (blind). For the visually impaired, a medical examination is currently the only part of classification. The physical examination/testing for all other disabilities is then followed by sport based tests to determine the competitor's function or ability in a sport. Final confirmation of the class occurs during observation during competition.

CURRENT CLASSIFICATION SYSTEMS FOR PARALYMPIC SPORTS

The Summer Paralympic program consists of 18 sports, all with a classification system. Team sports require the competitor to be classified with some competing in an open class, and others allocated points contributing to a team total. The following gives a brief overview of each sport.

ARCHERY

There are three overall classes with subclasses depending on the competition. Athletes are placed in classes according to whether they can stand (ARST) or sit (ARW 1 & 2). The sitting class is differentiated by disability involving the arms.

ATHLETICS

This sport faces the biggest challenge and criticism for its inability to embrace a functional system or sports specific approach. There are many remnants from the disability based systems that exist, with disability federations still exerting control over the direction of classification. This has meant that there are several classes and quite often at the Paralympics level this then has an impact on the competition rules. The sport has a unique mix of some sports specific and disability based classification. The IPC rules govern competition for a Paralympics and dictate that events must have a minimum of 6 competitors from 4 countries. The consequences are that often an athletics event is cancelled or combined using a points table to award performance based on a percentage of world record for the individual's actual class. An athlete can come second after setting the world record when there have been not enough competitors in some categories to constitute an event.

Reform is greatly needed. Previous authors have suggested changes based on performance levels (Higgs, Babstock, Buck, Parsons, & Brewer, 1990). Tweedy (2003) is proposing a fresh approach to athletics based on the principle of force generation and force control.

BASKETBALL

Eligibility is based on a competitor having an objective and measurable permanent physical disability in their lower limbs which prevents them from running, jumping and pivoting as an able-bodied player. Players are assigned a point value from 1.0 through to 4.5 according to their level of physical function. These points are then added together in a game situation where a team is not permitted to exceed 14.0 points for the five players on court at any given time. The classification is based on function not medical diagnosis.

BOCCIA

This sport is governed by the body for Cerebral Palsy Sport (CP-ISRA). There are four classes defined by the amount of assistance required. This sport is predominantly played by competitors requiring much assistance in day to day functioning and all use wheelchairs for mobility.

CYCLING

This sport has three basic divisions: visually impaired; locomotor disability and competitors with cerebral palsy. The sport is investigating combining some of the locomotor and cerebral palsy divisions. The sport of handcycling made its appearance at the Athens Paralympic Games 2004. Handcycling is for competitors who require a wheelchair for general mobility or are unable to use a conventional bicycle or tricycle due to a severe lower limb disability. They compete in three functional divisions in IPC cycling competitions.

EQUESTRIAN
The system used for equestrian was grounded in a profile system developed by Meaden (1991). The approach is essentially based on the requirements of the sport and has 4 classes.

FENCING
A combination of medical and functional tests are used to place competitors in 3 separate categories A, B and C with only A and B being eligible for a Paralympics games.

FOOTBALL
7 a side
Ambulant athletes defined by CP-ISRA criteria are eligible to compete. A player from the two lower classes must be on the field at all times.
5 a side
Athletes qualify according to the rules governing visual impairment (IBSA) and compete together in an open event. The competitors' eyes must be covered for competition. However, goalkeepers may be sighted and in such cases, must not have been registered with FIFA in the last five years.

GOALBALL
Eligibility for this unique Paralympic Sport is established by IBSA definitions with competition in an open event. During competition all competitors have their eyes covered.

JUDO
Eligible athletes under IBSA classification criteria compete together in an open disability class being placed in the same weight divisions that operate in Olympic judo.

POWERLIFTING
Competitors with amputations and other (Les Autres) disabilities can compete together with athletes with Cerebral Palsy, Wheelchair Athletes and short stature athletes (dwarfs) and are then divided into different weight classes.

To become eligible in International Powerlifting competition, the athletes have to meet minimum disability criteria as outlined for the relevant disability groups. Additionally the competitor must have the ability to fully extend the arms, with no more loss than 20 degrees of extension in either elbow, to perform an approved lift according to the IPC Powerlifting rules.

SAILING
Sailing is a multidisability sport where athletes from all the disability groups with the exception of the Intellectually Disabled can compete together. The system is based entirely on the functions required to compete in Sailing.

The Sailing System has identified four main functions

(a) Compensation for the movement of the boat (Stability).
(b) Operating the control lines and the tiller (Hand function).
(c) Ability to move about in the boat (Mobility).
(d) Ability to see whilst racing (Vision).

In each functional class the athletes are categorised under one of several categories depending on their functional limitations, and are finally rated according to a point system, from 1 point describing the most limited functional ability, up to 7 points describing the highest level of functional ability. Each crew of three sailors is allowed a maximum of 14 points. In Individual contests sailors must meet the minimum criteria for disability; that is, upon evaluation of their functionality they must be awarded 7 points are fewer.

SHOOTING
The Shooting classification is divided into two main classes, those than require a shooting stand and those that do not. These classes are further defined by subclasses

SWIMMING
Swimming combines the conditions of amputation (limb loss), cerebral palsy (coordination and movement restrictions), Spinal Cord Injury (weakness or paralysis involving any combination of the limbs) and other disabilities (such as Dwarfism) and major joint restrictions, across classes. The range is from the swimmers with least ability for the stroke (severe disability) to those with the most physical ability (minimal disability). In any one class some swimmers may start with a dive or in the water depending on their condition. This is factored in when classifying the athlete.

TABLE TENNIS
The Table Tennis classification System is comprised of 10 functional classification classes based on a sports specific approach.

WHEELCHAIR TENNIS
The only eligibility requirement for individuals to become competitive wheelchair tennis players is that they must be medically diagnosed as having a mobility-related disability that would prevent playing competitive able bodied tennis. There are two classes, one for lower limb disability according to a set list of requirements by the International Tennis Federation with the other class for individuals with an upper limb disability eg. equivalent to a C8 tetraplegic with defined functional limitations with their ability to serve and perform arm strokes.

SITTING VOLLEYBALL
Athletes in Sitting Volleyball only need to reach the criteria for minimum disability level related to the skills or functions to perform volleyball. Examples include amputation of fingers, shortening of one arm/one leg to a certain percentage, fusion of ankle or wrist and other comparable disabilities. Sitting Volleyball is played by amputees and athletes with other disabilities (Les Autres). Each team may have a maximum of one minimum disability player on court at any one time; the rest of the team must all have a higher level of disability.

WHEELCHAIR RUGBY

The athletes are grouped within a point system ranging from 0.5 points, describing the most limited functional ability, up to 3.5 points describing the highest level of functional ability. A maximum total of 8 points (for four players) is allowed on court during a game. Wheelchair rugby players show different levels of limitations of movement, strength and control in arms, trunk and legs. It is mainly played by athletes with spinal cord injury involving both their arms and legs to some degree or other disabilities causing different levels of paralysis like Cerebral Palsy, Polio etc.

VISUAL IMPAIRMENT

Competitors with a visual impairment are examined by an Ophthalmologist and classified into one of three classes according to criteria defined by IBSA. This testing has no relationship with vision requirements for a given sport. The same classes apply across all sports. When required by a sport, in an open class situation eg Goalball or for the most visually impaired class in an individual sport, the eyes are covered to ensure competitors are on the same terms.

WINTER SPORTS

Previously, In Alpine skiing, there have been eleven classifications for athletes with a physical disability (seven for standing and four for seated) and three for athletes with visual impairments. When classifications are combined in competition due to an insufficient number of athletes in a class, a formula is used to "factor" athletes' times according to their classification status. For Torino, in 2006, a new approach that combines Alpine skiing classes will be adopted. It is based on three categories, sitting, standing and visually impaired/blind skiers. Other sports such as Wheelchair Sled Hockey and Curling follow a sports specific approach. The number of classes, the approach to classification, categories and numbers are listed in Table 1 at the end of the chapter. Most sports, although using a sports specific approach include a medical examination.

THE ROLE OF TECHNOLOGY

Technology complicates the issue of classification. A clear example of this is a below elbow amputee runner for 100m and 200m distances. The disability results in a lack of balance at the start and during the race with a diminished arm drive. If the runner then wears a specially designed lightweight prosthesis designed to remedy the problem are they still at a disadvantage? Equipment used in sports can make a significant difference to performances. The sport of swimming prevents the use of any assistive devices while swimming – this is despite the fact that floats, flippers etc would assist some disabilities greatly. Sport rules need to keep pace with technology and its impact on classification.

INTELLECTUAL DISABILITY

Competitors with an intellectual disability were granted full medal status at a Paralympics for the first time in Sydney 2000. Unfortunately the classification system was subject to an incident which caused a scandal at the 2000 Paralympics. This has had long lasting implications for competitors with an intellectual disability (Williamson, 2004). The Spanish

Basketball Team was made up of players whose IQ (one of the key criteria for this group) had been falsified. The team was largely made up of players without a disability. Due to the International Federation (INAS-FID), the group representing athletes with intellectual disabilities being ultimately responsible for validating all athletes, they were held accountable. Appropriate safeguards expected for all other disabilities were not in place for this group. INAS-FID was requested by the IPC to provide a more secure system based on a sports specific approach with the capacity for protest. The time lines were not met and the 2004 games in Athens were without full medal events for INAS-FID athletes. Currently the IPC is working with INAS- FID to resolve this issue. The challenge is to provide a system that considers the intellectual disability from a sports function view point. The relevance of IQ to sport and the appropriate cut off level is under scrutiny. Additionally, it is quite possible that if IQ is relevant to sport, the level will be different depending on the requirements of the sport. If IQ is considered not to be appropriate, the challenge is to find the best approach to validate an individual's intellectual disability (Williamson, 2004). At stake here is quantifying the disability and developing a system suitable for the sport.

THE FUTURE

The Paralympics is proposed as a movement that parallels the Olympics. It represents an elite level of competition. With the exception of weight categories, able bodied competitors are not further separated into divisions by height, biomechanics and race, all of which can impact on winning. Not all able bodied competitors, regardless of how hard they train will make an Olympic Games – the same should apply for those aspiring to be a Paralympian. The Paralympic movement started with its roots in rehabilitation but it has well and truly moved beyond this now. For some sports, it is now a lucrative source of money and sponsorship. An allocated classification can have an enormous impact on the financial rewards available to a competitor.

The notion of fairness is supposedly at the heart of most classification approaches (Tweedy, 2002). This really needs to be defined and further challenged as classification will never be entirely "fair" when it primarily exists for elite competition. DePauw and Gavron (1995) suggest that emphasizing ability tends to eliminate the more severely disabled from competition. Since the emergence of more functional systems, competition numbers have increased, standards and performance levels have improved dramatically and competitors are now forced to be more selective in their choice of sport or event. At the beginning of the Paralympic Movement it was not uncommon for a competitor to represent their country in a variety of sports at the same games when schedules permitted e.g. Wheelchair Basketball, Track and Swimming. The Paralympics is a serious sporting endeavor, and can never attain "fairness" for all – some sports will simply never be an option for some disabilities.

Making an Olympics depends on numerous factors – naturally inherited attributes (e.g. body shape, height, arm span) superior technique and training, the "will" to win, being able to remain injury free at the "right" time and the presence of a large field of strong competitors. These very same factors apply to competitors with a disability. Making it to the "top" depends on many variables. In classification, competitors should never be penalized due to natural endowments and training. It is easy for people to blame the classification system for their inability to make a games, rather than looking at all the components that go into making an elite competitor.

The IPC is faced with the task of constantly reviewing the classification systems that are in place. Performances once thought impossible for some disabilities are now easily achieved. Classification has to take this into consideration and be prepared to monitor and modify systems as required. Having too many classes in any sport lessens its credibility as a true competition.

The other challenge that the IPC must meet is explaining and selling the idea of classification to the general public when faced with the spotlight of the media. Not all of society is comfortable with the idea of disability on full display in the sporting arena and complicated systems are also harder to explain. The current systems for all sports need continued research and review. The Paralympic movement is still relatively young with performance levels yet to stabilize. For the movement to continue to grow and adhere to the principles of high level competition, classification should be closely monitored in the role it plays.

REFERENCES

Daly, D. J., & Vanlandewijck, Y. (1999). Some criteria for evaluating swimming classification. *Adapted Physical Activity Quarterly, 16*, 271-289.

DePauw, K. P., & Gavron, S. J. (1995). *Disability and sport.* Champaign, Ill.: Human Kinetics.

Higgs, C., Babstock, P., Buck, J., Parsons, C., & Brewer, J. (1990). Wheelchair classification for track and field events: A performance approach. *Adapted Physical Activity Quarterly, 7*, 22-40.

International Paralympic Committee (2005). Classification. Hypertext Document. (http://www.paralympic.org/release/Main_Sections_Menu/Sports/Classification/ - Accessed - February 27th 2005.)

Legg, D., Emes, C., Stewart, D., & Steadward, R. (2004). Historical overview of the Paralympics, Special Olympics and Deaflympics. *Palaestra, 20*(1), 30-35,56.

Meaden, C. A. (1991). Assessing people with a disability for sport: The Profile System. *Physiotherapy, 77*(6), 360-366.

Richter, K. J., Adams-Mushett, C., Ferrara, M. S., & McCann, B. C. (1992). Integrated Swimming Classification: A Faulted System. *Adapted Physical Activity Quarterly, 9*, 5-13.

Shephard, R. J. (1988). Sports medicine and the wheelchair athlete. *Sports Medicine, 4*, 226-247.

Strohkendl, H. (1996). *The 50th Anniversary of Wheelchair Basketball.* Münster: Waxman.

Tweedy, S. M. (2002). Taxonomic theory and the ICF: Foundations for a Unified Disability Athletics Classification. *Adapted Physical Activity Quarterly, 19*, 220-237.

Tweedy, S. M. (2003). Biomechanical consequences of impairment: A taxonomically valid basis for classification in a unified disability athletics system. *Research Quarterly for Exercise and Sport, 74*(1), 9-16.

Williamson, D. C. (2004). Sports Classification for Persons with Intellectual Disabilities: A general purpose proposal to demonstrate impact functionality. *Palaestra, 20*(3), 26-29,46.

Wu, S. K., & Williams, T. (1999). Paralympic swimming performance, impairment, and the functional classification system. *Adapted Physical Activity Quarterly, 16*, 251-270.

Table 1: Summer Paralympic Sport Classifications

Sport	Approach	Categories	No. of Classes
Archery	Sports specific	ARST Standing ARW Sitting	1 2
Athletics	Mixture of disability based with partial sports specific	T Track F Field (Both track and field are further categorized by the traditional disability groupings of wheelchair, cerebral palsy and visually impaired)	20 23
Basketball*	Sports specific	Points awarded from 1 to 4.5	8
Boccia	Mixture of disability based with partial sports specific	BC 1- 4 All are Cerebral Palsy classifications with the exception of class 4, the only class for non-cp diagnosis	4
Cycling	Mixture of disability Based with partial sports specific	CY – (blind classes combined) LC 1-4 CP	1 4 4
Equestrian	Sports Specific	EQ	4
Fencing	Mixture of disability based with partial sports specific	A B C	3
Football	Disability based	7– a-side Ambulant Cerebral Palsy 5 – a-side Visually Impaired Players	4 1
Goal Ball	Disability based	Open Class for Visually Impaired	1
Judo	Disability based	Open Class for Visually Impaired Categorized by weight divisions	1
Powerlifting	Sports specific	Open Class for all disabilities Categorized by weight divisions	1
Sailing	Sports specific	Points awarded from 1 – 7	7

Shooting	Sports specific	SH1 not requiring a stand	1
		SH2 requiring a stand	1
Swimming	Sports specific Visual impairment is disability based	S – Freestyle, Butterfly, Backstroke	10
		SB – Breaststroke	9
		SM – Medley	10
		Classes 1-10 – are allocated to swimmers with a physical disability Classes 11-13 – are allocated to swimmers with a visual disability	
Sitting Volleyball	Mixture of disability based with partial sports specific	Open Class with minimal disability criteria applied to team combination rules	2
Table Tennis	Sports Specific	TT – 1 -10	10
Wheelchair Rugby	Sports Specific	Points awarded from .5 – 3.5	8
Wheelchair Tennis	Sports Specific	Lower Limb Disability Class	1
		Quad Class	1

* Only Wheelchair Basketball rarely medically examines the players.

9 COACHING AT THE PARALYMPIC LEVEL: IF ONLY THE ADMINISTRATORS UNDERSTOOD!

Chris Nunn

"Never judge success against others, but on your ability to reach your full potential in any given moment!"

Chris Nunn 2006

INTRODUCTION

Coaching is the effective manipulation and management of resources in the endeavour to create an environment in which an athlete, or a group of athletes, can optimise their chances of reaching their goals. This applies equally to club level coaches and to those striving for elite international performance. In this chapter we will look at the effect quality coaching has had on the international Paralympic movement, and then at the effect the administration of international Paralympic sport has had on coaching.

A COACHING BACKGROUND HELPS!

I am fortunate to have been involved with the Paralympic movement since the 1988 Seoul Paralympic Games. My introduction to athletes with disabilities occurred when Nigel Parsons, an arm amputee, asked me to coach him at the beginning of 1987. Nigel was frustrated and felt he was not being given due consideration by the coach he was previously working with. The coach was a former Olympic coach who had welcomed the athlete into the squad, however not a great deal of consideration was given to the strength and conditioning components of the training program. As a result the athlete felt neglected.

My athletics background had been as an international decathlete, and was fortunate to experience the exhilaration of an Olympic Gold medal when married to 1984 Olympic Heptathlon Champion Glynis Nunn. The experience taught me the commitment, persistence and planning required to be successful at the highest level of sport. As a result, I felt I could offer something to Nigel and therefore began my career as a coach of athletes with disabilities.

The task for me was to develop a strength-training program that would enable Nigel to develop his upper body. Upper body strength is crucial when running and necessary for body balance. As a coach I began to really understand the necessity to treat each athlete as an individual. A strength program for Nigel could not include a great deal of explosive upper body work as he was unable to hold an Olympic bar in order to perform power cleans, over head presses and other similar exercises which could be incorporated into a program for a sprinter. We attempted to develop a device, which would enable attachment between the arm and the bar, but at the time we did not have the technology of the resources to complete such a task. Instead we focussed on using resistance machines which enabled Nigel to train without needing to grasp a bar. The need for me "to look outside the box" as a coach had been entrenched well and truly when working with Nigel.

Within months of beginning to work with Nigel, Kerry Cosgrove, the executive Director of the Amputee Association of Australia approached me and asked if I would like to be one of the Paralympic Coaches for the Seoul Games. I was flattered, but declined to accept the offer, as I knew nothing at the time about athletes with disabilities or the Paralympics. I was however single at the time, following the breakdown of the marriage with Glynis Nunn, and agreed to travel with Nigel to assist him in his sprint events at the Games.

THE FIRST APPROACH

I have noticed on repeated occasions that qualified coaches who are approached to coach an athlete with a disability are hesitant and often reluctant to take on the athlete. This reaction indicates a lack of understanding as to what is required, and is a reflection of the training a coach receives when undertaking their studies.

What the coaches fail to remember is that they have been approached because of their sports specific knowledge and not their understanding of disability. The disability knowledge can be learnt very quickly relative to the many thousands of hours required for many years to become a coach capable of preparing athletes for international competition.

Personal experience with athletes with disabilities has enhanced my coaching expertise and enabled me to become a better coach of able-bodied athletes, knowing that all athletes require a great deal more individual preparation than the textbooks and lectures indicate. It has also taught me to think "outside the box" when coaching and this has led to changes to prosthetic legs and throwing frame designs which had never previously been tried.

So what are the principles a coach should use when coaching an athlete with a disability? An excellent understanding of the sport and the events that the athlete wishes to contest is essential. Sports specific knowledge is crucial for providing an athlete with the environment and program that will enable them to progress, develop and perform anywhere near their potential.

The challenge for the coach who has come from an elite sports background is to gain an understanding as to where the Paralympic movement is at and where it can be taken.

TALENT AND EVENT IDENTIFICATION

A coach may also need to suggest to an athlete that although they are currently enjoying a particular sport and gaining reasonable success, they may be better suited to another sport or event. This is knowledge gained through an understanding of the requirements of a specific sport or an event within a sport such as athletics or swimming. In my career I have twice suggested event or sport changes for athletes I was coaching and both have gone on to win Paralympic Gold medals.

The first to do so was Hamish MacDonald who came to me as a sprinter. Hamish contested the final of the class T35 100m at the 1992 Games, but was much shorter than the other athletes in the race, and although his leg cadence was very good he had a significantly smaller stride length. He was also probably the best physically prepared athlete in the event and it was clear to me that he had limited potential as a sprinter. Hamish did however, have a very strong upper body after considerable time and consideration I eventually convinced him that he should take up the shot put, where he could utilise the strength and speed. I also explained that together we would develop a throwing frame that would suit his body and enable him to utilise his maximum functional ability.

We spent 18 months developing a frame with a sloping seat and footplates in positions that forced Hamish into a throwing position. This was a new innovation as all the previous frames were simply flat seats for the athletes to sit on. During this period my experience in coaching and the application of biomechanics was crucial. I knew that we needed to replicate as closely as possible the actions of an able-bodied thrower, where the summation of forces and the application of technique determined the outcome. We also studied the rule book very carefully and determined that we could interpret them to our advantage and provide Hamish with an edge going into competition.

At the 1996 Atlanta Paralympic Games Hamish not only won the shot put but also broke the world record by 1.50 metres. The decision had been justified.

The second athlete I suggested swap to another sport was a visually impaired athlete Anthony Biddle. Anthony had begun competition as a high jumper and had experienced mixed success at international level and like Hamish he had made finals, but never won a medal. Another athlete with an excellent training ethic, Anthony was also not physically suited to the high jump. He had relatively short legs and was much shorter than the athletes from other countries he was competing against. His strengths were his ability to train and his thighs, and therefore I suggested that he take up cycling and put him in contact with the national cycling coach. Anthony made a successful switch to cycling and won the gold medal in Athens in cycling.

I have cited these two examples to support the notion that coaches need to be mindful that many athletes with disabilities have been introduced to sport due to opportunity and access to local coaches. They have enjoyed the independence and success that sport can provide and have therefore stayed with the sport they were introduced to. Coaches need to implement their own "talent identification" process and be honest with each athlete regarding their suitability to the chosen sport.

Physical Fitness for Athletes with Disabilities

One of the areas I have noticed many coaches struggling with has been the development of fitness for athletes with disabilities. The necessity to undertake cardiovascular fitness components is often compromised due to the biomechanical inefficiencies of leg amputees and athletes with cerebral palsy in particular. My experience has been that conditioning work for athletes in all sports can be undertaken through a combination of resistance training in a strength and conditioning facility and in a swimming pool. It is also imperative that athletes with disabilities are trained in such a manner that they can use any facility anywhere in the world that is accessible. I have always been opposed to the development of specialised equipment for athletes with disabilities because once the athlete does not have access to any "special machines" or equipment, they feel compromised in their training. However, it is appropriate to develop strapping for hands and to look for alternative ways of using equipment, as the athlete may need some "mobile" assistance.

Once again the techniques I developed in order to provide a physical base for athletes with disabilities have been transferred across to become an integral component of programs I put together for able-bodied athletes. The result has been increased fitness levels for all athletes and a reduction in injuries due to the recovery components which the water-based training provides.

I mentioned earlier the necessity to develop modifications which have not previously been tried for athletes with disabilities. Many coaches are in the habit of looking for the answers through other people's research. I believe there is a great deal more which can be done to enhance the level of performance of athletes with disabilities. For example, I have witnessed the dramatic improvements athletes with cerebral palsy can make when encouraged to train the affected limbs, and therefore believe a great deal more research is required before we can understand the capacity many athletes have for improvement. The difficulty is that many researchers are not interested in studying elite athletes with disabilities because they cannot secure a large enough number of subjects to enable the data to be tested and validated. As a result most of the studies conducted remain "case studies", but these are very useful for coaches looking to understand their athletes.

It is also my belief and experience that biomechanical and physiological testing for athletes with disabilities should only be undertaken once the athlete reaches a reasonable level of fitness. Many resources are required to undertake such tests and most athletes with disabilities will not have a high degree of fitness to begin with and therefore they will show great improvement initially regardless of the testing undertaken. Therefore field tests provide an adequate level of feedback for each athlete. Once the athlete is capable of performing in a consistent manner then the testing procedures can be introduced.

My final word on the physical conditioning of athletes with disabilities is that not enough coaches push these athletes to their limits. Many athletes with disabilities have grown up in a relatively protected environment and need to be taken out of their comfort zones. Each of the athletes I have coached has experienced a "Hell week" where the two objectives for the week have been to firstly physically exhaust the athlete and secondly to mentally exhaust them. This can be done effectively and safely when utilising the safe environment of water. The pride and exhilaration the athletes experience once they have successfully completed the training sessions for the week enables them to move to another level of training and ultimately performance.

THE MODERN ERA IN COACHING

The Seoul Paralympic Games should be seen as the beginning of the modern era of Paralympic Sport when coaches and athletes realised that most athletes were underachieving. There were two groups of people competing at the Games. The first group had a disability, but it could be argued it wasn't physical, but attitudinal. They believed they had the right to be there because they had a disability. I believe strongly that No one **individual** has the right to represent their country, the privilege must be earned!

The second group was made up of athletes attempting to perform their sport or event to the best of their ability and were extremely competitive. However, many of the athletes knew little about preparing for competition, and several of them did not work with a coach at all. Few did more than several weeks training prior to a competition, even fewer understood the concept of planning over several years or even a year, generally they were technically deficient and fitness was poor.

That said, it should also be noted that of the athletes competing the wheelchair group were certainly better prepared and understood the requirements of their events in greater depth than athletes from the other disability groups. This is not surprising considering that the Paralympics began with the rehabilitation of men with spinal injuries following the Second World War and Games which were recognised as the equivalent of the Olympics were first conducted for wheelchair athletes in 1960. Therefore, by 1988 this group had a 28-year history behind it and was much more advanced than the others. To the credit of the wheelchair athletes and coaches this group has continued the search for improvement.

THE TRANSITION FROM CARERS TO COACHES

The 1988 Australian Seoul Paralympic Team was typical of many of the teams for other countries. "Coaches" were appointed to cater for disability specific sections of the team, i.e. wheelchair, amputee, blind and cerebral palsy. As a result, the "Team Coach" was required to care for the athletes in each section and had to cover all the sports in which these athletes participated. This meant a "Section coach" was needed to travel between swimming, athletics, weight lifting, table tennis, basketball, etc. This clearly was a logistical nightmare and a very inefficient method of catering for athletes needs during competition.

Within Australia a movement began which would ultimately see each sport move to "sports specific coaching" appointments and therefore a better understanding of the athlete's needs.

The debate began in earnest between those who had been on teams under the 'section system' and those who had come to sport for athletes with disabilities from an elite sports background. The debate came to a head quickly and at the 1994 World Championships for athletes with disabilities in Berlin when, yet again, the team positions were being allocated under the section system. Finally the Australian Paralympic Committee decided that a new "Sports specific" system would be tried for the 1996 Paralympic Games in Atlanta. This decision was only reached when those who had previously been away as Section Managers, were promised other administrative positions within the Australian team! Fortunately, and not surprisingly, the Australian Team performed better than it ever had previously and the Sports Specific system was claimed as a triumphant success by the APC.

This was a significant turning point within Australian Paralympic Sport. With the next Games being hosted in Australia it was a chance to "shine" and show case sport for the disabled in Australia. For the first time Head Coaches were appointed early in the 4 year cycle and effective planning was able to take place. This did not happen for all sports, but for the "big 3" in Australia, athletics, swimming and cycling, early appointments were critical to the ultimate performance of these teams in Sydney.

Whilst there was much dissention and discomfort from within Australia, particularly from those who had come to the sport from a carer background and could clearly see that their "days were numbered", the way forward was clear. Sports specific teams are here to stay. This concept was also being encouraged in other parts of the world and similar fights were being fought and won. By 2000 almost all the large teams represented were using a sports specific approach to sport.

The significance of this change was enormous. Athletes were being asked a vastly different set of questions and undertaking a change in mind set which was not possible under the "section" system. Whilst it is important to understand what an athlete needs to eat, what their room requirements are and how much assistance is needed when travelling, these questions do not constitute the major focus of athlete performance. Athletes and coaches were now looking for hundredths of seconds and centimetres in improvement.

THE IMPROVEMENT IN COACHING, ATHLETE PERFORMANCE AND ATTITUDE!

The progress made in the areas of athletic performance and coaching expertise has been dramatic in the period between 1988 and until now and warrants a comment on how far the high performance end of sport for athletes with disabilities has come. It was during the 1990's that athletes and coaches began to explore boundaries that were previously thought impossible and as a result records in all sports fell with regularity.

My belief and experience is that improvement occurred once coaches began to treat athletes with disabilities as athletes first and foremost, but more importantly, the athletes began to train, think and behave in the true manner of elite sport. The parallels with elite able bodied sport and elite sport for athletes with disabilities now exist.

Elite coaches are now heavily involved in research and development. Thus the training regimes, skills and techniques used by elite athletes with disabilities competing at international level is exceptional. Each effective coach has incorporated the skills of biomechanists, physiologists, psychologists, physical therapists, engineers, mechanics, talent identification and any other professional who may be able to provide answers or support to an athlete.

During this period coaches were planning regional and domestic training camps where athletes could come together and learn about their events. Overseas trips were used for the purpose of athlete development and competition opportunities. Coaches were interacting across the globe to enhance and share their knowledge, endeavouring to improve athlete performance. Athletes and their personal coaches were being assisted with the preparation of the 4 year and yearly periodised training programs. Systems were implemented which enabled the progress of each athlete to be monitored. Team selection criteria were written to ensure athletes adhered to the expectations of the high performance coaches.

In short, athletes were treated as elite and therefore expected to think and act like elite athletes. The days of getting on the team after a few weeks training were gone and the rate of improvement in athlete performance was incredible. Implementing a sports specific approach and a change in attitude had brought this about.

THE COACH'S ROLE

What role then does the coach play in such a team? Is the coach the most important individual within the team? The athlete should always be the most important part of the team. Without them, there is no need for anyone else. However, it is the coach who is given the critical role within the team of implementing and creating the appropriate environment for success, and must have an understanding of the skills which each other member of the support staff brings with them. It is only then that the effective coach can develop a plan that will see the athlete progress towards reaching their full potential. With the implementation of the plan it is the coach who must ensure all parties remain disciplined. It is the level of discipline provided by each individual that will determine success!

Successful training will not always mean winning, but should always mean growth! Through sport the opportunity to learn about the individual, regardless of the position they hold within the team, is enormous.

Effective coaching at Paralympic Level will require an understanding of a myriad of complexities, ranging from the individuality of an athlete, the complex classification system to the limiting and inhibitive entry system.

COMING TO TERMS WITH ELITE EXPECTATIONS AND CREDIBILITY

The change in mindset was difficult to accept for many athletes who had been travelling for several years and had achieved a certain level of success. Questions such as, "Why should I train more when I am already the world record holder?", "Why should I attend these training camps?", "Why do I need a training plan?" were asked. The answers were simple, "How good do you want to be?" and "Do you really want respect from the able-bodied sports people?". With this in mind the truly elite concept began to emerge from within the international Paralympic community.

Many of the athletes now competing at the Paralympic Games train at equivalent levels to their Olympic counterparts, however, there remains a group of athletes who would struggle to be competitive in club and regional competition given their level of training. They are able to compete at the Paralympics because there are limited numbers of athletes in their classification groups and their chosen events. Whilst the Paralympic movement was in the period of growth during the late1980's and 1990's, it was expected by most athletes and coaches involved, that fewer of the "club level" athletes would be competing as the level of coaching and athlete commitment improved. This has been the case.

The Paralympic Games is now for elite athletes, and provides the opportunity for them to compete against the very best. Medals are won by the best of the best. Coaches push the limits with their athletes, athletes push the limits with their bodies and their equipment, and this is what places Paralympic sport above all other international competitions for athletes with disabilities. Participation in the Paralympics should be the result of years of hard work. Athletes are now performing beyond what would have seemed possible in 1988. The world records 'as I write' for leg amputee 100m is 11.08 seconds, the wheelchair marathon is 1hr 20:14mins and in swimming well inside 60 seconds for the 100 meter event. These performances establish credibility amongst the able-bodied environment.

For the truly elite Paralympic athlete, "credibility" is everything! Therefore, coaches are expected to train these athletes in a creditable manner, accepting no compromise in the pursuit of excellence. As the athletes return to the community their performances at the Paralympic Games are "judged by the public" and often result in sponsorship and scholarship assistance in many countries throughout the world.

The evidence indicates that athletes at the Paralympic Games are "elite" and deserve the kudos associated with being elite, it the reward for years of hard work. The desire to achieve optimal training and competition opportunities provides the focus and application of coaches throughout the world. Collectively they spend hundreds of thousands of hours each quadrennium preparing athletes for their chance at success in the cauldron of international competition, which is the Paralympic Games.

THE EFFECT OF ADMINISTRATION ON ATHLETIC PERFORMANCE

Given the overview provided above, is it then reasonable to suggest that the International Paralympic Committee (IPC) has been successful in assisting athletes and coaches realise athletic potential?

Far from it! In fact, it is more reasonable to suggest that many athletes and coaches have been able to succeed "in spite" of the IPC competition systems which have been put in place for Paralympic competition. Much of the administration behind the Paralympic Games remains at "emerging development" level, and thus affects the credibility of the performances of the hard working dedicated group of coaches and athletes who must bear the brunt of administrative decisions which do not consider the needs of the most marketable Paralympic product, the elite athletes.

Coaches endeavour to look at the "big picture" as they strive to develop the holistic athlete. The nature of coaches is to look for areas of improvement and eliminate weakness, whilst improving strengths. Ultimately the coach is looking for the "weakest link in the chain", knowing that when under pressure it is this link which will limit performance.

The spacecraft "Challenger", although the most technologically advanced machine in modern times, exploded when two O-Rings worth $1.50 each lost resiliency. Seven lives, millions of dollars and thousands upon thousands of man-hours came to an end because of the "weakest link"!

So what is the weakest link that the coaches of Paralympic athletes have to deal with? It is simply International Sports Administration!

The growth of the Paralympic movement has been limited by the IPC's administrative decisions. Growth and depth of numbers at the elite level was essentially "put on hold" when former president Dr Bob Steadwood signed an agreement with the IOC which limits the total number of athletes who can compete at each Paralympic Games. This was a short sighted approach to getting the International Olympic Committee (IOC) "on side", and the adverse effects of this decision are now impacting on the placings achieved by athletes training for individual events in the sports of athletics, swimming and cycling at the Paralympic Games. Team sports now have in place a qualifying system that ensures that the best teams get to compete at the Paralympics, as should be the case.

> The Sydney 2000 Paralympic Summer Guide stated:
> "The Paralympic movement requires a fair and equitable system to meet three key components: *Quality, Quantity and Universality.*" It goes on to state "*Quantity... provides opportunity for increased participation and evolution. At the same time, a maximum size or limit to the Games needs to be established to avoid the financial and logistical problems associated with gigantism.*"

Clearly this demonstrates that decisions have been made considering the needs of the administrators and not the athletes! Let us consider the Paralympic sport of athletics. Athletics, a sport that measures performance by centimetres, and hundredths of seconds, has two major flaws in the manner in which it conducts its business.

For the first we turn again to the Sydney 2000 Paralympic Summer Games Qualification Guide", it has written in the "General Conditions" the following:
> "2. ... the number of athletes......at the Sydney 2000 Paralympic Games will be 1050."
> "3. ...This number will be made up of a first allocation... based on their performances in events listed on the IPC calendar....
> "4. ...a further allocation...... will be made by the IPC Athletics Section.....Countries will be encouraged to bid for places on this allocation"

A system has been put in place, which encourages bidding! This is outrageous, foreign to athletics and is more akin to an auction where price determines the outcome! Perhaps the intention is deliberate to associate with the price of conducting the Paralympics!

This system of allocation applies for other individual sports. During the 2004 Athens Paralympics cycling experienced the most bizarre case, which indicates how this restrictive agreement affects athlete preparation. The case involved Australian visually impaired cyclist Keiran Modra OAM.

Whilst in the final stages of preparation for the Athens Games Keiran, the defending Paralympic Champion and World record holder, was the centre of a dispute between the Australian Paralympic Committee and the Athens Organising Committee (ATHOC), which was the committee responsible for conducting the Paralympic Games under the rules of competition established by the IPC sports committees.

For several months prior to the Games ATHOC argued that because of Modra's decision to use an alternative guide on his bike, his ranking was therefore changed and he was not ranked as highly as the other Australian athletes and could not be included in the Australian Team, as the quota had been filled.

Despite several attempts to reason with ATHOC, the APC was unsuccessful in their application for an additional place for Modra. As close as three days prior to his competition beginning Modra was ordered to leave the Paralympic Village. It was only due to the persistent efforts of the Australian Team staff that common sense finally prevailed and Modra was granted accreditation and thus access to the competition he had been training for over many years. The end result was that Modra went on to win 2 gold medals!

This system outlines very specifically the weakest link for a coach! Whatever happened to the system where an elite or emerging athlete could train for several years with the expectation that if they became good enough they would be able to contest their event at the Paralympics? Isn't that why qualifying performances were introduced, and were they not effective in maintaining appropriate levels and numbers at an event? It is the method used by the IOC to effectively limit numbers.

WORLD RECORDS BUT NO GOLD!

The second "flaw" is the "Points system" within athletics that borders on the ridiculous and has had a profound effect on the competition results, an area that should be quarantined from administrative decision-making.

The general public, as well as most coaches and athletes, does not understand that an athlete can train for many years, go to the Paralympics, break the world record in their class and be beaten into 4th place by three athletes who do not break the world record! It is beyond a coach to explain this to an athlete and their support staff. It is beyond an athlete to explain this to their sponsors and funding agencies!

The situation outlined above occurred in the class F35-38 women's javelin at the 2004 Athens Paralympics where Australian athlete Katrina Webb broke the class F37 world record by 4metres and did not place in the top three! Similarly, in the class F33-44 men's shot put, Hamish MacDonald, the only athlete to break a world record, finished 2nd. In the class F37-38 men's long jump, Darren Thrupp of Australia broke the class F37 world record and finished 3rd. Clearly the system devised to restrict the number of athletes has not worked and needs significant adjustment.

It is impossible to explain to the general community, and many of the representatives within the funding organisations, that an athlete can break a world record and finish fourth. The implications for funding are evident, and a lack of funding brings about a more restrictive approach to competition and training if the athlete does not have access to training venues, facilities or medical support. It has been an executive, administrative decision that has lead to this situation!

The alarming and disturbing aspect of this scenario is that coaches throughout the world have been detailing the potential for problems since 2002 when the system was first used at the World Championships and nothing has changed!

IPC CLASSIFICATION FRUSTRATIONS

It is not only the coaches and athletes who feel the frustration of administrative decisions. In a damning email sent to the IPC by the Classification Commissionaire Athletics, Mats Laveborn made these comments:

> *"As a chief classifier of wheelchair athletes it has been a great disappointment not being able to do my job properly at the Paralympic level.....I have seen athletes in the wrong classes winning medals they should not have. I have seen world records broken by the wrong athletes. These records will stand and make it impossible for the right athletes to win in future Games where classes are combined and results are scored by pentathlon points systems.*
>
> *Why has this happened? Well, in the Paralympic Games the classifiers are not allowed to follow the protest procedure of IPC.*
>
> *...the conclusion is that we cannot do our job and this has caused very much frustration amongst us. The coaches and athletes have not been aware of this procedure and of course they blame the classifiers.*
> *All NPC's (National Paralympic Committees) are concerned, it could happen to anyone that they lose their medals because of this.*
> *.....Please let us fulfil our tasks as classifiers for the sake of the athletes.*
> *Sincerely yours*
>
> *Mats Lavenborn "*

The problems outlined have arisen as a direct result of the archaic agreement between the IOC and the IPC and the decisions made by the IPC executive. Coaches are now unable to train athletes with surety that the events will be contested in a fair and equitable manner. Growth – Stunted or Progressing?

There will be those who would argue that significant growth has occurred within the Paralympic movement and will attempt to support this argument by showing that the number of participating countries has increased consistently since 1960 when the first Paralympic Games were contested. The counter argument is that with an increase in the number of countries competing at the Paralympics there is desperate need to remove the limit to the number of athletes competing, in order to avoid elite athletes missing the chance to compete in their chosen events and to showcase the expertise they have developed.

Modra's experience, and those outlined for the class F33-38 athletes, highlights the difficulties coaches face in preparing elite athletes for Paralympic competition. At a time when an athlete should be in competition mode and the coach ensuring that the "environment is conducive for success", many coaches and athletes are embroiled in battles simply to access Paralympic competition. When there, they are competing under a system that does not ensure the best athletes win.

STRENGTH IN NUMBERS

Another implication of the current quota system for the individual sports is that the "stronger" countries will dominate the Paralympic Games in the future and the opportunities of developing countries will not be available unless their athletes can reach the elite levels of their sports. This is contrary to the ideals of the Olympic Games.

The number of Chinese athletes competing at the Paralympic Games is evidence of this already occurring. The future looks good for those countries that are strong and have large numbers to draw from, but it is not so bright for the smaller developing countries.

THE FUTURE

Let us consider the concept of an International Centre of Excellence (ICE) that caters for athletes with disabilities. Such a centre could bring together many of the leading coaches, and research scientists, to work with the developing coaches and athletes from around the world. The ICE would cater for a variety of sports, house the best sports science facilities and offer specialised and generic principles of training for all to access. Athletes and coaches could apply for funding or use the facility on a fee for service basis. It would also provide an opportunity to undertake some studies in the area which would have large enough subject numbers to validate results, something which has been lacking in most research conducted to date.

The ICE would enhance the development of Paralympic Sport throughout the world and assist with the enhancement of the regional areas where athletes and coaches are often disadvantaged. The establishment of scholarship programs would enable coaches and athletes to visit at regular intervals where their progress could be monitored and their knowledge base broadened.

This would also provide a unique opportunity for a classification division to be established where the current classification systems can be reviewed and refined.

This is an exciting possibility and would not require huge amounts of money to implement. Therefore, a major sponsor, a host country and a director with an athlete focus are all that is required.

CONCLUSION

It must be emphasised that the quality of the elite Paralympic athlete and the coaching they are receiving cannot be questioned and is first class. Today's modern athletes, Olympic and Paralympic alike, are better prepared than their predecessors. That is, they have the ability and have chosen to train under the guidance of a coach, in the pursuit of excellence, and most coaches are able to create the right environment where excellence can be repeated and success achieved. The unfortunate aspect of elite performance for athletes with disabilities is that they are required to **fight battles with administrators** in order to save their "spots on the team" and to compete in a fair competition.

In order to gain respect from the able-bodied sporting community, the Paralympic movement has to do better than replicate what was being done in the "Able-bodied" environment. It is not enough to follow others when change is needed. As I write there are some deficiencies within the Paralympic movement, these might change for the better rapidly.

If not a vision must be put in place, an assessment made of what is good and bad, and a strategy implemented which will ensure the appropriate changes take place. When problems occur they should be seen as an opportunity for improvement, and a succession plan should be implemented in order that corporate knowledge and understanding is maintained. It is time for the International Paralympic Committee to make the necessary changes to the administration of the Paralympic Games. Once this has been achieved and all athletes have fair and equitable competition opportunities the Paralympics will reflect the professionalism of the athletes and coaches.

10   SPORT SCIENCE AND THE PARALYMPICS

Brendan Burkett

THE HISTORY OF SPORT SCIENCE IN PARALYMPIC SPORTS

Paralympic sports evolved from rehabilitation programs in the 1950's, and as such were built on medical science knowledge with an application to exercise. These programs initially focused on spinal cord injured athletes and the competitive sports program was an extension of the rehabilitation program. The evolution of the exercise sciences in Paralympic sports has followed similar paths as that of Olympic sports. That is many of the pioneers in the Paralympic programs were medical doctors, particularly as the person with a disability normally grew out of rehabilitation programs. The "rehabilitation practitioners" who developed these initial programs in fact could be argued as pioneers of the modern day exercise scientist because as with any rehabilitation program the objective is to regain a level of function to the human being. This rehabilitation is applied under the name of "performance enhancement" as part of the modern day Paralympic exercise scientist role.

Within the majority of Paralympic sports, the coaches, athletes and scientists take the knowledge and experience of Olympic performances and then apply and modify these to the Paralympic sport. For example in designing the training program for a Paralympic cyclist, the coach and sport scientist would use the Olympic cyclist's training regime as the start point. Then based on the adaptation process of the athlete, the monitoring of human and performance indicators by the sport scientist, the coach would then make modifications to the training program. Again as with Olympic sports, the Paralympic Games have seen a growing increase in the number of official sport scientists as part of each countries Paralympic team. At the 1988 Seoul Olympic Games the first international sports science project was conducted. This sports science project analysed the swimming race analysis and measured important factors such as start time, stroke rate, stroke length, distance per stroke, turn time, finish time, and the swimming velocity within each of the 25m segments. From this data the coach and athlete are able to evaluate their swimming performance and determine how to enhance this swim for future events such as the final that night, or which components to work on in their training (e.g. stroke count, swim pace, race strategy, aerobic fitness, maximum speed work).

At the 1992 Barcelona Paralympic Games the first international swimming race analysis was also conducted. This analysis has continued at the 1996 Atlanta Olympic and Paralympic Games, and at the 2000 Sydney Olympic and Paralympic Games exactly the same analysis was conducted for Olympic and Paralympic swimmers. Unfortunately there was no analysis conducted at the 2004 Athens Olympic and Paralympic Games. This was considered a major loss to furthering Olympic and Paralympic sporting performance. Despite the lack of a coordinated international program, the need for further sport science information was demonstrated as in Athens several countries conducted their own individual sports science analysis. This growth in sport science within the Games is also reflected at the highest level, with the Medical Committee of the International Paralympic Committee (IPC) forming the Sport Science and Education committee. This committee coordinate the applications for sport science research projects that are now being conducted at Paralympic Games and World Championships.

The demand for exercise science to the Paralympic athlete is the same for the Olympic athletes. Basically the sport science requirements for the Paralympic athlete start off the same as that for the Olympian, but then this unique population applies a new set of variables to extend the currently accepted principles of exercise science. These applications have been divided into the disability specific requirements as well as unique sport requirements.

When studying the unique movement patterns of the Paralympian, it is critical to correctly identify the barriers that are experienced by the Paralympian. From this knowledge solutions on how these can be overcome can then be developed. For example, a person who is visually impaired has a fully functional musculoskeletal system, and therefore should follow a similar pattern of gait as a sighted person. But due to their visual impairment their feedback loop is different and as such they depend more on the proprioception feedback on what is happening in their immediate environment. This "modified" feedback mechanism has evolved from personal experience of "bumping" into objects and after a while the bruises and cuts to the shins result in the person being more tentative in their walking gait. The end result is although they have no difference in their musculoskeletal and nervous system, and therefore should have a similar pattern of gait, the loss of vision then results in a unique pattern of gait. It is these types of applications that the exercise scientist can provide an immense difference to the quality of life for the Paralympic athlete.

TECHNOLOGY AND THE PARALYMPIC ATHLETE

Understanding how and why the human body moves, and more importantly the factors that limit and enhance our capacity to move, is critical to any sporting performance. Olympic and Paralympic athletes depend on this knowledge as part of their pursuit of excellence at their respective games. In reviewing exercise science and the Paralympian this chapter briefly defines what is exercise science? As this text is focused on technology and the Paralympics there is slightly more detail on the biomechanics discipline, when compared to exercise physiology and sports psychology. The chapter finishes off with the history of exercise science at the Paralympic Games, and major achievements for the future.

As the Paralympic athlete often depends on some form of technology to carry out their activities of daily living, such as a wheelchair for the spinal cord injured or lower limb affected athlete – the technology utilised by the athlete can be essential. Throughout other industries there have been tremendous technological developments, from exploration in space, under water, agriculture, manufacturing, and medical science. What is currently lacking is the "application" of this technology to the Paralympian. It is not a case of needing to reinvent the wheel, but rather to look around at what has been already developed and then determining how this can be applied to the problems at hand. It is when this lateral thinking approach is applied to the current issues for people with disabilities the future use of technology will really make the world a better place for the person with a disability.

Technology has played a major role within the Paralympic movement as the athlete can use technology to replace their lost function to enable them to carry out daily tasks through to the elite sporting performance. To this end the Paralympic movement has struggled with the introduction of technology into the sporting arena. The dilemma facing the Paralympic movement is "how much technology to allow", as to what point does technology that replaces functional anatomy become performance enhancement. There is also the equity issue with accessibility to technology. Developed countries have access to both the materials and the knowledge behind the technology and therefore can modify the technology to meet their specific requirements. This has far reaching effects on the Paralympic athlete. Not only will they be "more functional" with their new anatomy, but this new level of function can lead as previously suggested to an improved efficiency in daily tasks thru to a more effective performance in the competition arena. To date the Paralympic movement has loosely provided guidelines on the use of technology. If these guidelines are too restrictive then this can stifle future progress in the technology area – but then to provide an even playing field for the different resources within the countries around the world is a challenge. In sports such as swimming the athlete is not allowed any device to improve their functional anatomy, in athletics there are guidelines but to date these are reasonable open.

In some cases there is no immediate application of technology develop from exercise science for the Paralympian. For example, the current rules within swimming do not allow the swimmer to use any assistive devices so in this application the simpler the best way to solve the problem.

This leads us to ask the pertinent question:

What is sport science?
Sport science grew out the specialisations within physical education around the 1960's. Many of these pioneers in exercise science were medical doctors who realised the need for science based principles to guide the development of exercise science. Some of the prominent landmarks in the history of exercise science include:

- 1831 - Christian Braune, for conducting early studies on human gait
- 1882 - Claude Douglas, for the pioneering research on oxygen in breathing and the development of the Douglas Bag for collecting respiratory gas.
- 1931 - Kenneth Cooper, known as the father of aerobics and founder of the Cooper Institute in USA.

In discussing exercise science within the Paralympic family it is useful to consider some of the prominent landmarks in the history of the Olympic and Paralympic Games:

- 1896 – inaugural Olympic Games,
- 1948 – Sir Ludwig Guttmann organised the inaugural sports competition involving World War II veterans with a spinal cord injury in Stoke Mandeville, England – this lead to the Paralympic Games.
- 1989 – formation of the International Paralympic Committee (IPC), Dr Robert Steadward president

Over the decades there has been the need to develop methodology for optimal health and fitness. Exercise science has become the catalyst for this development. Despite the numerous successes, several questions remain unanswered for the able-bodied population which cover issues such as:

1   Potential benefits of exercise?
2   Prevention of cardiovascular disease, metabolism, and weight control?
3   Influence of physical activity on growth and development?
4   The relationship of age and exercise, and exercise and the immune system?

All of these questions, which have been developed from research in the able-bodied population, are also applicable to the disabled population as they are facing the same issues. More importantly an entirely new bank of questions can be raised for the disabled athletes who are extremely physically active – such as the Paralympian. To address these issues the exercise science profession broadly includes the disciplines of biomechanics, exercise physiology, and sport psychology. The relationship between these three disciplines and the Paralympian are discussed in the following section.

BIOMECHANICS

Biomechanics has many definitions, and the author's preference is for the study of the human body in motion. Essentially there are four areas within the biomechanics discipline: developmental biomechanics, biomechanics of exercise and sport, rehabilitative biomechanics, and occupational biomechanics. Each of these disciplines relate directly to the Paralympic athlete in either their activities of daily living (when they are not competing) and ultimately in their competition. In order to study the human body in motion the biomechanists rely heavily on technology to measure and quantify motion.

Alternatively, developmental biomechanics concentrates on evaluating movement patterns across the lifespan. This has particular application to motor skills and movement patterns in the fundamental movement activities such as walking, kicking, jumping, throwing and catching. From this information baseline profiles are developed to enable the current movement pattern to be compared to a reference point. Currently this works fine for the able-bodied population as there has been sufficient numbers of data collected to build a statistical reference point. However, there has not been the same number of data collected for people with a disability to enable a suitable reference point to be created. The same process and technology can be applied to both reference groups, highlighting an area for future research. For example, what are the movement patterns for fundamental daily task such as locomotion (walking for those that can, or propulsion of their mobility device), regaining function of an impaired limb, through to executing a skilful athletic performance.

As an extension of developmental biomechanics, there is the area of sport and exercise biomechanics. This discipline specifically focuses on the intra-body segment relationships, or posture, in order to minimise risk from injury and to enhance sporting performance. To often the exercise science profession concentrates on enhancing sport performance through the training, at the expense of reducing the risk of injury. Ultimately the "net gain" from training is the sum of the negative consequence of injury added to the positive outcomes from performance enhancement.

Technology in this area has improved the functional performance of machines, or created new devices, and activities such as plyometrics to reduce injury risk and enhance sports performance are utilised. Biomechanical technology such as load cells has allowed the high frequency measurement of "what forces are actually being developed and transferred" as a consequence of the sporting activity to be measured. Classic examples include the impact forces on the foot when running, or on the hand when catching a cricket ball. This scientific knowledge allows for modifications to be made to the sporting equipment, and/or the technique for addressing this issue.

The Paralympic athlete has a greater dependence on this knowledge due to their disability any lost bodily function needs to be compensated with support coming from another area. Examples of biomechanical applications in Paralympics include the "functional" design of wheelchairs. The function design of wheelchairs for tennis is different to road racing, which is again different to wheelchair basketball. Likewise, the prosthetic design for highly active amputees through energy absorbing carbon fibre Flex feet is different to the amputee sailor's peg leg.

Other examples of technology in Paralympic sport can be viewed when analyzing the swimmers start. This combines the kinematic analysis of segment movements such as rate of arm swing, path of the movement of the head, and the explosive power of the lower limbs. Collectively this movement pattern is analysis via the kinetic link chain to determine the summation relationships between timing variables like the drive from the legs, arm movement, and head position is very important. All of these relationships with the human segments then need to be compared with reference to the starting block and water surface. As the swimmer moves their upper limbs their centre of gravity naturally changes, if they are poised with the line of gravity right near the front of the starting blocks any change in movement pattern will alter the centre of gravity relationship and cause the swimmer to loose their balance. When controlled this can be a benefit to the swimmer as they can then use the natural acceleration forces of gravity to propel them into the water. Some work has been done in this area on the Olympic swimmers start, and is currently being conducted on Paralympic swimmers start. Paralympic swimmers who have reduced balance control, such as lower limb amputees or cerebral palsy, can find balancing on the starting block difficult. To understand the relationships requires specific understanding of the forces generated on the starting block and the position, velocity and acceleration of the human segments as they leave the block and enter the water. This requires the specific technology of mounting the force plate to the starting block and synchronising above and underwater video cameras.

Rehabilitative biomechanics is defined as the study of the movement patterns of injured or people with disability. One of the key outcomes from these studies has been the modification or development of machines to retrain the movement pattern. This also includes intermittent mobility devices such as canes, crutches, walkers, through to complete permanent devices such as prosthesis and wheelchairs. As the majority of people with a disability are aged the development of assistive devices has naturally focused on this market. The Paralympic athletes have then created a whole new market, not only are they significantly younger than the traditional aged person with a disability, they are also highly active and as such place far greater loads on the assistive devices. This new market demand, in the long term, will result in a better understanding of the relationship between human, activity, and the artificial aid – but there is still a fair amount of ground to cover in this area.

The final discipline is occupational biomechanics, and as the name suggests this evaluates work environment and scientifically provides a safer and more efficient work place. The industrial design for people with disabilities is evident in modern day buildings with wheelchair ramps, and Braille for the visually impaired and blind to allow access in and around buildings. Other examples in the built environment include providing ramps along the scenic pathway and wheelchair lifts in and out of swimming pools to ensure the people with disability can have access. The creation of the Paralympic Games has enabled occupational professionals the unique opportunity in creating a built environment that satisfies the requirements of people with disabilities. For example, the transport issues of moving an entire population of people who may use wheelchairs, walking aids, prosthesis, have balance issues (from Cerebral Palsy), visual impairment, and intellectual disabilities. This is expanded into issues within the dining hall when selecting a meal, transporting that to a seat, and cleaning up, as well as sleeping accommodation, and recreational activities. As with all areas these problems can be solved often times by using, or slightly modifying, existing technology and philosophy – all the Paralympian does is extend the thinking required to solve the problem.

Underpinning the understanding of biomechanics is the sub discipline of functional anatomy, which scientifically describes the relationships between the musculoskeletal system and how this applies to human movement. As with the other sections within this chapter the reader is directed to further information on the principles of the functional anatomy as this text is specifically focusing on the application to the Paralympic athlete.

In studying functional anatomy the scientist answers a range of questions; such as what adaptations occur when a person begins a regular exercise program? Is there an optimal type and level of exercise for maintaining the integrity of the skeletal system? The key feature in functional anatomy is the musculoskeletal systems combines to produce outcomes of "strength". This strength is defined as the force generated by muscular contractions and the leverage of the muscle at the joint. This produces a "moment of force". The key difference for the Paralympic athlete, and coach of the Paralympic athlete is there are a range of factors due to the different functional anatomy that cause the Paralympic athlete to use different mechanics to produce the "moment of force". Due to their disability, such as spinal cord injury or muscular-dystrophy the athlete may use a modify method of gripping the object to be moved in the traditional manner, or may not be able to modify their grip to focus the force to a different part of their anatomy, or to modify the application of their force in a different plane.

In other cases, such as amputation, the athlete may not posses the limb to grip and therefore will need to completely modify their process of movement – for example use their feet or a combination of head and shoulder to hold a tennis ball prior to serve. There are some other less obvious relationships unique to the Paralympian, such as for the lower limb amputee. At first glance the impact of loss of the lower limb is assumed to be confined to the lower limb only. When looking at the image of an amputee skeleton you can see how the amputation has caused the orientation of the pelvis to be modified. As the pelvis is connected to the vertebral column this change in pelvic angle results in a scoliosis of the spine. The altered vertebral column in the cervical region causes the shoulder to change alignment as well as the orientation of the skull. So the "compensatory" mechanism from the disability can have far reaching consequences for the person with a disability. The end result is more knowledge is required in this area to firstly understand the process and then to rectify the problem.

EXERCISE PHYSIOLOGY

Exercise physiology has been defined as the study of muscular activity, functional responses and adaptations during exercise. To understand the relationship between the human body and exercise requires knowledge of the cardiovascular, pulmonary, nervous, muscular, endocrine, immune, and skeletal systems. It is widely accepted that exercise can enhance the quality of life, but for the aged (Gerontology) the unique response of exercise in this specific population is of much interest. For the Paralympic athlete similar relationships are slowly being established, particularly with specific disability groups. For example, following spinal cord injury the human could be restricted in the exercise they could perform. This decrease in physical activity can increase the risk factors for cardiovascular disease for this population.

To design the training session the Paralympic athlete and coach seek advice from the exercise physiologist to determine the appropriate intensity and duration for training. The most common measures are heart rate and blood lactate. Established relationships currently exist between heart rate, blood lactate and the training intensity, or training zone. Using this knowledge the coach and athlete have a scientific measure that their training will result in the desired performance outcome. Of the limited studies that have been conducted on the effect of exercise on a person with a disability there exists a wide range of variability in the suggested recommendations for exercise. There are also limitations in following the current methods of analysis. For example to determine oxygen uptake (VO2) with an Olympic athlete the most common method is to measure the oxygen uptakes as the subject runs on a treadmill, or cycles on a cycle ergometer. A spinal cord injured athlete, or any athlete that does not have the function of their lower limbs (amputee, CP, les autre) will not be able to pedal the cycle ergometer. Some research studies have then modified the oxygen uptake tests and get the athletes to use a hand crank. The reliability of this method of assessment needs further investigation. In addition, for those confined to a wheelchair or who cannot not fit on a conventional treadmill, will require a specifically built wide treadmill that can safely accommodate the wheelchair.

A branch of exercise physiology is bioenergetics and metabolism. In some cases this topic on how the body generates energy for muscular work falls under the discipline of dietetics. Regardless of the aligned profession, the measurement of anthropometric profiles (or the net result of energy intake and expenditure), and the development of "legal" ergogenic nutritional aids are of particular interest to the Paralympic athlete and coach. With the difference between gold and silver, or bronze and fourth, being as small as 0.35%, or 0.01 second, anything that can make a difference to the athletic performance is eagerly sought by the Paralympic athlete.

Thermal adjustment is also a very important component of exercise, particularly as the chemical reaction of converting energy intake into muscular activity produces a by-product of heat. Looking at the preparation for the past Paralympic Games, the control and adaptation to a hot/humid environment such as Athens was a major issue for Olympic and Paralympic athletes. As with other applications the Paralympic athlete follows the same guidelines and principles as found with Olympic athletes, but with some modifications to the guidelines due to the unique characteristics of the athlete with a disability. With reference to heat adaptation, the able-bodied athlete dissipates their heat through their limbs. How does an amputee or short stature athlete respond to heat as they have a reduced limb area? Likewise the response or adjustment mechanisms to heat variations, or extreme ranges of heat, are of importance to the cerebral palsy and spinal cord athlete as their mechanisms for maintaining temperature homeostasis are different.

SPORT PSYCHOLOGY

Sport psychology involves the study of human behaviour in exercise or sport environments. Essentially sport psychology addresses 'how does exercise affect one's psychological makeup, and how the principles of exercise physiology can be used to improve performance?'. As with Olympic athletes, the Paralympian is confronted with the similar issues of the psychological effects of exercise, the problem of exercise adherence, motivation, and the anxiety pre competition and then when in the middle of the major event. The established process of proactively controlling the athlete's mood state, visualisation, and pre-competition thought process is of particular importance to the outcome of the sporting performance.

In some cases the Paralympic athlete can apply similar processes as the Olympic athlete, but for some disabilities this is not possible. For example, some, and there are only a small number, of cerebral palsy athletes can also have an intellectual disability. This could restrict their ability to use the power of the mind to modify the mood state or follow the race plan. In using visualisation techniques the athlete often will watch a video of a past performance, usually their best performance, so as to "visualise" the perfect race. For the visually impaired or blind athlete this is not possible so they need to resort to other techniques. Like wise when using muscle relaxation techniques to bring the athlete into the desired mood state the common procedure of systematically contracting and relaxing muscle groups within the body to create an overall level of relaxation needs to be modified for the amputee athlete who is missing limb segments, or for the spinal cord injured athlete who in the case of quadriplegia may only have limited control with their upper limbs only. The athlete who has an intellectual disability may have a different response mechanism to the "burn out, or staleness" that is common in athlete following long periods of training and competition. Using sports psychology the indicators of overtraining and more importantly the mechanisms for dealing with these issues can be solved using sports psychology.

The following table makes a summary of comparisons and highlight the current status of sport science in Paralympic sport.

Table 1: Summary of comparisons highlighting the current status of sport science in Paralympic sport.

Question	Application to Olympic (able-bodied) population	Application to Paralympic population
What function do bones perform?	Mechanically to provide framework for body to move. Physiologically – the development of blood cells.	The same applications as to the able-bodied population.
What adaptations occur when a person begins a regular exercise program?	Depending on the load applied, ultimately an improvement. This has been based on well document and resourced studies.	The start point is to assume the same relationships from the able-bodied situation apply. Still unknown the reaction to exercise?
Developmental biomechanics – defining movement patterns across the lifespan.		

Research Domains	Past	Present	Future
Outcome Based - Health, Fitness, Lifestyle and Quality of Life	Impact of retirement from disability sports on athletes with disability - adjustment issues	Perceived benefits of physical activity in persons with MS. Direct and indirect costs of MS in active and sedentary individuals. Application of theoretical modes of behaviour change on physical activity and lifestyle issues in persons with disability.	Continued research in the area of outcomes of health, fitness and lifestyle programs in persons with disability.
Applied	Physiological responses of persons with disability to exercise stress and training program.	Determining relative contribution of central and peripheral factors to increased oxygen consumption under hybrid exercise conditions in spinal injured using near infrared spectroscopy (NIRS).	Continuing research on impact of FES assisted exercise technologies on health-related fitness parameters.
Biomechanics	3 dimensional analysis of the free throw in wheelchair basketball. Analysis of the swimming performance of B1, B2, B3 (visually impaired) athletes at the Paralympic Games. Biomechanical analysis of a new adaptable wheelchair for sports use.	Biomechanical analysis of the gait in persons with cerebral palsy.	Future studies in Biomechanical analysis of performance enhancing technology in athletes. Biomechanical analysis of FES rowing technology.
Psycho-social	Experiences of women athletes with disability.	Perceived benefits of physical activity for persons with Multiple Sclerosis	Impact of physical activity programming and the Centre experience on health-related quality of life in persons with physical, intellectual and sensory impairment.

Research Domains	Past	Present	Future
Clinical	Autonomic Dysreflexia using functional electrical stimulation. Attenuation of the Autonomic Dysreflexia effects of FES using surface anaesthesia.	Surface anaesthesia as a mechanism of providing FES services for persons with incomplete lower extremity paralysis.	Applications of FES technology for rehabilitation. Analysis of shear forces on skin integrity on FES rowing
Technological	Technological Development of FES technologies: • ROWSTIM 1. • HYDRASTIM 1 (Prototype - Supported by AHFMR).	Development of ROWSTIM III: • (Closed loop FES control rowing for SCI).	Commercialization of FES Technologies for SCI and other neuromuscular disease: • ROWSTIM III.
Industrial/ Co-operative	Evaluation of new wheelchair design technologies: • Better Made Wheelchair Co.	Development of ROWSTIM III with: • Supercorp Inc. • Body Point Designs Inc. • Supported by AHFRM Technology Commercialization Fund.	Continued solicitation and cooperation with industry in development and assessment of biomedical and rehabilitative devices

11 FROM THE OUTSIDE LOOKING IN AND THE INSIDE LOOKING OUT:
A COACH'S PERSPECTIVE OF INTELLECTUAL DISABILITY IN THE PARALYMPICS

Peter Corr

INTRODUCTION

With fifteen years direct involvement with Paralympic athletes, I am here to tell you that the whole experience has '**blessed my life**'. The first ten were heavily focussed on wheelchair athletes, so I guess my interaction with and understanding of other disability groups was largely as an observer. However, through my opportunities and observations grew an empathy with all Paralympic athletes and coaches who strive at the top level. This is particularly true of those who are inspirational in that they show the world that they can not only excel in their mental commitment and physical achievements, but they can do so whilst overcoming adversity every day. As a coach of wheelchair athletes, my ignorance of athletes with intellectual disability reflected that of most of our society. We ignore or look on from a safe distance. Over time, my apprehensions and fears have diminished and this gave me the opportunity to work along side intellectually disabled people. This transition has enabled me to experience a somewhat unique transformation from **someone on the outside looking in to a person on the inside looking out.**

I experienced overwhelming highs and lows at my first Paralympic Games in Barcelona during 1992. The excitement of competing at my first ever Paralympic Games, coaching the Australian Women's Wheelchair Basketball Team, the anguish of the shock birth of my beautiful daughter, Alyce, [10 weeks premature and 960 grams] and the exhilaration of walking into an Olympic/Paralympic Stadium to the roars of 120,000 cheering fans. These images are as indelible as they are blurred, but I clearly recall a story related to me during team debrief by Dr. Susan White. It seems strange that I recall it as Sue was in charge of our intellectually disabled team members who competed in Madrid, away from the main Paralympic Games site. It related to a discussion she'd had with the whole ID contingent prior to their departure. Needing to clearly spell out the team's medical guidelines she reinforced in her intense discussion on sex, condoms and responsibilities to each other, that "no-one was to have sex" whilst representing Australia through the campaign. "Before any athlete was to consider such any sexual encounter" they were instructed to report to the Doctor and discuss the situation. From the ensuing silence, a strapping young male athlete at the rear of the meeting, sitting beside an attractive young lady with whom he clearly had an interest in, raised his hand to ask the only question raised on the topic. "What do we do about sex considering we are married?"

To this day Sue swears she has not yet devised an adequate response to such a simple question and I, as a rookie coach at the time, was never brave enough to raise the question of sex, safe or otherwise, with the Paralympic wheelchair girls team. The importance of open direct discussion of sex and responsibility with intellectually disabled athletes was highlighted to me through this amusing episode and has become a tool which I have utilised in my later coaching career.

Four years later during my next Paralympic campaign in Atlanta, another unusual memory is clear in my mind. Atlanta represented the first time in which some athletes with intellectual disabilities were granted status alongside other athletes from more established disability groups. More on the implications of that later. With six years senior coaching experience behind me, I became fascinated by the refreshingly simple honesty of ID athletes. This was highlighted through an encounter with a young intellectually disabled male swimmer who won a gold medal on the second night of competition. He became an instant hero within the Australian Women's Wheelchair Team, The Gliders. For him competition was over, so to pass time he gradually and ever so politely manoeuvred to become the Gliders number one groupie. After each training session and game, he escorted us back to our accommodation and became a fly on the wall to many of our team discussions and post-mortems. We went about our business without realising he had assumed part of the team's everyday Paralympic lives. Whilst passive and indeed silent, for the most part, such attachment was deemed odd to some team members and to my staff. We had little clue on how to manage either him or his flattering support. We were certainly in no way equipped to dismiss or reject his innocent yet passionate interest. The memory that lingers today is his melancholy, or was that drunken, contribution on the final night of competition after we had been defeated by the USA for the bronze medal. To highlight his understanding of the disappointment we were all feeling, he confessed that indeed we should not worry about losing as his victorious Gold medal was not all it seemed.

"I cheated to win my medal" he confessed in a sombre tone.
"How?" we all asked.
"Well" he started hesitantly, "because I have an IQ of 76".
With some puzzled glances amongst those present he continued, "the cut off point for us IDs is 75".

In our state of morose self-pity, which had beset us since losing the Bronze Medal, he had given us a new perspective. His comprehension of "cheating" by having an IQ score "so far" above the cut off mark had us falling about the floor laughing. Despite his heinous crime and his confession, we collectively refused to expel him from our midst and in the process learned a little more about tolerance of one of our lesser-known team members. Sydney 2000 was the first time I had experienced the full integration of athletes with intellectual disability in preparation, in organisation and in the complex building process of a Paralympic Team on home soil. At that time we had nothing but our own vision and dreams of the successes that this team was about to experience. The anticipation and the excitement in the athletes' village, on the first night were palpable. As an experienced coach for this campaign my team was focussed on solving our own issues, accommodation for my wheelchair athletes in the modern double storey accommodation, team politics over the captaincy and the pressure of expectation to win medals at your home Paralympics. I was suitably self absorbed with team management when at 10.30 p.m. on the second night an urgent alarm was raised. One of the ID track and field athletes had run off and his head coach and manager demanded all hands on deck, to assist in the search for him. He was most unhappy about his roommate, so had decided to quit, leave the village to go home. The sketchy early reports were that Chris Nunn, track and field head coach, himself a half-reasonable athlete in his day, was in hot pursuit. The problem was that as good as Chris Nunn used to be on the track, the escapee, one Tim Sullivan, went on to break many Paralympic sprint records. So in reality we had little chance of catching him anyway. By midnight we had found him, returned him and convinced him he was a valued and vital member of the Australian team. Throughout this mini emergency, I did find myself asking, "what the hell is going on here" as competition had not even started yet and Tim went on to show the world over the next few weeks and indeed years what a fine athlete he was and still is.

History shows that the Sydney 2000 Paralympic team was one of the most successful teams to ever represent Australia at a World event and whilst time with this exceptional team taught me great respect for the abilities of athletes with Intellectual Disability and Physical Disability alike, it is the images from "left field" that remain amongst the strongest in my memory as an outsider looking in on these athletes. The facts are that intellectually disabled athletes contributed proportionally more to this Australian team's success than any other disability group. It was an Athlete with intellectual disability who was recognised as our Paralympian of the Year in 2000. While we were willing to accept their successes on the track and in the pool, I am far from convinced that we have ever afforded them the respect they deserve. Perhaps because we were ill equipped to acknowledge the simplicity of their expression. But for some wheelies (wheelchair athletes), blinkies (visually impaired athletes), storks (amputee athletes) and dribblers (cerebral palsy athletes), I am sure it was because they wished to ask some burning questions.

What the Hell are Intellectually Disabled Athletes Doing at our Paralympics?

Why are they Receiving Equal Recognition or Funding?

Underpinning these questions were the belief amongst many athletes and coaches that "they" don't train like us, "they" don't talk like us, "they" are not elite like us, in fact "they" don't even understand what being elite is!!! These may be harsh questions and assertions, but they are questions that are still being asked and are relevant to the movement today. The Paralympic movement still faces uncertainty when dealing with intellectually disabled athletes. Furthermore, the Paralympic movement appears reluctant to properly address these questions in a thorough meaningful way. They surround such discussion with politics and clouds of political correctness, which when added to our society's uncertainty with regard to intellectual disability, set the stage to ensure that the road ahead for these athletes remains a minefield. Fortunately and conveniently for the International Paralympic Committee, the Spanish Basketball Team in Sydney confessed to cheating in the competition for athletes with an intellectual disability. As many of us are now aware, a journalist from a Spanish newspaper disclosed in his own newspaper that he and a number of others in the Men's Basketball Team, had competed in Sydney with no intellectual disability. The International Paralympic Committee's reaction was one of shock, horror and outrage. Therefore the decision was simple. Intellectually disabled athletes cheat so all were excluded from the Paralympic Games until further notice. The decision was made with a simple vote and accepted with little more than a whimper. No ID athletes competed for medals at the 2004 Greece Paralympic games, full stop.

But who cares really? The Spanish did cheat, but were they the only ones? As someone who has been involved in three Paralympic Games, one does not have to dig too far to discover examples of other athletes crossing the same line. Indeed, are all blind athletes blind and correctly classified? What is the practice of "boosting" discovered by some wheelchair athletes to enhance their performance? But perhaps this is another chapter or indeed a book! The questions I believe to be most relevant include the following:

1   Why were all ID athletes expelled when only the Spanish basketball team were "outed"?
2   What is the best classification system for Intellectually Disabled Athletes?
3   Is the system of classification to simply measure IQ valid?
4   Are the measures for IQ consistent across all countries and are they universally applied?
5   What have INAS-FID done to ensure the validity of their athletes and what are they doing now?
6   What does having an IQ of 75 or less mean?

So without answers to these and many other questions, I found myself re-motivated. Therefore in 2001 I transformed from 'an outsider looking in to become an insider looking out'. I took over as National Coach of the Australian Men's Basketball Team for Athletes with an Intellectual Disability, the Boomerangs. Just as the images I discovered looking in from the outside, amused me, many of my newfound perspectives put a smile on my face or in some instances further confused me. But many a challenge indeed lay before me.

My knowledge of the Boomerangs could be traced back to their preparation for the Sydney 2000 Paralympics where I had been introduced to:

1.   A lumbering 120 + kilogram giant, "waddling" up and down the court but indeed talented around the basket.
2.   A handsome and motivated Lebanese man with a warm smile but too scared to shoot the ball.
3.   An effusively friendly 6'5" player, who reminded me of "Lurch" from the Adam's Family and who was unsure of which hand he shot with but could advise me on how to coach.
4.   An athlete with such athleticism and silky basketball skills that he was invited to play with the Australian Under 18 Squad in an international practice match and upon sinking his first three, three point shots, was asked "how are you intellectually disabled?"
5.   A balding 21-year-old who knew more about the NBA than anyone I know and who believed he would one day play in the NBA.
6.   An athlete who could not come to training without his mum and who expected her to bring his drink bottle to him in every break during individual practice sessions.
7.   A talented basketball player who could dunk, drive and shoot, but who would go 'off his brain' at his team mates if he wasn't given the ball to dunk, drive and shoot.

8. A captain, who understood the game, but wasn't sure whether he had picked the right sport. According to him he had run 100 meters in 11 seconds flat when he was 15 so "should he be chasing an athletics career".

9. Two midgets (in basketball terms), one who claimed that he should be an automatic selection but shouldn't have to practice and the other who practiced for hours but didn't believe he should play.

10. Lastly an exceptional young talent who was a coach's dream, but who was convinced that he would lose his girlfriend if he played for the Australian team.

This was just my first squad and with them I attempted to use my canvas and paints. I found that I had fallen under a magic spell and I thrust myself into the challenge of creating a real, human sporting masterpiece, The Boomerangs. My first team meeting was overwhelmingly positive. I had never felt so wanted by a group of athletes. I outlined my goal to help them win their first medal at a World Championship and then take them on to the Athens Paralympics. I promised to improve each of their individual skill levels so we could play as a team, at a higher level in the future. I committed to teaching them a simple style of play, which they could remember instinctively, and without having to remember "plays" for 25 different situations. The power and intensity of their focus was palpable. The enthusiasm and support of each player in that room gave me a sense that we could not fail. There appeared nothing that they would not do, or sacrifice they would not make to venture down this new pathway together. But reality hit home when I asked a simple question. "Tell me what you remember about your basketball experience in Sydney?" A simple and non-confronting starting point, or so I thought. The passionate enthusiasm drained away in an instant and was replaced by a confusion that only surfaces when your mind goes totally blank. So in an instant I was face to face with 15 totally blank faces intimidated by the question I had posed. Why? Because it became obvious that they retained nearly nothing of their Sydney playing experience. More alarming was that it emerged that they were embarrassed to tell me that they were didn't really understand the question. From that moment I recognised that I had to commit myself to never assuming, that either my questions or explanations were fully understood. Perhaps, my most important lessons in coaching intellectually disabled athletes occurred in that room. Always check and recheck that each individual understands. Do it in a way that least embarrasses the individual and create an environment where your athletes feel comfortable in asking or checking anything they don't fully understand. These pivotal lessons provided a starting point to more effectively communicate with athletes who have become masterfully adept at hiding and deflecting the many things in life that they find difficult. They do this to be accepted and to not expose themselves to a sense of reinforced failure that our society has helped ingrain into their brains. Nobody wants to feel like a "dumb-arse". I have never treated them as such.

I felt almost instantly connected with the team and they followed my every word almost religiously at first. Why? Because they "loved me" or so they told me. I have a suspicion that it was because they were sure I would lead them to the Promised Land, a Paralympic medal. Today those dreams are still there but they are based on trust, honesty, reality and no false expectations.

MY PHILOSOPHY INCLUDES:
1. Improving each individual's physical ability and skill level.
2. Encouragement far in excess of criticism from coaches and from team mates.
3. Teaching the game, 'on court', with simplicity.
4. Learning from mistakes without fear of making them.
5. Playing the game in an uninhibited way.
6. Revisiting our team concepts as many times as is necessary.

Managing athletes who would work themselves into the ground at one training session, and skip the next session without a word is a complex balancing act for a coaching staff. They will train to exhaustion because the national coach has asked them to, whilst at other times show no understanding of the concept of elite training. They are athletes who struggle to comprehend or implement a full game plan and will never solve why some teams who beat them play with players who have no intellectual disability. Yet they play with joy and instinctive passion along with an overwhelming pride in representing their country.

Many of their struggles are born out of the ignorance of those looking in and only seeing that they appear so "normal", whatever that is. If they look and behave so normally why is there any difficulty in matching actual performance with what they picture in their own imaginations? The lack of understanding of the implications of playing sport with an intellectual disability is an enormous obstacle. They face the testing frustrations of not understanding, yet trying to implement what is taught, without losing face. Many have encountered the highs of representing their country at an early age and feeling overwhelmingly successful in doing so. But they then come crashing back down to earth when they return to "normal" life and the same community who cheered for them, shun them when it comes to giving them a permanent job opportunity. They encounter the indignity of being accepted as the warmest, friendliest "most huggable" people on one hand, but hearing some refer to them as "dumb arses" when they don't think they're listening. By the way, that is the politest of the translations that I have heard. I could bore you with stories of arduous preparations and hours of blood, sweat and tears, culminating in an inspirational rise from the ashes performance to win a Gold Medal. Incidentally, we did go on to win our first medal at the next World Championships in Madera, Portugal. It was a Bronze Medal and we won it by one point in the last thirty seconds of the match and it felt 'gooooood'.

Nevertheless, the fairytales are not everyone's reality and besides there are many better books around on that subject. I prefer to share with you some of the realities and obstacles that are faced by these athletes every day. The thought processes behind these episodes, I struggle to understand and I am sure the athletes involved, understand them even less. So I raise some questions and thoughts on what is difficult about understanding intellectual disability. For example, what motivates an Australian player recognised as one of the premier players in the ID Basketball world, to prepare for eighteen months and quit two weeks prior to leaving for a World Championship? How does he reconcile this decision after inspiring his team mates with his 198 cm athletic frame and his capacity to score 25 plus points per game and a ten year commitment to standing along side his team mates? Well it's simple! Add new girl friend, whose idea of support is to explain to her new man that if he pursues this career as an elite intellectually disabled athlete she can forget about staying with her. "I won't live with anyone with that label". From there the excuses no matter how obscure kept flowing and no logic, no loyalty, no financial incentive and no support would move. So we left for our first World Championship without him. Despite the gaping hole in our preparation we stuck by our simple principles and the "Boomerangs" learnt in two weeks how to "come back" from adversity.

We all dream of contact from loved ones back home, when we are travelling overseas but when that phone call from a loved one to one of my team was to tell him that his girlfriend was not able to be at the airport upon his return from Sweden, all hell broke loose. To this athlete this consumed him with thoughts that they were breaking up. His obsession with this notion despite clear messages to the contrary, resulted in him spending $1300 on mobile phone calls in ten days. All just to reassure him that he was not being dumped. No hours of patient counselling, no explanation from his parents, who had paid thousands to come watch him play, not even the confiscation of his phone could heal his emotional trauma. Yes, he did pay the telephone bill and yes his girlfriend found her way to the airport and they are still together. I only hope it is not all he remembers from his first opportunity at representing his country.

Help me in my advisory and counselling techniques please. The coaching staff had identified that one of our most experienced players was undermining the calm approach that we had adopted to training sessions, by yelling frantically on the court at almost every play. Whilst attempting to quietly address the negative effect of this behaviour on his teammates, he stormed from the court hysterically. After two hours of individual counselling we had made no progress. In his mind we were trying to destroy his passion for the game and had no faith in his ability to one day play in the NBA. It was nearly two weeks later that he did return to the team and proved to be a vital part of our successful World Championship. I also think he now understands that we do believe in him, but that might change next training session and he is still waiting for his call up to the NBA.

More importantly you might explain to me and my team of athletes how a simple show of hands in some far away meeting can banish their 2004 Paralympic dream in a moment? They sacrificed the hours, years, employment opportunities and personal relationships, to climb their sporting mountain, only for the IPC ban to create an earthquake beneath them and shattering their world. They could not and did not compete at the Athens Paralympics and to this day they don't understand why. You were not there to help me wipe away their tears. I have not, to this day found a rational answer or justification for this decision and my athletes, all intellectually disabled athletes, appear to be simply pawns in a political sporting game. Mmmmmmmmmmm food for thought.

In November 2004 the International Paralympic Committee passed a motion that "Despite INAS-FID's lack of development of a watertight, reliable, valid and proven eligibility and verification system, this General Assembly agree not to exclude athletes with an intellectual disability from IPC sanctioned competitions, but instead, while recognising that INAS-FID has the primary responsibility, requires that the IPC actively directs the process by which mutually acceptable eligibility and verification systems are developed (e.g. eligibility criteria, sport specific criteria and protest procedures). During this process, INAS-FID's membership status is reaffirmed and, in consultation with the IPC Sports, athletes with intellectual disability should be able to progressively return to IPC sanctioned competitions as a means of testing the sport specific components of the eligibility and verification process".

This motion is conditional and if read closely states that they agree not to exclude and not that they agree to include athletes with an intellectual disability. Will we get to Beijing? I assure you that there is a long road ahead and after the events of the past years I won't be making any promises to my team, but I will continue to coach, fight and give my athletes something to hope for.

I HOPE THAT YOU MIGHT REFLECT FOR A FLEETING MOMENT.

Intellectual Disability is one of the least noticed, least understood, least cared about and most politically ignored groups in our society. My coaching experience has highlighted that it is difficult to recognise, challenging to manage, diverse in its presentation and to many people demanding to make the effort for. My athletes present so normally and in many ways are so. They have learned to be masters of disguise when it comes to showing the world what they don't understand. **They are easy not to notice.** So might I suggest that **YOU TRY TO NOTICE?** Take the time to ask a simple question that might help both you and me understand their lot a little bit better. Make a little effort and it will help make a little difference. I'm lucky because I have in the past noticed, I will in the future and I'm better for experiencing life with them.

12   PARALYMPIC COMPETITION OR TECHNICAL SHOWDOWN?

Katrin Koenen

INTRODUCTION

Athens, Greece, September 2004: The Paralympics are a great success - 4.000 athletes from 136 countries being judged in 19 types of sports; 72.000 visitors at the splendid opening ceremony, world records, emotions and a noticeably increased media interest. Also Otto Bock [the company which this chapter is really about] is breaking all records: 2299 deployments during eleven days of competitions; 107 technicians from 25 countries helping athletes from all disciplines, regardless of whether a carbon spring foot, a modular knee joint or a wheelchair is broken or just needing a final adjustment. Major deployments are done by the orthopaedic technicians at the Otto Bock Service Centre in the Paralympics village, while smaller teams are present on all sites of competitions. This statement and the figures, however, can possibly raise the question, as to whether the athletic performances and records are more dependent on technical devices rather than on constant and intense training, or on the strong will and motivation of the athletes. For example, the 200 meter race for male below-knee amputees that a double below-knee amputee, Oscar Pistorius, finished with a new sensational world record of 21.97 sec, could support this thought. Indeed, it seems that the imagination of a technical showdown is growing with the improvement of the performances and the extension of the development of prostheses and wheelchairs in the competing countries.

Throughout this chapter we will try to find an answer to this question by discussing the development of technical service at the Paralympics, its impact and its justification. This will be achieved by giving an overview of the history of Otto Bock [the company] and its relation to the Paralympics and also by illustrating, what the Service Centre and the work done by the technicians is all about, the increase of technical service, its procedure and its meaning to the athletes will be revealed.

Now, first of all: Who or what is Otto Bock?

THE OTTO BOCK COMPANY GROUP

"Otto Bock" is a group of companies with its headquarters in the ancient town of Duderstadt, Germany. Under the Otto Bock Holding GmbH Co. KG umbrella, the group subdivides into three core sections: a) Otto Bock HealthCare, b) Otto Bock Kunststoff (Foam Plastics), c) Information and Communication Technology (ICT). In 1919, i.e. after World War I, Otto Bock, an orthopaedic technician, began what turned into a unique success, by founding a company in Berlin that would supply thousands of war victims with prosthetic and orthotic devices. He achieved this because it was impossible to meet the demand for these devices with traditional methods of craftsmanship, Otto Bock manufactured prosthetic components in serial production and delivered them directly to the local prosthetists, thus laying the foundation for the orthopaedic industry, now the Otto Bock HealthCare section. From the very beginning Otto Bock was interested in using new materials for manufacturing and even tested and used aluminium for prosthetic components as early as the 1930s. Since the preferred type of wood, poplar, was difficult to obtain, he looked for substitutes in the chemical industry and developed plastic components, which were first employed in the 1950s - some of which are still in use today. Based on this success, it became clear to Max Näder, Otto Bock's son-in-law, that these new materials had great potential, so he founded Otto Bock Plastics in 1953. Today, this company is an important technological partner for Otto Bock HealthCare, but also a developer and producer of plastics for the automobile industry, among others.

Back to Otto Bock HealthCare: Innovation continued to be the principal source of corporate growth: For instance, the introduction of the modular leg prosthesis in 1969 set an international standard, while its patent contributed decisively to the present market position of the company by securing an uncontested market status in leg prosthetics for more than twenty years. Another milestone of the sixties was the development of myoelectric arm prostheses that can be controlled through muscle signals. By applying such complex technology, Otto Bock evolved from a manufacturer of individual components into a producer of complete prosthetic systems.

Since 1990, the family-owned company has been guided into its third generation by Hans Georg Näder – grandson of the company's founder – who took over the management of Otto Bock at the age of 28. And over the last ten years, besides orthopaedic technology, the business field of "Rehabilitation/Mobility" has been established in the HealthCare section. Today Otto Bock is the world market leader in prosthetics, as system provider of high-quality and technologically sophisticated products and services. It consists of more than 50 operative sales and production facilities worldwide, with export business into over 140 countries in the HealthCare section. It is positioned all over Western Europe, in North America and in Japan. In growth regions around Asia and the Pacific Rim, in Eastern Europe, in Central and South America the company is established with sales and service corporations and manufacturing plants. Indeed, since the social significance and integrating power of sports concerns people with disabilities as well as those without, Otto Bock began to sponsor sporting events, starting with the Paralympics in Seoul, 1988. And from the beginning on the concept was not just aimed at financial support: Repair shops were deployed complete with technicians, not only in form of a Service Centre for products of their own making, but performing also on-site service and repair of wheelchairs and prostheses of any make. As global player and with its operative sales and production facilities all over the world, the Otto Bock Company is - so far - the only one worldwide that can offer this high quality service on basis of substantial material know-how within an international service team and at the same time provide the entire logistic process that is needed.

THE JOURNEY FROM SEOUL TO ATHENS

It is clear that the year 1988 represented a positive turning point for the Paralympics altogether. For the first time, the host city of Seoul was hosting both, Olympic and Paralympic Games, and even in quick succession of a 9 day turnaround. Consequently, spectators and media interest for the Paralympics reached a new level. The Paralympics became a media event with international coverage, even though to a less degree than the Olympic Games. Other important trends also became apparent: Prostheses were used more and more in sports, and as a result the athletes began to look for prostheses that were fit for top-level sport and competition. Through this development many world records and other high-grade performances were achieved. But, of course, the use of technical devices – as everywhere – include the possibility of their break down: A prosthesis that does not fit perfectly or turns out to be unstable in some way, a wheelchair with a flat tire or with some kind of irregularity - just reason enough to miss a competition, to lose. Therefore Otto Bock began to provide technical service for the athletes on the spot. About five technicians went to Seoul to offer assistance during the Paralympic Games. The idea of a "Service Centre" was born and was very well accepted and called upon by participants of all teams.

From that period onward Otto Bock became the Sponsor and Official Provider for all Paralympic Games. Barcelona 1992, known as the 'Paralympics of emotions! More top athletes demonstrated their abilities in public. Thousands of thrilled spectators in the stadium could be seen, cheering and doing "la ola" every day. It was the first time that media such as the BBC would broadcast live from the Paralympics. And it was for good reason that this occurred: The "handicapped" athletes demonstrated a substantial improvement in their performances. A long with this Otto Bock expanded their support enormously: In two Service Centres near the entrance to the Olympic Stadium, ten technicians performed about 700 deployments. Whether it involved changing modular components or repairing prostheses, whether the task was to build a structured steel side for a throwing wheelchair or a bench for a wheelchair-bound markswoman, the range of items and operations was endless. By 1994, the Winter Games had also become a regular Paralympic event. Skiing with prostheses for example, which had previously drawn scepticism, had become normal. But, of course, the downhill trails still would cause problems for prostheses and their wearers. Accordingly, on-site service was required. During the Winter Paralympics in Nagano, for example, 53 complex repairs were done only at downhill trails.

In 1996, at the Paralympic Games in Atlanta, about 250 new world records demonstrated the improvement of the athletes' achievements as well as the improvements of their prostheses and wheelchairs and also the repair service increased again: 25 technicians performed a very broad range of work, altogether 1.100 deployments. Next, in the year 2000, the Paralympics "down under": At the magnificent opening ceremony a record number of 3843 athletes from 125 countries participated, all of them contributing to a most impressive, breathtaking event. Importantly the pictures of the excited spectators, watching incredible athletic performances were going around the world and once again Otto Bock offered full technical service: This time sixty orthopaedic technicians from 11 countries did more than 2,000 repairs during these Games.

With the ever growing number of athletes and the further development of sports-prostheses also for winter sports, the number of Otto Bock's technicians and their deployments continued to increase as well: At the Winter Paralympics in Salt Lake City 2002, 20 technicians were on duty, in the Service Centres at the Paralympic Village and its satellites.

Then, at the Paralympic Games 2004 in Athens, all records were broken! No less than 4,000 Athletes from 136 countries entered the stadium during the grand opening, then to achieve 304 world records and 448 Paralympic records. Fifty television stations and a total of 3,200 accredited journalists reported on the Games and 107 Otto Bock technicians gave their best at the Service Centre in the Paralympic Village and at 16 satellites at the sites of competition, all in all 2,299 deployments were completed.

TECHNICAL DEPLOYMENTS: SUPPORT OF ATHLETE'S PERFORMANCES OR SIMPLY A TECHNICAL SHOW DOWN?

So far I have emphasized the number of deployments but what stands behind all that? A deployment means, that an athlete was actively assisted by an orthopaedic technician, ranging from the exchange of a flat tire (most frequent repair during Summer Paralympics), to the repair or fine adjustment of prosthetics and to the full replacement of a sports device. This may involve changing of modular components, improvement of carbon spring feet, reinforcement of orthoses, welding of wheelchairs and also lending of spare parts (e.g. wheelchairs, crutches). Before we were talking more specifically about the deployments of technique, however, what follows is a short overview of the technical equipment needed. From the invention of the wheel to jet airplanes, mankind's progress has been marked by innovative ideas for increasing mobility. Dreams have turned into plans, plans have led to innovation, and innovation has led to fundamental changes in the way we live, causing distances to dwindle and making boundaries less significant if not disappear. Today, more than ever before, people believe that mobility is vital for their quality of life. In regard to prosthetics, this means a continuous search to provide prosthetic devices to individuals with limb de?ciencies, and to make them as functional as possible. Similarly, orthoses are designed to support permanently or temporarily impaired bodily functions, both for therapeutic or prophylactic purposes. Another area for mobilization is the production of manual and electrical wheelchairs and after handicapped people were conceded the right to drive and to train their bodies just like non-handicapped, the development of sport devices started to increase likewise. Athletes began to work on individually adjusted functional prosthetic devices and thus gained considerable advantages for their performances. Out of everyday prosthetics, special equipment was created. Standard issue knees, for example, previously designed as a useful tool for walking, in combination with titanium and a hydraulic control, with a change of configuration and by a carbon fibre flexible system allowed "record" sports prostheses for sprinters. Lighter arm prosthetics were developed in order to give the athletes a slight advantage on the starting block and during the completion of the race the anatomical simulation of the arm provided obvious competitive advantages. Different wheelchairs were created for the varying needs of each type of sport. For example, racing chairs, wheelchairs for basketball, for tennis or for rugby.

Over the years a wide range of complex new technologies and materials evolved and this development certainly has not reached its ultimate heights as yet. However, while all this can and in fact does improve the achievements of the athletes, it also deepens the technological gap between the developed and the developing nations, and at the same time it demands if not enforces an extraordinary qualification of the technicians in the service team, as they must be able to deal with any kind of technology - no matter which material and what problem. With all those new, sometimes self-designed constructions on the one hand and very old technologies on the other hand, also with a high number of unforeseen break downs, the need of professional service is enormous and still growing. No doubt, assistance in all kinds of situations will always be required for handicapped athletes, no matter if dealing with high tech devices or very simple, self-made models. This, after all, is the normal course in the development of sports, whether the athletes are handicapped or not. If we look, for example, at the history of cycling or automobile sports, we see that technical standards and its service have improved immensely in recent years. But also in any other sport that needs specific equipment, be it a sport device, a special shoe or even a swimsuit, technical development has never stopped, neither has it ever been questioned.

On returning to the Paralympics and to the Otto Bock people: Besides the above mentioned "normal" requests for deployment, we understand that the technician must be ready to meet any challenge at the different sites of service. Whether it involves a manufacture of some prosthetic device, quick repairs or searching for highly specialized information, the demands are very high in regard to technological and material know-how, to the entire logistics process and, of course, the orthopaedic techniques. The key to successful team work is a combination of experience, precision and also speed. The time allowed to repair prosthesis during a competition is limited to just a few minutes – again, just like at a cycling or car race. A good example is the experience of Fany Lombaard from South Africa: In the pentathlon event of the above knee-amputees at the Paralympics in Sydney, the axis of his modular knee joint broke. Technicians in the Paralympic stadium had to provide prompt and expert assistance with just a small selection of tools, since the on-site satellites consist of only a workbench. If they could not have helped straight away, the champion would have been out of contest. Instead, Fany Lombaard won the gold medal, establishing a new world record.

Obviously, the art of improvisation also is required in the process: For 30 rugby players the competition at the Paralympics in Sydney could have been over before they started, as their wheelchairs - due to a rule change for international rugby games – were not in accordance with the regulations. It was a 24-hour job for two orthopaedic welding experts to remove the irregular safety devices for their legs, to design and build new ones that were acceptable. Perhaps even more impressive is the story of the German cyclist Michael Teuber in Athens: On the day before the finals the special carbon orthoses supporting his ankles broke. This seemed to end the competition as far as he was concerned but after a nightshift of two technicians, his first fitting of the new orthoses was called for 7 a.m. on competition day; two hours later he won the gold medal in Individual pursuit, and in the end Michael Teuber was one of the most successful athletes on the German team, winning two golden and one silver medal! Finally, fine-tuning must not be underestimated. On the day of the 100-meter race for male below-knee amputees in Sydney, four participants came to the Service-Centre, requesting final adjustment. These athletes finished in the top four positions.

However, it must be stated that, the main body of "clients" calling on the service of the technicians are not medal winners, world champions and record holders. The main group consists of ordinary athletes, many of them from third world countries, which profit from a technically fully qualified service with quality spare parts - a service that for many of them would be unattainable in their country - thus enabling them to take part in the competition. For example, the Iranian National Basketball Team had lost the washers for all wheelchairs on their flight to Athens. Since it would take three days to get correct spare parts, while their first competition was scheduled only two days later, the technicians improvised with some kind of wire. The team took part in the match and came back afterwards to get the chairs fixed for the rest of the Paralympic Games.

CONCLUSION

Whether a Paralympic athlete is out to set a new world record, a Paralympic team is fighting for a medal or individual Paralympic participants running for a new personal best, it is clearly [flesh and blood] the human being at centre stage. It can be clearly stated that at this elite level any kind of success requires a combination of different factors. As far as handicapped sports are concerned, even though technology developments support athletes very effectively – from the energy-storing carbon spring foot and the modular knee joint with hydraulic control to the high-tech basketball wheelchair – the leading group of athletes owe - as their new world records show, their medals to technology. However, their performance can never be attributed to orthopaedic technology alone. In Athens, the winner of the women's long jump for above knee amputees was a Chinese participating without prosthesis, proving that the athlete herself or himself is the deciding factor after all. It is obvious that there are combinations of factors for Paralympic success these include: the human spirit, human will power, human motivation, hard training and dedication which appear to be the key factors to Paralympic success. Naturally, any orthopaedic or technical aids have to function fully, like in any sport - handicapped or not; therefore technical service should be offered to all athletes, in all disciplines, no matter what kind of prostheses, orthoses or wheelchair they require. In this regard the Paralympic Games, the largest international sport event after the Olympic Games, is the only event, though, where an equivalent technical service is offered to all athletes - **free of charge**. Technical deployments then, not only help athletes from developed countries to increase their achievements, but support participants from developing countries to enhance their technical equipment and extend the chance of successful participation. Thereby the gap of technical standards is getting smaller, bit by bit. The offer of deployment free of charge is what organizers of sports events can do to help provide the utmost fairness for all competitors.

Furthermore: If we want the Paralympic Games to go on, growing in all directions – increased number of athletes, world records, participating countries as well as spectators and press media - there is a need for even more progress. In spite of all the success in the past, athletes have to work even harder for more improvement in the future. Yet, it is just as important to continue setting new standards in orthobionics, and learning more about the solutions nature has to offer. If we combine this information with technical expertise, the development of highly functional devices for sports as for everyday life can go on and an interdisciplinary cooperation between orthopaedic technology, universities and institutes for applied science, with physicians and therapists cooperating, is a prerequisite for the Paralympic Games, to continue its success story making the event even more exciting for all. Indeed, it could be argued that by providing free advice and technical assistance Otto Bock has become the 'backbone' of the Paralympic Games.

13   THE PARALYMPICS: HORSE POWER

Donna deHaan & Jo Winfield

INTRODUCTION

The only equestrian discipline currently represented at the Paralympics is Para-Dressage which became a recognised Paralympic sport in Atlanta in 1996. As a sport, Para-Dressage has to date been wrongfully neglected in relation to research and text, yet Para-Dressage is currently making a smooth transition from the introduction stage to the growth stage of the Paralympic lifecycle. As of January 1st 2007, the Fédération Equestre Internationale (FEI) became the first governing body to represent both able bodied and disabled athletes, demonstrating that even in a comparatively short Paralympic history, equestrian sport has evolved as a forerunner in relation to equality and representation.

Para-Dressage is often wrongly perceived by the UK public as being an additional activity offered in conjunction with the Riding for the Disabled Association (RDA). The RDA is primarily concerned with the therapeutic benefits of riding, but often provides a good grounding in dressage training at grass routes level through its own regional and national competitions. Equestrian sport is unlike any other sport and as such Para-Dressage deserves to be identified as an exceptional case study within the Paralympic paradigm. Both horse and rider are athletes and as such come with their own entourage, for example, every team doctor is matched by an equine equivalent, a team veterinary surgeon; for every human physiotherapist there is an additional equine physiotherapist; just as human athletes' can be tested for drugs, so can their equine counterpart, and horses have their very own stabling equivalent to the athletes village. There are also other practical difficulties entwined around equine based events which make them notoriously difficult to manage, for example, climate influence on horse performance and welfare and legislation surrounding disease control (hence Hong Kong and not Beijing will host equestrian competitions in 2008). Furthermore, equine sport in general precariously balances sociological issues such as equality (gender) against inequality (elitist sport). As a sport this situation offers so many unique characteristics to be studied and therefore it should be at the forefront of Paralympic discussion. What follows is an attempt to give greater clarity and explanation of this unique Para-Equestrian sport.

GOVERNANCE AND DEVELOPMENT OF THE SPORT

The Fédération Equestre Internationale (FEI) was founded in 1921 and is the international body governing equestrian sport recognised by the International Olympic Committee (IOC). Currently the FEI represents 134 national federations and is the sole controlling authority for 8 equestrian disciplines; Jumping, Dressage, Eventing, Driving, Endurance, Vaulting, Reining and Para-Equestrian, which is subdivided into Para-Dressage and Para-Driving. The IOC recognises the equestrian disciplines of Jumping, Dressage, Eventing and Para-Dressage. Although Para-Dressage has only been represented at the summer Paralympics since 1996, the FEI Para-Equestrian sports have been developing for over 20 years with World Championships being held every four years since 1987.

In 2006, the FEI became the first International Federation to govern and regulate equestrian sport for both able bodied and disabled riders and Para-Equestrian became the eighth FEI Discipline. The FEI now officially recognises Para-Equestrian as a full discipline, with national and international competitions held in both Dressage and Carriage Driving for individuals with a disability, although Para-Dressage remains the only Paralympic equestrian sport. To keep Para-Dressage as an Olympic sport it is necessary to maintain at least 24 competing nations across three continents. There are currently approximately 36 nations competing in Para-Dressage. Within Paralympic competitions there are normally 70-80 individual available places, which can represent teams of three or four members or individual riders (78 Para-Dressage places have been allocated at Hong Kong). A team is made up of three or four rider places but each team must have a Grade I or II rider within it (see subsequent Classification of rider). Some nations may not have sufficient riders to meet this criterion and can therefore put forward riders on an individual basis.

Para-Dressage is one of only five disciplines from the twenty five Paralympic disciplines represented in Athens in 2004, in which men and women compete as equals and hence can share the winning podium. Indeed Para-Dressage riders could also share the winning podium with able-bodied dressage riders, whilst this has not happened at the Olympics, some Para-riders do compete in able-bodied classes to gain experience at a competitive standard within the sport of dressage. This is possible because in laymen's terms, Dressage scoring and hence placing is based on the quality of the horse's individual required movements, in other words how horse and rider achieve this is to all intents and purpose irrelevant. It is therefore, not unusual to have Para-riders winning classes and qualifying to compete in able bodied national level, such is the standard of the Para horses and riders. This is generally an exception to the other Para disciplines where the Para athletes compete only in their own categories. Whilst the sports of Dressage and Para-Dressage are separated at Olympic level, this equality through the lower ranks helps not only develop horses and riders; it also helps promote Para-Dressage as a recognised sport.

Dressage and Para-Dressage events have often been run simultaneously at the same venue, however, in 2006 the first ever Combined FEI Dressage and Para-Dressage competition was organised in Moorsele (Belgium). The competition involved national teams made up of a Dressage and a Para-Dressage rider and was the very first FEI competition whereby the combined marks of both riders produced a team score, the highest of which produced the winning pair. Not only did this provide a unique opportunity for Para and able-bodied riders to compete together, it also assisted in raising the profile of Para-Dressage riders and the sport of Para-Dressage. Increased exposure and awareness of a Para sport will undoubtedly have a knock-on effect in relation to spectator numbers, media coverage, sponsorship and so on. Raising the profile of Para-Dressage in the context of national and international competition can only have a positive effect in regards to the sports Paralympic profile.

CLASSIFICATION OF A RIDER

In order to provide fair competition for all competitors who may have varying degrees and types of impairments, a 'Profile System' is used and the assessments allow the rider to be classified into the appropriate grade, these assessments are unmounted and relate entirely to the athletic impairment and a Profile number is given which can be applied to any Paralympic activity. Before any Para-Equestrian competitor can be eligible to compete at an international event, he or she must be assessed by accredited classifiers and be allocated a Profile number; this is reassessed every three years.

Para-Dressage is a multi-disability sport, open to athletes with a physical disability or a visual impairment (FEI/IPC). Traditionally, according to the International Paralymic Committee (IPC), riders are classified according to the six different disability groups in the Paralympic Movement: amputee, cerebral palsy, visual impairment, spinal cord injuries, intellectual disability and a group which includes all those that do not fit into the aforementioned groups (les autres). The classification of impairment into easily recognised categories, and the grouping of these categories into grades, facilitate and ensure fair competition. There are five Grades for Para-Dressage, which range from Grade I for the most severely impaired riders, to Grade IV for the least impaired. The competition within each Grade can then be judged on the skill and performance of that competitor on that horse regardless of the competitor's disability. Classification follows IPC guidelines these are:

> *Grade Ia and Ib*: mainly wheelchair users with poor trunk balance and/or impairment of function in all four limbs, or no trunk balance and good upper limb function, or moderate trunk balance with severe impairment of all four limbs. Grade Ia and Ib may be combined in competition classes due to similarities in the performance requirements of the dressage test.
> *Grade II*: individuals are mainly wheelchair users or those with severe locomotor impairment involving the trunk and with good to mild upper limb function, or severe unilateral impairment.
> *Grade III*: are individuals who are usually able to walk without support. Moderate unilateral impairment or moderate impairment in four limbs, may be evident and hence they may need a wheelchair for longer distances or due to lack of stamina. Total loss of sight in either eyes, or intellectually impaired individuals are also categorised into this grade for national competitions. Blacked out glasses or blind folds must be worn by Grade III visually impaired riders.
> *Grade IV*: individuals who have impairment in one or two limbs, or some visual impairment.

Riders are grouped according to their functional profiles. Riders compete in two Dressage events; a Championship Test of set movements and a Freestyle Test to music. There is also a third Team Test for nations who field a team of riders. Competitors are judged on their peformance as they ride their horse using a series of commands for walk, trot and canter. Riders may use permitted assistive devices which include, dressage whips, a connecting rein bar, rubber bands and other aids.

SELECTION OF HORSES

Probably the most fascinating aspect of any equestrian sport is the unique relationship between two athletic entities, horse and rider. Not only are the human athletes selected for teams because they are the world's elite sports men and women in their chosen discipline, their performance and consequent medal hopes are based on the selection, training and performance of elite horses. As previously mentioned, for every member of the rider's support team there will be an equine equivalent support member. Costs must be covered, not only for supporting athletes but also the horses as competitors prepare for and arrive at the Games. In the Olympic equestrian disciplines of Dressage, Show Jumping and Eventing, teams are selected on horse and rider partnerships, partnerships which may have taken years to develop. In order to help develop Para-Dressage as a Paralympic sport the selection and use of Paralympic horse power has changed as the sport has matured. Whilst many nations may be able to provide a Para rider or indeed a team of riders not all nations are able to provide horses due to various logistical issues such as transport across continents, welfare and quarantine concerns. Therefore for the first two Paralympic appearances in Atlanta (1996) and Sydney (2000), the Para riders all used borrowed horses, this applied to all nations in order that a level playing field was maintained. Borrowed horses are selected on their performance and experience in dressage tests; the level that the horses are required to compete at in Para-Dressage will related to the Grade of the rider. For instance, a Grade Ia rider will perform their test in walk, therefore a horse must be capable of maintaining a good walk for the duration of the test (approx 4 minutes), this often requires a horse that has excellent concentration and training and would be competing at advanced or international level. A Grade IV rider will need to have the horse power to perform movements that are seen in advanced level dressage tests.

Within the sport of Para-Dressage, riders within the UK will usually be competing on their own horses or horses that have been lent to them with the view of competing for an agreed length of time, for example until the next Olympics, or World Equestrian Games (WEG). This allows the riders to build up and establish a relationship with a horse and trainer over a period of time. The recent trend of riders using their own horse power enables them to develop their competition skills in able bodied classes as well as Para competitions and gives them the edge in Paralympic competition. For example in the World Para Championships which were held at Hartpury College in the summer of 2007 (a qualifier for the Beijing Paralympics 2008) the majority of teams provided their own horses, however, due to the limitations as mentioned earlier, some nations found their horse power from a pool of horses that the host nation has sourced. This system generally supports nations new to the sport of Para-Dressage who may only have individual riders at this point. Borrowed horses are put forward into a pool with details of the horses capabilities; these can then be matched to the requests received from nations wishing to find a horse. It is up to the nation to visit and assess the suitability of the horse for their individual rider's needs; often these nations are those who are relatively new into this sport and may only be putting one or two riders forward as they are not yet established at a team level. Horses are available at an individually agreed date prior to a competition.

Whilst it is predicted that 90% of competitors at Beijing will provide their own horses, this figure still indicates that 10% of competitors are able to experience this Paralympic sport in spite of limited resources! The support system of borrowed horses has clearly helped develop the international appeal of Para-Dressage as the numbers of competing countries continues to increase, whilst the trend towards 'own' horse power also indicates solid growth and commitment as countries become more established in the sport.

TRAINING OF HORSES

As previously mentioned, the horse is an athlete and as such needs the same level of training and competition preparation as you would expect of a human athlete. Every horse is an individual athlete and every rider will have his or her own style of riding, it is therefore paramount that each horse and rider combination develop an individual training programme. Able bodied riders will spend hours training their horses and are often reluctant to allow others to ride their horses for any prolonged period. During the normal everyday training of the horse, the physical needs of the horse have to be met. Dependant upon the effect of a Para rider's functionality, the horse's needs may be met by the Para rider, but there is often the need for the Para rider's horse to have the training supported by an able bodied rider. Asymmetry in a rider can have a detrimental effect upon the horse's movement and consequent performance and as, such an able bodied rider or trainer will often be used to maintain postural stability in the horse.

At any competition (National to Paralympic) there are restrictions as to who can ride the horses during the actual event itself. Dependant upon the grade of the Para rider some of the horses can be worked in by an able bodied rider (often the horse's trainer or the team trainer), this allows the Grade I and II riders to be mounted on a horse that has been worked in (warmed up) and is in a relaxed and safe state for riders of this category to ride safely. Other grades of riders may have their horse lunged (worked from the ground) for them before they get on. The working in period before a class is timed in order to provide a fair length of time for all competitors.

COACHING / MANAGEMENT

The training of the riders is important at all levels and particularly to develop the coaching aspects that are needed in a competition environment. Within the RDA there are training qualifications that educate the trainer on the therapeutic aspect of working with horses but these do not meet the needs of the competitive Para-rider. In the UK, The British Horse Society (BHS) provides a system of training riding Instructors that have more skills related to developing the performance of the horse and rider, across a range of equine disciplines. The Para-Dressage riders have been utilising Instructors from this background who have then adapted their skills to meet the needs of the Para-riders and who work alongside the sports physiotherapists to provide the coaching that these athletes require. Riders can search for and find suitable BHS registered Instructors through the BHS database, however there is currently no system in place to identify that an Instructor is specialised in coaching Para-riders.

In Britain, the United Kingdom Coaching Certificate (UKCC) qualifications are being developed across all sports and equestrian is one of the twenty one priority sports leading this initiative. The BHS system is including the UKCC qualification in its examination system from 2007. In this new system, individuals at the first level of riding instructor, BHS Assistant Instructor (BHSAI) can also complete a portfolio for submission for the UKCC Level 2 coaching certificate. In time this structure should enable the training and development of coaches to Level 4, which would allow a coach to extend their coaching practice and skills and refine their coaching practice. Once the Para-riders are at an international level their requirements become predominantly coaching led. These coaching skills are developed in the same way for equestrian sport, as for any other sport.

Para teams are managed by a Chef d'Equipé, who is responsible for the performance of the whole team in exactly the same way as the other equestrian disciplines.

THE FUTURE OF PARA-DRESSAGE

Para-Dressage is still a relatively late starter in comparison to the evolution and development of other Paralympic sports. Approaching its fourth Paralympics, Para-Dressage has certainly come out of the starting gates with pace and is continuing to develop in relation to participation numbers. To date however, this sport has been somewhat neglected in terms of research attention. Individuals interested in equine science have studied the horses from a physiological perspective, those interested in sport psychology are beginning to study rider psychology but in researching for this chapter we were hard pushed to find any studies relating to the sport itself. This area needs to be addressed. Those of us interested in sport, in the beauty, the power, the politics and the freedom of sport, should sit up and take an active interest in the sport of Dressage, for there is no other discipline that truly encompasses the beauty, the power, the politics and the freedom of sport. In what other sport will you witness men and women, able bodied and Para athlete competing side by side? The FEI is one of the only governing bodies that jointly represents an Olympic and Paralympic discipline. This is a sport that embraces equality and unity. Once again we need to reiterate that there is a need to carry out research relating to this sport and learn from this unique discipline. As a sporting community preconceptions need to be shed of equestrianism as elitist and not worthy of being categorised as a sport. In short, whilst Para-Dressage is evolving as a sport, individuals who profess to be interested in sport need to take a closer look at this sports unique characteristics.

SOURCES

British Dressage (BD) and Para-Dressage www.britishdressage.co.uk
British Equestrian Federation (BEF) www.bef.co.uk
British Horse Society (BHS) www.bhs.org.uk
Fédération Equestre International (FEI) www.horsesport.org
International Paralympic Committee (2002) Equestrian Classification Manual.Bonn:IPC.
Riding for the Disabled Association (RDA) www.rda.org.uk
United Kingdom Coaching Certificate (UKCC) www.ukcoachingcertificate.org

SECTION 3

OLYMPISM VERSUS PARALYMPISM?

This section is perhaps the most controversial as it attempts to provide answers to the age old question as to whether Paralympians should be included in the context of the Olympic Games. It reviews a wide range of perspectives and attempts to truly mix the academic and practical perspectives of the Paralympic Games. Conclusions are drawn which are developed under sound reasoning and include important ideas such as volunteerism for the Paralympics and the notion of terrorism and the benefits of Paralympic sport and acknowledging the wider social needs of athletes in the Paralympics.

14   A KALEIDOSCOPE OF COLOUR & VIBRANCY: REFLECTING ON THE PARALYMPICS

Lisa O'Keefe

INTRODUCTION

In Sydney, Australia, on October 18th 2000, the 11th Paralympic Games opened amid the dramatic and colourful backdrop of Home Bush Stadium which was attended that evening by over 100,000 thousand people. The opening ceremony of the Paralympic Games unveiled a ritual awash with a kaleidoscope of colour and vibrancy. Australian pop icon, Kylie Minogue sang for the crowd and athletes from all over the world entered the stadium to cheers and cries of delight from the watching supporters. The Paralympic Song written by Graeme Connor, 'Being here is what it's all about' (Paralympian, Oct. 2000) rang out, and when brought together, the different elements of the occasion seemingly became symbolic of the culture and traditions of Australia. This coupled with the ideal that the Games are a complex interaction of passion, courage, strength, athleticism and fun perhaps leads us to argue that the Paralympics is the only remaining 'Games' that really encompasses the true Olympic Ideals and spirit as espoused by the early sport researchers and indeed, De Coubertin himself.

The Sydney Paralympics was a very special event for so many reasons. Never before had the southern hemisphere hosted the world premier showcase for disabled athletes. These were the Games which clearly hoped to encapture the Paralympic motto 'Mind, Body, Spirit' and help to work toward the ultimate goal of integrating elite athletes with a disability into able bodied sport. How then did the 2000 Paralympics compare to the 2000 Olympic Games? This question is interesting as when attending the Olympics, one feels honored to see the world's elite athletes performing at their best, for example watching the fastest men and women on the planet. However, the Paralympics aroused different emotions and feelings for us. It too delivered great performances from many athletes, 550 gold medals won and tales of ecstasy and agony from the track, swimming pools and sports halls which conversely, made us have feelings and emotions which were deeper than those felt at the Olympics. There was not a sense of pity, as some might suggest, but a heart felt passion and admiration for the sport stars, which was often accompanied by thoughts of being ashamed. Ashamed in that the small things that we moan and grumble about continuously seem so insignificant compared to some of the problems that the athletes faced on a daily basis. They are indeed inspirational and make you want to go home and change your life, do those things you always wanted to do, but never did, and accomplish things for yourself. The lessons to be learned from the athletes are many and varied; they taught me discipline, determination and a willingness to work hard against all odds. But what else did the Sydney Paralympics represent? What else did they give us and why were they in the words of the IPC President, at that time, Dr. Robert D. Steadward, 'The best Games ever?'

Firstly, the cooperative agreement signed four years earlier between the IOC and IPC, had brought both Games together in terms of shared facilities and workforce. All core services in Sydney were delivered by the same staff and both Olympic and Paralympic athletes lived in the same village and enjoyed the same catering services, medical care and venues. Ticketing, technology and transport systems for the Olympics were seamlessly extended to the Paralympics. Getting too and from the facilities was relatively pain free and despite intense security, lines into events and competitions were kept to a minimum. In fact the train ride out to Homebush and the entrance to facilities all added to the atmosphere of the occasion. Spectators, all making for the stadium, included a multitude of nationalities, a rich diversity of languages and you found yourself talking to complete strangers about the Games, the events, what motivated and led them to be a part of the Games. Above all else you could feel the anticipation, the excitement and the warmth that brought everyone together. You felt part of a great event, a great occasion, which made you smile at the world and made you proud to be part of a piece of sporting history.

Many of the volunteers from the Olympics were also working at the Paralympic Games and seemed just as happy, involved and exhilarated by the experience as they had some two weeks previous. Those that I spoke too said that the whole experience had changed and enriched their life and that the Paralympics was just as incredible and stimulating as the Olympics had been. Many commented that it had been 'the best bit', as these athletes were in it purely for the competition itself and not for million dollar contracts or endorsement deals.

Since the first Paralympics was held in Rome in 1960, with just 400 athletes and staff including 23 countries. (Canadian Wheelchair basketball association, Jan 1996), the event has grown dramatically. From 3,053 at the Seoul Games in 1988, the Games have increased in size to 3,824 in Sydney (IPC, 2004). The number of staff including coaches, medical staff and administrators also rose from 1,000 in Barcelona (1992) to over 2,000 in Sydney (IPC, 2004). Sydney also became the largest Games ever in terms of the number of participating countries with 123 delegations, including the independent athletes of East Timor. Most participating nations also brought more athletes than in the past. For example, the National Paralympic Committee of South Africa fielded the largest team in their history, a contingent of 88 athletes and officials. However, this was not the only 'first' for the Sydney Games. For the first time, 18 full medal sports were on the program and the debut for the sports of wheelchair rugby, which had been a demonstration event in Atlanta and women's power lifting, along with sailing. Along with this there were over 300 new world and Paralympic records set. Of course other records were set in Athens 2004.

This trend continued throughout, as Sydney also became the biggest Games in terms of those attending. The fantastic weather coupled with the selling of day passes, which allowed entrance into any event, rather than 'set' competitions, meant that people could come in and visit any of the venues. Everyone had a chance to see any and every event and this encouraged many to attend and helped to promote different sports, which people may never have previously attended had others not been full. The affordability of the tickets at only $15 Australian dollars or $8 for concessions meant that people could spend the whole day at the Games and also get the opportunity to visit a number of the events and any of the 15 venues hosting them. This allowed people, who could not afford tickets to the Olympics to still be part of the whole experience, visit the facilities and witness and be part of the largest world wide sporting event.

Many visitors from within Sydney and the surrounding area attended because they wanted to support their nations bid and help to make the Games a success. The Australian public clearly demonstrated their national pride, coming out in droves to support their Games. Everyone was a sea of yellow and green and chants of 'Aussie, Aussie, Aussie, Oy, Oy, Oy' were to be heard wherever you went. In the stadiums, the arenas and even on trains, buses and in the street, the chorus of voices sang out, supporting not only their home grown athletes but their very own, Paralympic Games. The success in terms of attendance was obvious. A record number of 1.2 million tickets were sold, more than double the 500,000 for Atlanta. On the Sunday, over 88,500 spectators attended the biggest attendance for any competition day to date. (CNNSI.com, October 23rd 2000). The opening ceremony itself sold over 92,000 seats with some observers putting the figure closer to 110,000. (ABC coverage of the 2000 Games). Steadward argued that 'Ticket sales far exceeded the International Paralympic Committee's expectations and certainly doubled the goals set in the early stages' (CNNSI.com, October 28th 2000). Ticket sales were expected to generate about $9 million but demand was far greater than had been anticipated and over $11 million worth of tickets were sold. Together the athletes, with the supporters helped turn the Paralympics in Sydney into a great spectacle. The Games were exciting, there were no household names, no real superstars but we were still impressed by the athletes that ran, jumped, threw, played and swam in front of us. There was a sense of achievement and pride not only for the athletes but the spectators who witnessed the events.

PROBLEMATICS

Regardless of previous comments regarding the better aspects of the Games 'sport is still sport' and the Games were not without its fair share of controversy. One of the unfortunate similarities between the Paralympics and the Olympic Games was the use of performance enhancing drugs and materials. In a negative way, the two are now both on a par, and just as in the Olympics, which had taken place two weeks earlier, there were drug allegations later substantiated with positive samples. This became one of the main discussion topics heard around the stadium and differing venues of the Games: Who were the athletes who had tested positive for drug use? Many people were extremely shocked about this, and often more so than with the doping cases at the Olympic Games themselves, which many witnesses said were expected. However, doping cases at the Paralympics, seemed to upset and surprise spectators greatly. Many felt that disabled athletes would not resort to such tactics, perhaps the evidence of not only doping but categorization problems, which will be discussed later, demonstrates the competitiveness and the increasing importance of success at the Paralympics.

It was the first time drugs were detected since the Barcelona Games and the most ever during a single Games. As the IPC President Dr. Steadward commented, 'Never before in Paralympic histories have we witnessed such a number of doping offences'. It could be argued however, that although no drug cheats were found in Atlanta, out-of-competition testing was not introduced until the Sydney Games and so it can be assumed that athletes may have been taking banned substances and only remained uncaught because of a weakness in the testing mechanism of the system. Ten power lifters were found to have used performance-enhancing drugs following out-of-competition tests before the Games opened and US sprinter Brian Frasure was stripped of his silver medal in the F44 200m for amputees after testing positive for steroids. He was banned for four years.

This was astonishing for many spectators. The image for many people is that athletes with disabilities are not 'real' people; they do not see that just because someone has only one arm, they can still be just as competitive, just as ruthless, determined and willing to do whatever it takes to get to the top, as someone with two. For those who had expected a 'clean' Games, many went home disappointed and let down. Even disabled sport is corrupt in this way? Is nothing still sacred in the sporting arena? However, perhaps even more disturbing, and something that I found difficult to grasp, are the tactics employed by some athletes, which are feasible due to their disabilities. One technique that I was made aware of, dubbed 'boosting' but technically known as autonomic dysreflexia, involves the athlete, through various means causing the body significant amounts of pain, in order to gain a reaction, which may help in competition. It can be done through sitting on a ball bearing, filling the bladder to a dangerous level or pricking a pin to the flesh, ingesting great amounts of fluids prior to the sporting event to distend the bladder or tightening garments. It is described as a normal response to pain that is regarded as a medical emergency in a hospital. On a sports field it could cause a surge of adrenaline that might help the individual win a gold medal. Those using "boosting" technique attract attention by their startled expression, sweating, goose bumps and high blood pressure. That is why the athletes are checked before they take the field. The benefits of such a technique are reported to be 'increased cardiopulmonary effects, oxygen utilization and noradrenaline release' (Malanga and Filart, 2004). This malpractice is common among spine-injured competitors even though "boosting" exposes them to the risk of suffering a stroke.

This technique obviously undermines the credibility of the Games and does nothing to improve the public image of disabled sport. It should be with great consideration that athletes make the decision to involve themselves in such practices. Not just solely because of the medical consequences but also because of the social ramifications that this triggers. The Paralympics and its athletes often struggle to gain recognition, to be taken seriously as elite athletes and to obtain and secure funding and sponsorship for themselves and their sport. Incidences such as drug taking and boosting, can only hurt and hinder the Paralympic Movement in the long run. Rumors of these performance enhancing techniques were strong in and around the Paralympics and horrifying stories of what athletes were prepared to do to themselves were repeatedly heard. People were appalled by these suggestions and even some of those competing expressed their disgust and repulsion for what they knew was taking place.

Another major talking point of the Sydney Games was about categorization. Protests and counter protests were lodged after questionable performances by many athletes who it seemed may have been competing in the wrong category. There were many stories of unfair competition, debates and discussion about the criteria for each category and how accurate the screening process for athletes was. One of the most outstanding memories I had from the Games was the 5,000meters T-11 race for totally blind runners. The final, won by Kenyan, Henry Wanyoike was protested by the GB team after their runner Bob Matthews came second. It was believed that the appeal was on the grounds that the winner was not totally blind and had dragged his guide throughout the last three laps of the race. In fact after the race, he broke from his guide and jumped over a hurdle barrier. The appeal was quashed by the Court of Arbitration despite a number of raised eyebrows about the sight of Wanhyoike when he collected his gold medal. I personally could not believe the decision or what I had witnessed on the track but it highlighted both the problems of categorization and the questionability of some of the criteria for determining the categories. The thought of all the hard work put in only to be taken away by others who are no more than cheats, is heartbreaking at any level, but especially when four or more years of dedication and hard work are unsatisfactorily and unfairly rewarded. This demonstrates nothing more than a total disrespect for not only the Games themselves but their fellow competitors and a total disregard for the spirit of the Paralympics.

Another question posed by viewers of the Games was why can't the Olympic Games be an Olympic Games for all athletes rather than have 2 Games segregated along able/disabled lines? This call for 'vertical integration' is based on the idea that competition would be organized around the sport and not the disability. It is felt by some that this would help the Paralympians to be seen as athletes not just as courageous and determined people. From the mainstream athletes the argument is always that it would weaken their competition and have the potential to cause a loss of sponsors. Nevertheless, even those involved in disabled sport have concerns. Logistically, how would the Games be able to cope with the increased number of athletes, staff and officials etc during the same two week period, plus how would the schedules and venues be able to accommodate the competitions? Also, the Paralympics gives those with disabilities the opportunity to show the world how they are capable of performing. If the Games were compressed into one, those with disabilities may well lose their chance to be the focal point for the world and would have to share the stage with their able counterparts. This way, the athletes get to have their own time, their own moment, ensuring that the whole world is focused and watching them and no one else.

Finally, a main contention within Sydney was the inclusion of the 'intellectually disabled' category. First included in Atlanta, with events in swimming and athletics, the numbers of athletes rose dramatically, with 244 competing in Sydney (Slot, 2001). During the Games, many of the disabled athletes that I spoke to disapproved of the 'intellectually disabled' athletes being there at all. They said that they did not understand the concept of competition and winning was not necessarily their prime motive for taking part. I did witness this myself in a Men's T20 Track event. One athlete had a significant lead on the rest of the field but slowed down to look behind and as he said afterwards, 'let the field catch him'. He felt bad to be winning by such a margin. This demonstrates the difficulty in determining whether to admit the category into the Games. Disabled athletes insist that it weakens the Paralympics and that these athletes do not understand the concept and therefore should not be allowed entrance into an event, which is for elite competitors. Along with this is the question of how accurate is the categorization process? Athletes qualify for this category by having an IQ under 75 and by providing documentation illustrating social dependency and they have to have been mentally disabled prior to age 18. Many expressed concern that this was just as difficult if not more so to accurately test for and so may be open to issues of wrong categorization.

Unfortunately, after the Games, it was found that the Spanish Men's basketball team and gold medal winners had only 2 out of the 12 players on their squad who were actually intellectually disabled. Carlos Ribagorda, a journalist said that he played for the team for over two years and he and nine team mates were not subjected to any medical or psychological tests to check their eligibility. He alleges that athletes in other sports were also not disabled and also did not meet the eligibility criteria (The Paralympian, No.4, 2000). Although only a small number of athletes were actually found to have abused the system and feigned handicap in this way in order to compete, we can be unsure as to how many really were involved in the deception. This fraudulent use of the classification system has had far reaching repercussions for the Paralympic Movement. The IPC banned all intellectually disabled athletes from the Paralympics, including the winter Paralympics in Salt Lake City in 2002.

As I write the case is still ongoing but I have two initials reactions; firstly, spare a thought for those in the intellectually disabled category, who were not cheats, who competed fairly and are now being punished because of the selfishness of others. Secondly, when did winning in the Paralympics become so much more important than fair play, honesty, and pride? It seems that the very nature of the Paralympics has changed. Perhaps we can blame the increased sponsorship of the Games, which suggests that they are viewed as a viable event for companies to market their products. Big name corporations lent their voice to the Games, including Mercedes-Benz, Nike, Adidas and Vodacom or maybe the increased media coverage, with over 2,300 media representatives from all over the world on-site to cover the Games made a difference? Web casting was also introduced, with an estimated 300 million hits during the two week period of the Games. Is the pressure to perform in disabled sport now reaching the heights previously only seen in the 'able bodied' world? Is the competition now been viewed with more legitimacy throughout the world? Did the fact that the IOC during its 11th Session where it elected the President of the IPC to be a member for the first time prove significant?

We could answer yes to all of these questions, and highlight how that interestingly the Games are beginning to display many of the characteristics of its bigger and older brother. Questions about the fairness of categorization and the appropriateness of those with intellectual disabilities being able to compete alongside those with physical limitations will long continue to be debated. The Games raised many questions, had a share of controversies and can if we look closer teach us a number of lessons for the future. The Sydney Paralympics were a demonstration of quality sport in the 21st century. They had everything, the drama, the ideals, the sadness and bitterness stemming from the cheats; they displayed elite athletes performing at their best for the whole world to witness. What do we take from it? That not everything is rosy, hard decisions needed to be made and policies changed. Those in the highest echelons of the Paralympic organization need to work together to strive towards categorization policies that are accurate, that are fair, and that eliminate the opportunity for those willing to take advantage and inveigle the system. The out of competition drug testing needs to continue and be strengthened, to reduce if not eradicate the possibility of athletes beating the doping policies.

But on a positive note, what were the greatest moments of the Sydney Games? The warmth and camaraderie of both athletes and spectators? The openness of everyone involved and a willingness to socialize with strangers, who later became friends for life. I remember standing proud for the national anthems with individuals from opposing countries and the realization that good can come from the world being brought together and working together. What seems clear is that for those who were lucky enough to witness them, the Sydney Paralympic Games were for many people a life changing experience. The kind of experience that that can live with you your whole life, that gives you goose bumps just thinking about it and makes you smile as you recall the memories. The 2000 Paralympics encapsulated both the good and bad evident in life and sport but overall they demonstrated that elite disabled athletics can work. Indeed, people do want to watch the Paralympic Games and are willing to spend time and money watching and more importantly that these athletes are elite athletes, now more so than ever before, in every sense.

15   TWO GAMES ONE MOVEMENT? THE PARALYMPIC VERSUS THE OLYMPIC MOVEMENT

Peter Kell, Marilyn Kell & Nathan Price

INTRODUCTION

Every four years the Paralympic and the Olympic Games combine to become the largest single sporting event on the globe. The combination of these two sporting movements is characterised by a complex and often contradictory relationship. The Paralympics are intended as a parallel event to the Olympics and it is a relationship that often sees the Paralympics as nothing more than a "side show" to the Olympics. This relationship introduces questions about whether the holding of the Paralympics is in the best interests of the disabled sports people and Paralympic athletes. There is also a concern that aspects of the Paralympics reinforce outdated notions about the abilities, status and place of disabled people in society and within sport.

This chapter briefly documents progressive moves in the last 50 years of the 20th Century to develop a closer relationship between the two sporting movements and organising bodies while exploring some of the dilemmas and contradictions that emerge between them. The authors argue that while the Paralympics has led to significant beneficial outcomes, not least developing a positive profile of the achievements of disabled athletes, the association with the Olympics has some troubling aspects. The authors question the need for a parallel event suggesting that the current dual format only perpetuates outdated stereotypes about ability and disability and reinforces a paternalism and devaluation of the achievements of Paralympians. The chapter argues that much of protocols and systems of classification in the Paralympics contradict contemporary thinking about sportsmen and women by concentrating on the notion of disability. This use of a medical model reliant on "deficit" theory as the organising logic of the Paralympic games contradicts the obsession of the Olympics with human performativity that challenges boundaries of 'faster, higher and stronger'. The authors suggest that the success of the Olympics has been based on the imagery of the perfect athletic body. Olympic mythology and culture has been underpinned by fantasies about bodily perfection and can traced through the work of Leni Riefenstahl's Olympia movie in 1936 to commercial coverage of today. This Olympic obsession with the imagery of bodily perfection contradicts much of the contemporary theorisation about disabilities and reverses many advances made in rights for disabled people.

In addition this chapter briefly documents and explores a selection of issues concerning the links between the Paralympics and the Olympics and identifies the inequalities in financial support, athletic careers, media profile and status and prestige as elite athletes. The Paralympics have largely avoided the controversies and scandals associated with the excesses of the Olympic officials but the relationship has not always been in the best interests of disabled sports men and women. It goes further by arguing that supporters of disabled sports have three possible choices for the future in the linkages with the Olympics.

They can remain locked in a co dependent relationship with the IOC, conducting parallel games, or argue for a total integration of the Paralympics into the greatest show on earth. The chapter argues that another alternative is to seek to develop a different approach that is oriented to the needs of the disabled sporting community that does focus as an elite event but values participation.

THE PARALYMPIC JOURNEY: PARALLELING THE OLYMPICS

The Paralympics emerged as a direct consequence of the rampant nationalism that spawned the Olympic movement in the early 20th century. Part of the Olympic ideal articulated by Frenchman Baron Pierre de Coubertin was an affirmation of the nation state and the preparation for military conflict through the rigors of sport. More particularly it was preparation for war against Germany after the indignities of losing the Franco-Prussian war. In the wake of the cataclysmic wars of 1914 -18 and 1939 -1945 the dimensions of injury and trauma meant that rehabilitation and sport were linked as expressions of nationalism, sacrifice and stoicism.

The first Games were attributed as being organised by Sir Ludwig Guttmann in 1948 at the spinal injuries clinic at Stoke Mandeville in England. The Institute opened in 1944, during the war, incorporated sports as part of the treatment of war casualties. The link with the Olympics was established early with the Games, started on the same day as the opening of the 1948 London Olympics. These first Games attracted 16 competitors but the event repeated throughout the 1950s grew in popularity with 360 competitors from 24 countries competing in 1957 (Adair & Vamplew 1998). The progress towards the integration of what was to become the Paralympics and the Olympics really commenced at the end of the 1960 Rome Olympic Games when 400 disabled athletes participated in Olympic style events in 8 disciplines. By 1988 at the Seoul Games the relationship expanded to include the same venue for the Paralympics as the Olympiad. This practice has become accepted with the exception of the Soviet Union in 1980 where organisers refused to host the Paralympics and justified this lapse with the claim there were "no disabled citizens in the USSR" making the Games unnecessary. From 1960 the categories of participants expanded from exclusively wheel chair athletes in 1948 to include the vision impaired who were admitted in 1972, amputees admitted in 1976 and intellectually impaired athletes who were admitted in 1992. The categories have expanded to include recognition of Cerebral Palsy athletes and non-specific disabilities as les autres (the others) (Hughes 1999 p173). This expansion of eligibility has resulted in steady growth in participation so that by the Athens Paralympics in 2004 with 3,696 athletes coming from 136 countries. This growth meant that more athletes competed in the Paralympics in both Sydney and Athens than participated in the 1956 Melbourne Olympic Games.

The interrelationship between the two Games includes the participation of athletes in both events. Most notable Pal Szekeres, a Hungarian fencer, won a bronze medal in 1988 in Seoul. He was in a car accident in which he sustained spinal injuries. In the 2004 Athens Olympics he created history by winning a bronze medal in the individual foil (IOCa 2004). The integration of the Paralympic and Olympic Games saw the adoption of many of the rituals and symbols of the Olympic movement including the torch relay, athletes and official's oath, medal presentations, the extravagant opening and closing ceremonies and the importance of the marathon event as part of the sporting calendar. The Summer and Winter Games format has been replicated in the Paralympics as well. In the sports there has been a mix of "niche" disabled events such as wheelchair rugby as well as generic events such as judo, cycling and archery adapted to the needs of disabled sportsmen and women. The Summer Paralympics in 2004 included 18 sports. The Paralympic 'Winter Games' emerged after the 1976 Toronto Games and includes ice sled hockey, cross country skiing, Alpine skiing, the biathlon and ice sled speed skating.

While the Paralympics were the largest single 'multi sporting event' behind the Olympics recognition and profile remained static until the televising of the Paralympic Games at Barcelona in 1992. These Games broke records for attendance, attracted over 1.5m spectators on a no charge admission basis. However, the figures were surpassed by the Sydney and Athens events that were characterised by large and enthusiastic paying crowds. Indeed, while the integration of the Paralympics and the Olympics has been a progressive development and has lifted the profile of disabled sports the path has not been without its dilemmas. These dilemmas suggest that there are still lingering questions about the wisdom of integrating Paralympic and the Olympic competition? Part of the dilemma is also a theoretical issue about how contemporary concepts of ability and disability are represented.

PARALLELING THE OLYMPICS! CONTRADICTING CONTEMPORARY VIEWS OF INCLUSION

Initially, the name "Paralympic" referred to an event for paraplegic competitors. However, with the inclusion of more disability categories, the prefix "para" has taken on its Greek meaning of "parallel" that is an event run parallel to the Olympic Games. The reality of parallelism is that no matter how good the performance of a disabled athlete he/she can never compete in the Olympic Games by seeking special consideration, such as specialised equipment, support or facilities. This does not prevent disabled athletes from competing in the Olympic Games. One of the more recent examples is Frank Bartolillo, a profoundly deaf athlete, who represented Australia in fencing at the 2004 Athens Summer Olympic Games on the same terms as all other athletes. However, this is an exception and the attitude of the Olympic movement is one of compete on our terms of compete in your own games.

The Olympic ethos specifies a number of roles that relate to these questions explored in the earlier section. The sixth role in the charter of the International Olympic Committee is to "act against any form of discrimination affecting the Olympic Movement". The eleventh is "to encourage and support the efforts of sports organisations and public authorities to provide for the social and professional future of athletes" (IOC, 2005, p. 10). While these two roles might seem highly appropriate in any consideration of the future of disabled sport they are in reality meaningless in terms of the Paralympics. This is because there is a separation at the peak level that contradicts the declared Olympic roles. The International Paralympic (IPC) is not actually a member of the Olympic organization and is a separate one that has its own vision, mission, goals and roles which has a very different mission and perceptions. So while the Olympic motto of

"Swifter, Higher, and Stronger" suggests pushing human physical capabilities to the absolute limit, the Paralympics motto of "Spirit in Motion" suggests vitality and excitement. While the Olympic Movement seeks to develop elite sport, logically an exclusive orientation, the Paralympic movement regards one of its roles as promoting "the concepts of health and human rights for athletes with a disability", a much more inclusive approach (Blauwet, 2005, p. 2).

By sanctioning a parallel system the Olympic Movement has failed to include disabled athletes in elite international competition and institutionalised exclusion as a taken for granted phenomena that is beyond challenging. Inclusion will not be a reality until athletes, disabled or non-disabled compete at the same events in the same teams. Inherent in this is the right to equal training facilities, coaching, funding, and media coverage. Any challenges to the status quo and any quest for inclusion are made more difficult by the use of the category and class system that the IPC uses to codify disabled athletes. It acts to exclude rather than include because classification follows a medical model and any classification deriving from a such a model assumes that "the problems that face people with disabilities are the result of their physical and/or mental impairments and are independent of the wider sociocultural, physical, and political environments" (Brittain, 2005, p. 430). In contrast to an exclusionary medical model a rights based inclusive approach celebrates difference and recognises diversity and is a shift from obsessive concerns with disability around often-constructed views about what people can't do (Kell, 2004). To make legitimate claims to being inclusive there needs to be real meaning behind celebrating the sports, people's participation in sport and not disability. To overcome this institutional discrimination the option is for the two sporting bodies to merge and recognise what has already occurred at national and event levels. To shift from a medical model to a social and rights based model of disability a combined IOC and IPC would need to consider how the world's most elite sporting event can remove the social, cultural and political barriers that currently force the majority of disabled athletes into a parallel and lesser competition. It is however; a challenge that needs to respond to the calls for equality in money, media and profile for disabled athletes.

THE CHALLENGES OF INCLUSION: MONEY AND MEDIA

While the relationship between the Olympics and the Paralympics has been assumed to be one that is parallel and equal, there have been periodic incidents that have challenged these assumptions. The relationship has often been typified by the sort of hitches that happened in 1996 at the Atlanta Olympics where parallel committees organising both Games experienced problems in the changeover. The observations of participants illustrate some of these problems.

> Atlanta was not ready for the Paralympic Games; the village was not ready and the venues were not ready, so we learned from that experience we extended the time between the Games – to get enough time to keep that momentum alive for the Paralympic Athletes. This was very important and it was highlighted in Atlanta. We got off the plane in Atlanta, there were no decorations. We went to Centennial Park, which I was so looking forward to seeing. It was rubble they had knocked it down (Hughes 1999 p174).

Rather than evidence of a parallel relationship with the Olympics the crossover problems are compelling evidence of neglect of the needs of disabled athletes and the subordinated status allocated to the Paralympics as an add on to the main event. These incidents in Atlanta contributed to the eventual integration of the planning of the Paralympics and the Olympics in 2000 with the Sydney Paralympics Organising Committee (SPOC) and the Sydney Olympics Games Organising Committee (SOGOC) combining to improve co-ordination and working together. This should not have been difficult because the precedent had already been established in 1994 at the Lillehammer Winter Games where the same organising committee operated both Games but the summer sports were much slower to make this change. However, the dilemmas that led the hiccups in Atlanta are not simply "co-ordination problems" but a deeper manifestation of the incompatibility of organising the Olympics centred on the logic of corporate global capitalism and the need for state support and planning for Paralympics.

The Atlanta Games were promoted as the "free enterprise Games" and the reliance on free enterprise models as the overarching organisational philosophy for the Paralympics is inappropriate because the Paralympics lack the marketing and pulling power of the Olympics in obtaining television broadcast revenue, corporate support and individual donations that typify the Olympic "free enterprise" spirit. The promotion, participation and production of Paralympic sports are heavily dependent on underwriting by governments and state and the Atlanta example is evidence of how the market philosophy left the Paralympics vulnerable. The paucity of any illusion about a parallel status with the Olympics is exposed most starkly where financial support, television coverage and the career structures of elite athletes are concerned. The renaissance of the modern Olympics in the late 20th century after the financial and public relations debacles of the Munich, Montreal and Moscow Olympics in the 1970-80 period was the product of the branding of the Olympics as a television event. Television rights secured the status of the Olympics with the biggest show on earth with 24 hour global coverage as well as news and highlights packages. In contrast the Paralympics have been a "poor cousin" and found it difficult to obtain the TV profile of the Olympics. At the 2000 Sydney Paralympic Games the network broadcasting arrangements were not concluded until March 2000 when the Australian Broadcasting Corporation (ABC), the state broadcaster, took over from the commercial host. The ABC ran a sixty-minute 5.30pm highlights package and a late news 45-minute summary as well as a broadcast of the Opening and Closing ceremonies. The reluctance of the commercial host to do a "free to air" service emphasis the difficulties the Paralympics have in securing the media spotlight. The coverage lacked the "saturation coverage" of the Olympics and resulted in the Paralympics using the internet to broadcast moving images that were not subject to the commercial copyright restrictions applied to the Olympics (Goggin & Newell 2005)

The profile of disabled sports in the wake of the Sydney Olympics receded even in the sports that are genuinely trying to pursue a policy of integration. The coverage of the Paralympics has been championed by 'Special Broadcasting Service' (SBS) and the Australian Broadcasting Co. (ABC), both state owned corporations. However, commercial networks committed to "free enterprise" continue to display a marked reluctance to broadcast disabled sports even when they are held concurrently with able-bodied sports. The 2004

PANPACS swimming had integrated disabled classifications in the international swimming meeting but there were virtually no disabled swimming events broadcast. In the 2005 Australian Tennis Open, a year which broke all viewing records for the Tennis 'grand slam' which was attributed to Australian Leyton Hewitt's appearance in the men's final, wheelchair tennis, at the same event also had an Australian finalist David Taylor but this event was not telecast. Unfortunately it is these commercial networks from which the funds for sponsorships vital to the sports are directed and this marginalisation by the media does nothing to assist in the building of the profile and opportunities for sponsorship for Paralympic athletes. It is also profile building which is essential in developing athlete careers.

The integration of the Sydney Paralympic Organising Committee (SPOC) and Sydney Olympic Games Organising Committee (SOGOC) benefited the organisation of the hosting of the Games of Sydney 2000 but the funding of participating athletes did not enjoy as much support. Even in Sydney where there was significant government funding for modified infrastructure, there was uncertainty experienced in government funding with two emergency rounds of funding being required to fund a "full" Australian team. The differentiated and unequal nature of financial support and opportunities to athletes in the Olympics and those in the Paralympics clearly identifies the extent to which professionalism has eroded claims of equality across the two organizations.

While successful athletes in the Olympic Games are virtual millionaires earning mega bucks as full professionals with full time managers juggling a portfolio of endorsements, media contracts, grants and performance bonuses Paralympians are mired in welfare and voluntarist structure dependent on charity and paternalism. Paralympians struggle financially to compete in elite sports and are dependent on the voluntary efforts of fund raising sporting associations, family members and the generosity and goodwill of the community. This support is not always guaranteed. For example a funding concert in 1997 for the 2000 Paralympics attracting only 250 people which was well below the anticipated 30,000 (Hughes 1999 p172). At the time of the Barcelona Games Australian government support for Paralympians amounted to $300,000 while support for Olympians totalled AUS $3 million. The pretence of parity and discrimination between Paralympians and Olympians was starkly evident when an offer by a car manufacturer of a free car for for each Olympic Gold medallist was publicly withdrawn from Paralympians (Adair & Vamplew 1998 p 82). This was however, principally because there are too many gold medals provided at the Paralympic Games and the car manufacturer could not afford the cost of multiple vehicles.

These dilemmas experienced by many Paralympians are evident in the career of the sole Australian Paralympic athlete who has enjoyed the part of the status and financial security of Olympic champions. Wheelchair athlete Louise Sauvage is a triple Paralympian and winner of 9 Gold medals in several Paralympic Games. Prior to her recent retirement she has been one of the few Paralympians who fulfils the requirements of a full-time athlete. Her status as a fulltime athlete is evident in her a six day a week training regime that included her covering over 150 kilometres per week in training. She was named Australian sports person of the year in 2001 - the only disabled sports person to win this award. Such is the esteem in which Sauvage and her achievements are held that along with Olympic champions Shane Gould, Dawn Fraser and Marlene Matthews, she has had a Sydney ferry named after her. Sauvage's success as a high profile athlete can be partly attributed to the fact that she actually participated in the "real" Olympics and her achievements were televised in prime time. She was the winner of the 400 metre wheelchair event included in the main Olympic program as a "demonstration" sport. She was also part of the torch relay and was paired with golfer Greg Norman to take the torch across the Sydney Harbour Bridge (Goggins & Newell 2005). The success enjoyed by Sauvage illustrates well some of the contradictions about the relationship between the Olympic and Paralympic Movements. Would Sauvage have enjoyed such a profile if she had not achieved star billing at the Olympics? And why were the medals she won not counted in the overall Olympic medal count? Sauvage has, through her international successes been able to obtain elite sporting grants, sponsorships and sporting association support and be a full time athlete over a ten-year period. Her iconic status, international record and what is referred to her "x factor" that has generated popularity with the media has meant that she qualified for state support and corporate sponsorship. However, she remains one of the few to achieve this status with most athletes dependent on the fund raising capacity of their sporting organizations, local communities and families.

The disadvantage concerning career opportunities is compounded when the expenses of the high tech wheelchair components and the materials for advanced prosthetics are required for athletes is considered. Superior technology occupies an important role in developing the competitive edge and the quest to develop superior technology is one that requires considerable resources that involve advanced research and manufacturing. This feature of the Paralympic Games, like the Olympic Games, explains why the medal tally sees the bulk of medals being awarded to American, European nations or the 2004 leading medal winner China where generous state support is maintained by the Communist state.

However impressive the progress at the most fundamental levels progress towards integration has been patchy and has experienced some notable setbacks. While the integration process has occurred in the Commonwealth Games, Goodwill Games and sporting events such as the Pan-Pacific Swimming Championships (PANPACS) there are sporadic disputes and controversies that indicate that the quest for inclusion is still unfinished business and acceptance by sporting authorities is subject to ambivalence and hostility. Acceptance of disabled athletes by the mainstream sporting Olympic establishment has not been easy with some administrators expressing discomfort at the trends towards integration. Former President of the Commonwealth Games Association, Mr Arthur Tunstall challenged the place of disabled athletes saying that it was "embarrassing to have them with able bodied athletes" triggering anxious moments in the Australian sporting community (Adair & Vamplew 1998 p.83).

A more recent barometer of attitudes is the controversy over the Australian Paralympic uniforms for the 2004 Athens Games where the precedent of having the same uniform as the Olympians that was established in the Sydney Games was broken. This one uniform policy in Sydney was hailed as a significant landmark by the Sydney Olympic and Paralympic organisers and the retreat from this policy was seen as a major snub to Paralympians. The controversy was also fuelled by concern that the sophisticated high fashion outfits worn by the Olympians were not evident in the less fashionable Paralympic uniforms. There was also controversy about the availability to disabled athletes of hi tech heat dispersing uniforms specially developed for the anticipated hot conditions at Athens. Indeed, it could be argued that uniform problems highlight the global inequalities associated with involvement in the Paralympics. At the Sydney Paralympics, for example the Cambodian team did not have uniforms when they arrived and were dependent on the charity of their Sydney hosts.

The absence of media profile, career structures for athletes and the ambivalence of administrators suggest that the Paralympics is not completely a parallel organisation to the Olympic Games. It suggests that while some progress has been made concerning the needs of disabled people and profiling the achievements and possibilities for them the Paralympics tend to reify notions of dependence, paternalism and marginalisation. How then, might these dilemmas and contradictions be resolved towards a more inclusive and equitable sporting environment? One of the more popular sports in the Paralympic program Wheelchair Rugby might give some clues on how this situation may be dealt with.

MURDER BALL: WHEELCHAIR RUGBY AS A PROTOTYPE IN INCLUSION?

Some of the contradictions of the role and status of special sports emerge from Wheel Chair Rugby, a comparatively recent entry into the Paralympics. A demonstration sport in the 1996 Atlanta Games, Wheel Chair Rugby became an instant success when given full medal awarding status in the 2000 Games in Sydney. Wheelchair Rugby, often called "murder ball" has all the features that make for excellent increased viewer levels. For example, speed, clashes between players and wheelchair collisions all make for great spectator and television action. The Olympic venues for this sport are sell-outs and it's a highly popular sport even amongst nations that are not recognised as Rugby nations. The sport also makes great television with a format of four quarters favouring breaks for advertising and sponsorship. In reality there is very little relevance to Rugby and it tends to look more like basketball without a basketball hoop. Indeed, the game emerged as a hybrid from wheelchair basketball for players with neck injuries making shooting difficult or dangerous (MSU 2002). Wheel Chair Rugby is a fast and robust sport that has some surprising features. It is a sport where men and women can play together and there is a keen interest from non-disabled people in participating. The Paralympic champions in Athens 2004 were New Zealand and their side had no less than 4 players who were former Rugby players who have Tetroplegia as a result of Rugby scrums where they sustained their spinal injuries (IOC 2004b). The game's appeal has expanded rapidly and the organisers are optimistic that the game will move into Asia in a big way.

Wheel chair Rugby, its popularity and the unique nature of the event suggest that it could be sustained as a stand-alone sport in any Olympic Games. There is a question about why it could not be included in the Olympics given its appeal and the fact that it has worldwide coverage and could be, along with equestrian, one of the only sports with men and women competing together. Indeed the classification system employed in Wheel Chair Rugby acts to level out any inequalities in a way that does not often happen in mainstream sports The idea might seem fanciful to "hard nosed" sports fans but it is a important to surmise if the Olympic movement is genuine about integration and equality it might consider going the next step and including some Paralympic sports in the Olympic Games. Arguments that suggest the performance of the Paralympians do not match up to elite non-disabled athletes appear flimsy when for example four categories of Paralympic weightlifting have superior results to Olympic winners.

Most importantly the linkage with Rugby that is now a professional sports may provide some hints on how disabled sports people might develop professional athletic careers. In order to do this there needs to be cooperation on the part of the sporting organisations. For instance it could be possible to integrate Wheel Chair Rugby with mainstream rugby. If we indulge in speculation that Wheel Chair Rugby was integrated with Rugby Union a lot more support and profile would become available to the disabled athletes through an internationally recognised organisation. For example, they would have access to superior sponsorship, professional management, career development, trained coaches and undoubtedly more media exposure. Furthermore, there is no reason why Wheel Chair Rugby could not become part of the Bledisloe Cup or even the World Cup events. There could be Wheel Chair Rugby at half time or as a "curtain raiser" thus exposing the athletes to the crowd and possible media coverage. Wheel Chair Rugby has what it takes to make a good spectator sport: violence, speed and skill. It was a sell out sport at the last two Paralympics. At the end of the 2000 Olympics the Australian Wheel Chair Rugby Team were introduced to the crowd at the Bledisloe Cup, a Rugby competition between New Zealand and Australia thus giving them an avenue for exposure and to build profile, and the reception they received suggests that fans are ready for such a development. It could make the next move to becoming part of one of the growing world sports. However, if this happens, sporting organisations have a larger responsibility in promoting and profiling their disabled competitors. This could possibly be achieved by including the athletes in regular events such as State Championships and Nationals, as is currently done by swimming but would go further to questions of opportunity.

Interestingly, part of this question is about equity for disabled athletes and directly relates to opportunities for participation. Continuous and prolonged opportunities for participation are a key part of a rights based approach to sport. Rather than the fragmented paternalistic and welfare based approaches that typify disabled sports there are lessons that can be learnt from Rugby, which has emerged from an amateur background. To help combat key dilemmas associated with this area Price (2004) suggests the implementation of an orientation package for family, coaches and administrators. The education and 'buy in' of parents and coaches to such a package of special importance. Recent research in this area in Rugby Union shows that parents and family assist the athlete the most in a wide range of needs and choices as well as provide advice and assistance especially in their career development, planning, education and life-skills (Price, 2004). Athlete mentors greatly assists the athlete in many areas of their athletic career and 'off the field' life. They have much to contribute and the experience of young Rugby players shows that regardless of whether the mentor is provided from the sporting organization or an outside source, the athlete greatly benefits from the trust relationship, motivation, advice and experience of the mentor (Price 2004). Should these approaches, and the co-operation of the sporting organization be applied to Paralympic athletes, they would arguably enjoy higher participation, access to professional and trained coaches, valuable advice and support, access to athlete programs that include career counsellors, education support, a well-structured athletic career and a lift in the profile of themselves and their sport.

Unfortunately, without great change, it is largely out of the individual athletes hands and this is where the continued help of the state is crucial. To build a profile and successful career structure the disabled athlete relies on individual sporting organizations and continued interest in them by the media This can be done by continued efforts of state sporting bodies and state run media organizations. If working for a state run organisation such as Australia Post and Qantas is good enough for Olympians why aren't Paralympians enjoying such support?

One clear way for the Paralympic movement to build profile is to ensure as many athletes as possible become involved. Participation requires a sound support structure from parents, family and friends and this profile boost is clearly dependent on all levels of government and the commitment of sporting associations to look towards community building and inclusion strategies rather than the elitism that accompanies the Olympic movement.

THE FUTURE FOR THE OLYMPICS AND THE PARALYMPICS: SEAMLESS INCLUSION OR DIVORCE?

While the Paralympics and the Olympics operate as parallel events the question arises about the extent to which this format actually contributes to the marginalisation of disabled sports men and women? It prompts the suggestion that participation in a "stand-alone" global event might be a better proposition than the subordinated existence as a parallel event. Some precedent can be taken from the success of niche sporting events such as the Gay Games and the Masters Games. Supporters of the parallel events suggest that the Paralympics provide a profile that would not be possible with a stand-alone event. Any argument that the Paralympics need the Olympics to profile sports fails to account for the success of non-Olympic sports such as women's netball which is one of Australia's and New Zealand's biggest participant sports.

Such arguments neglect the fact that disabled sports had existed as viable entities before the nation-state of Australia was founded in 1901. Inter-colonial cricket matches were conducted in Australia between the deaf as early as 1896 and it should be remembered that the Deaf International sporting movement commenced international games as far back as 1924 (Adair & Vamplew 1997 p 81). The case against divorce from the Olympics is also advanced by suggestions that the Paralympics has been largely immune from the scandals of the Olympics misunderstands the way in which blatant "free enterprise" approaches and the resultant outcomes corrode the ethics of both movements. Already there is evidence of this with complaints of sighted guides cheating, controversy over the truth about the Spanish men basketballer's status and disputes over athlete classifications suggesting that the Olympic legacy of cheating and corruption is also making an impact in the Paralympics.

There continues to be legitimating problems in being associated with a movement that glorifies the free enterprise spirit and reifies images of bodily perfection. The reliance on "free enterprise" contradicts the importance of the state structures to support the needs of the disabled where the market forces repeatedly fail them in all sphere of life. It is also counterproductive to adopt a rhetoric "the athlete and not the disability" when the Olympic movement persists with a fetish about bodily perfection and that perpetuates unhelpful stereotypes about what it is to be "normal". The answer partly lies in developing a sporting ethos that turns its back on the glitz and glamour of the Olympics and kick the habits of the Olympic movement. Regardless of what the future of the Paralympics might be any future sport for the disabled needs to meet the needs of all disabled people and not just an elite for both recreation and competition. This is not just a simple participation issues but a need to reclaim aspects of civil society to recognise and value diversity and difference in an inclusive way that promotes equality of opportunity.

REFERENCES

Adair, Daryl & Wray Vamplew. 1997 *Sport in Australian History.* Oxford: Oxford University Press.

Blauwet, C. (2005) *Promoting the health and human rights of individuals with a disability through the Paralympics movement.* Bonn, Germany, International Paralympics Committee www.paralympic.org/.../Development/Development_Tools/ Health_as_a_Human_Right_Final_Short_Version.pdf (accessed 05/02/05).

Brittain, I. (2004) Perceptions of disability and their impact upon involvement in sport for people with disabilities at all levels. *Journal of Sport and Social Issues, Volume 28,* No. 4, November, pp. 429-452.

Cashman Richard, 1995. *Paradise of Sport: The Rise of Organised Sport in Australia* Oxford: Oxford Press.

Cashman, Richard & Anthony Hughes.1999 *Staging the Olympics, The Event and Its Impact,* Sydney: UNSW Press.

Goggin, Gerard & Newell Christopher. 2005. *Disability in Australia: Exposing a Social Apartheid,* Sydney: UNSW press.

Hughes, Anthony, 1999. The Paralympics, Pp.. 170-183 in *Staging the Olympics, The Event and Its Impact,* eds. Cashman, Richard & Anthony Hughes. Sydney: UNSW Press.

IOC (2004a) *Unique Event: Only One Olympic and Paralympic Medallist* http://www.Olympic.org/uk/games/athens/full_story_uk.asp?id=11022 (accessed 19/1/05).

IOC (2004b) *Gold Medal Goes to the Kiwis* http://athens2004cm/en/Paralympics/ results?item=cbe87453e3c2ff00VgnVCM4000002b130cOa_&depnews+1&rsc+WR 0000000 (accessed 31/1/05).

IOC (2005) *Olympic Charter: in force as from 1 September 2004).* http://www.olympic.org/uk/organisation/missions/charter_uk.asp (accesse 06/02/05).

Kell, Marilyn. 2004. Pp 228-304 Whose Disability? Inclusion and Exclusion and the Ongoing Struggle of Identity and Difference, (ed) Allen, Jennifer, *Sociology of Education: Possibilities and Practices,* 3rd Edition, Sydney. Social Science Press.

Michigan State University, (2002) *Disabled Sports: Wheelchair Rugby* http;//edweb6.educ.msu.edu/kin866/srugby.htm (accessed 31/1/05).

Price, Nathan. 2004. *Game of two halves: The career development, planning, awareness and education of elite young rugby players.* Paper presented Sport management Association of Australia and New Zealand Conference (SMAANZ) Geelong.

16 OLYMPISM AND THE OLYMPIC ATHLETE WITH A DISABILITY

Eli A. Wolff, Cesar Torres & Mary A. Hums

INTRODUCTION

Olympism is a philosophical vision encompassing a set of values that in theory can be applied to people in all corners of the world. This chapter will address Olympism in the context of people with disabilities, disability sport, and specifically the Paralympic Movement. Olympism will first be outlined and then discussed in relation to disability sport and the Paralympic Movement. With Olympism in mind, the relationship between the Olympic and the Paralympic Movements will be reviewed and analyzed. Finally, after realizing the existing relationship, suggestions will be presented in order to bring athletes with a disability, disability sport, and the Paralympic Movement in a closer and much more fruitful alignment with the Olympic Movement.

OLYMPISM

In the early 1920s, Baron Pierre de Coubertin (2000a, p.477), the *rénovateur* of the Olympic Games, was concerned that the public "had only a vague grasp of the meaning and import of the [Olympic] Games". For Coubertin, the worth of the Olympic Games did not lie in the athletic events themselves but what he envisioned as the set of values that inspired and guided the Games. This set of values represented a complex philosophical vision he referred to as neologism Olympism. Coubertin wrote several articles discussing the philosophy of Olympism and mentioned it in many more but he never articulated a concise and clear definition. The International Olympic Committee's (IOC) definition purportedly reflects the centrality of Coubertin's vision. The *Olympic Charter's* (International Olympic Committee, 2004, 9) fundamental principles advance that:

> Olympism is a philosophy of life, exalting and combining in a balanced whole the qualities of body, will and mind. Blending sport with culture and education, Olympism seeks to create a way of life based on the joy of effort, the educational value of good example and respect for universal fundamental ethical principles.

It further pronounces that:
> The goal of Olympism is to place sport at the service of the harmonious development of man, with a view to promoting a peaceful society concerned with the preservation of human dignity.

It also adds that:
> The practice of sport is a human right. Every individual must have the possibility of practicing sport, without discrimination of any kind and in the Olympic spirit, which requires mutual understanding with a spirit of friendship, solidarity and fair play. The organization, administration and management of sport must be controlled by independent sports organizations'.

Although the meaning of Olympism is complex and open to interpretation, the *Olympic Charter* provides a clear outline of its core elements. The ideas of holistic human development, excellence, peace, and universal moral values such as fairness, equality, mutual respect, justice and non-discrimination are repeatedly emphasized. As sport philosopher Jim Parry (2000) has argued, Olympism is a theory of what an ideal human being ought to be and aspire to but also the actualization of that aspiration. Olympism is a moral project; it encapsulates a set of values that are to guide the decisions, actions, and judgments of those involved in the Olympic Movement.

It is important to highlight that under the precepts of Olympism lies educational technology, a means to advance and materialize the set of values mentioned above. Without these values, the Olympic Games would just be, to use Coubertin's phraseology, world championships, or "simply games." For Olympism, sport, and consequently the Olympic Games are means to help human capacities flourish. They simultaneously serve as reminders of human potentiality and as sites where human development and achievement can be celebrated. That is, the meaning and import of the Olympic Games, is to be found in Olympism's call to celebrate the human struggle to find coherence and promote the educational mission.

As a formulation for moral improvement, Olympism seems a worthy philosophy even when it has not been fully realized in practice. As sport historian Jeffrey O. Segrave (1988, p.159) has indicated, "at its best, Olympism presents a noble and honorable vision of sport dedicated to ideals of universal worth". Perhaps it is important to note that Olympism entails an ethics of intrinsic values, one in which sport is not only useful but, more precisely, worthwhile and meaningful in itself. After all, for the *Olympic Charter*, Olympism values the joy of effort. In this sense, Coubertin (2000b, p.581) treasured the idea "of effort opposing effort for the love of the effort itself". The allure of Olympism seems to be the healthy combination of putting sport at the service of lofty extrinsic purposes and enjoying it for what it is. Olympism provides a framework toward achieving a good, fulfilling, and happy life, but the achievement of such a life is the embodiment and actualization of Olympism.

OLYMPISM, DISABILITY SPORT, AND THE PARALYMPIC MOVEMENT

The scholarly investigation of the relationship between the Olympic movement and disability sport is in its infancy. Researchers have looked at the connection between the Olympic Movement's "Sport for All" ideal and disability (Hums & Grevemberg, 2002) as well as examined the role of Olympic education in the context of disability sport (Brittain & Wolff, 2003). Further, researchers have studied how the Olympic and Paralympic Movements intersect (Fay, 1999; Hums, Wolff & Legg, 2003; Wolff, 1999; Wolff, Legg & Hums, 2004). They have also looked into disability sport in relation to national and international sport federations (Fay, Hums & Wolff, 2000; Hums, Moorman & Wolff, 2000; Wolff, Fay & Hums, 2000; Wolff, Grevemberg & Hums, 2001; Wolff, Legg & Hums, 2004). In spite of this growing research, the implications that the philosophy of Olympism might have for sport with people with disabilities as well as their relationship have not been the focus of much inquiry (Landry, 1992; Schantz, 1996). This situation merits a brief comment on such relationship and its possible implications.

As mentioned above, the normative interpretation of Olympism found in the *Olympic Charter* affirms, much in line with UNESCO's *International Charter of Physical Education and Sport* and UNICEF's *Convention on the Rights of the Child*, that sport is a human right and that all individuals should have the possibility to exercise that right without discrimination of any kind. Furthermore, the *Olympic Charter* specifies that "any form of discrimination with regard to a country or a person on grounds of race, religion, politics, gender or otherwise is incompatible with belonging to the Olympic Movement" (International Olympic Committee, 2004, p.9). Interestingly, the *Olympic Charter* is silent when it comes to discrimination based on disability. Given the history of discrimination against people with disabilities, it would appear reasonable to assume that discrimination based on disability is also incompatible with the tenets of the Olympic Movement.

Although, discrimination based on disability is not explicitly identified, it could be convincingly argued that the spirit of the *Olympic Charter* does not permit this type of discrimination. This important Olympic document emphasizes the right of people to engage in sport without prejudice toward them as human beings. In addition to the spirit of the *Olympic Charter*, its non-discrimination clauses seem to imply including people with disabilities when stating that "every individual" has the right to practice sport without discrimination of any kind. Moreover, after listing incompatible forms of discrimination, one of its fundamental principles reads "or otherwise," suggesting discrimination based on disability is not allowed. It appears then that Olympism embraces people with disabilities within its tenets. Even if for Olympism people with disabilities have the right to engage in sports without discrimination based on their conditions, do the remaining postulates of Olympism fully apply to them? Disability sport has the same potential as able-bodied sport to foster holistic human development, excellence, peace, and the set of moral values advanced by Olympism. This is clearly illustrated by the ideals underpinning the Paralympic Movement and the Paralympic Games. The International Paralympic Committee's (IPC) mission is "to engage more people with a disability from around the world in sport" (International Paralympic Committee, 2003, p.6). It believes that "All athletes, without any discrimination, should be able to perform to the best of their abilities" (International Paralympic Committee, 2003, p.6). The IPC's message is that "through sport every person—with or without a disability—has the ability to experience success and to discover new horizons" (International Paralympic Committee, 2003, .2). The IPC's mission and message are undoubtedly aligned with Olympism. Indeed, the values of Olympism express what the Paralympic Movement stands for. With this synchronicity in mind, how would people with disabilities, and sport for people with disabilities, be part not only in theory but in practice of the fabric of the Olympic Movement?

DISABILITY SPORT, THE PARALYMPIC MOVEMENT, AND THE OLYMPIC MOVEMENT

The significance of an inclusive ideology has been recognized by individuals and institutions all over the world, including the IOC. Indeed, the IOC recognizes the Paralympic Movement as a partner of the Olympic Movement. However, in spite of this rhetoric it can be argued that people with disabilities and specifically sport for people with disabilities are currently not fully included within the Olympic Movement and the

Olympic Games. For example, Paralympians are not allowed to call themselves Olympians. It is important to examine the ideas usually used to argue that disability sport and particularly the Paralympic Games are different from able-bodied sport and the Olympic Games and therefore have to be separate and distinct from the Olympic Movement. These stances come from the Olympic Movement as well as the Paralympic Movement and disability sport. Prior to analyzing the arguments, it is relevant to define disability sport and explore the current relationship between the Olympic Movement and the Paralympic Movement.

DISABILITY SPORT

DePauw and Gavron (1995) define disability sport as sport specifically organized for persons with a disability. Similar to women participating or competing with other women in women's sport, people with disabilities participate or compete with other people with similar disabilities/abilities in disability sport. Disability sport hinges on equitable and fair categories, based on disability and ability, in order to provide even playing fields. Disability sport is essentially a category of sport, similar to women's sport (Hums &Wolff, 2003). The Paralympic Movement and its Paralympic Games ultimately serve the purpose of providing elite disability sport opportunities to persons with physical disabilities and also a limited number of individuals with intellectual or cognitive disabilities. The Special Olympics for athletes with cognitive disabilities and the Deaflympics for deaf athletes are also arenas of disability sport.

THE RELATIONSHIP BETWEEN THE OLYMPIC AND THE PARALYMPIC MOVEMENTS

The Olympic and the Paralympic Movements through the IOC and the IPC respectively have established a formal relationship to support each other (Hums, Wolff & Legg, 2003). For example, as a consequence of this agreement bids to host the Olympic and the Paralympic Games are no longer accepted independently of each other; cities must now bid for both Games simultaneously. Once the Games are awarded, the Organizing Committee oversees both the Olympic and the Paralympic Games, as illustrated by the efforts of the Athens Organizing Committee (ATHOC) in 2004. Additionally, delegates from the Paralympic Movement are able to serve on IOC committees. Representatives serve on committees such as the Athlete Commission, Games Selection Committee, Education and Culture Commission, and the Women and Sport Commission. Above and beyond the activities outlined in the agreement, the IOC and the IPC work together and communicate fluidly through each respective international headquarters on a regular basis. Finally, the IOC and the IPC have agreed to continue staging the Wheelchair Racing Exhibition Events during the Olympic Games. These events made their debut in the Games of the XXIII Olympiad in 1984 and have continued through the Games of the XXVIII Olympiad in 2004. Although there is a significant amount of cooperation and coordination between the IOC and the IPC, the two organizations continue to exist as separate entities with independent yet parallel Games. It is worthwhile to look at some of the reasons put forward for maintaining the separation between the Olympic and the Paralympic Movements Athletes Able to Qualify for the Able-Bodied Olympic Games

Olympic sports believe that individuals with a disability are not excluded from qualifying to participate in the Olympic Games and become Olympians. Those with this view are either unaware of disability sport as a unique form of sport and the specific disabilities/abilities of disabled athletes or choose to ignore them. It is true that a few individuals with a disability have qualified for able-bodied Olympic sports—like Neroli Fairhall in Archery in 1984, and Marla Runyan in Athletics in 2000 and 2004-but the majority of persons with a disability participate or compete in disability sport. The idea that people with disabilities are free to attempt qualifying for able-bodied categories of Olympic sport does not fairly account for the interests and abilities/disabilities of persons with disabilities. Taken into account these factors, disability sport seems to be the most appropriate arena for disabled athletes. Those who believe that disabled athletes are not excluded from participating at the Olympic Games appear to undervalue disability sport as a legitimate form of sport, and do not account for the athletic potential and varying levels and ranges of disability/ability of disabled athletes.

QUESTIONING DISABILITY SPORT STANDARDS

Along the same lines, some within able-bodied Olympic sports argue that since there are fewer persons with a disability and even fewer within each sport event, the standards for qualification into the Paralympic Games are not as competitive or stringent as for persons without a disability to qualify for the able-bodied Olympic sports (Hums & Wolff, 2003; LeClair & Wolff, 2002; Wolff, Fay & Hums, 2000). Regardless of whether this claim is true or not, critics of disability sport forget that this seems to be the case within able-bodied Olympic sports or events with a very limited number of competitors in specific countries. Most importantly, this view challenges the notion that athletes with disabilities are capable of achieving outstanding levels of excellence and be legitimate athletes in the context of their own disability sport. The critical challenge for disability sport appears to be the ability to develop appropriate categories whereby there is a significant pool of participants and contenders to establish an elite basis for athletes with a disability in the context of each sport event.

DISTINCT RECOGNITION

Some believe there is a need for disability sport, particularly the Paralympic Games, to maintain a "separate but equal" status in order to be properly recognized and acknowledged (Craven, 2003). This view postulates that disability sport can become more visible if the Olympic and the Paralympic Games are kept separate and organized under the supervision of the IOC and the IPC respectively. This way, athletes may become more marketable and are not to be lost in the mix of the able-bodied Olympic Games and able-bodied sports arena. The identity of the athlete with a disability is recognized as unique. The question arising here is whether the ideal of "separate but equal" will ever become true in practice, specifically in terms of resources and recognition.

DISTINCT PURPOSE

Others suggest the Paralympic Movement and its Games have a separate mission and vision from the Olympic Movement and their Games (Craven, 2003). It has been argued that the Paralympic Games are not aligned with Olympism and that distinct philosophies charter the Paralympic Movement and its Games (Landry, 1992). This view holds that the Paralympic Games have a unique identity distinct from that of the Olympic Movement. As stated above, the authors suggest that Olympism does in fact apply to disability sport and athletes with a disability. Moreover, the Paralympic Movement seems to embrace in theory and practice the philosophy of Olympism. In the next section, suggestions will be presented in order to bring athletes with a disability, disability sport, and the Paralympic Movement in a closer and much fruitful alignment with the Olympic Movement and its philosophy.

OLYMPISM AND DISABILITY SPORT: A POSSIBLE PARADIGM SHIFT?

If Olympism is a philosophical vision centering on moral improvement and including people with disabilities, then what can the Olympic Movement do to fairly recognize the potential of disabled athletes? Should the Olympic Movement recognize disability sport as a category within Olympic sport? Should the Olympic Games continue to be restricted to able-bodied athletes and the handful of disabled athletes who are able to qualify in able-bodied Olympic sport? Can the Olympic Movement recognize and accept disability sport as another category in the same way it divides Olympic competition in women's able-bodied sport and men's able-bodied sport categories? If indeed disability sport is a category of sport, how would this categorization of Olympic sport impact the organization of the Olympic Games and the Olympic Movement?

SYMBOLIC IMPLICATIONS

Incorporating disability sport into the Olympic Movement and its Games can have a positive impact on disability sport. Once this is done, Olympic symbols such as the Olympic rings, Olympic motto, and Olympic anthem would be applicable to disabled athletes. In turn, those disabled athletes who qualify for the highest level of competition in their own category could be rightly named Olympic athletes. The Olympic Games and the Olympic Movement would then more empathically embrace disability sport and athletes with a disability. The message would be clear and powerful, and have strong symbolic connotations for the ideology of inclusion.

LOGISTICAL IMPLICATIONS

The connection of Olympism to disability sport and the recognition of the latter as an Olympic category may lead one to wonder if the Olympic Games and the Paralympic Games will merge. In this sense, it is important to highlight the parallels to women's sports whereby at the sport-specific level there are separate World Championships for women (like FIFA Women's World Cup), yet still recognized and organized by the same sport federation. With respect to disability sport, the Olympic Movement and the Olympic Games could embrace and sanction the existing Paralympic Games as "Olympic" and include the event in the Olympic program. Within this framework, the Olympic Games could, for example, be extended to a month, and either has the competitions for able-bodied and disabled athletes at alternate times during that month or intermingle these competitions and fully blend them. In this way, all medals will be Olympic medals and valued the same way. In regards to the institutional aspect of these changes, the IPC as well as the National Paralympic Committees would become infused within the IOC and the National Olympic Committees and therefore became Olympic bodies.

FUTURE RESEARCH

Great opportunities exist to explore the relevance and implications of Olympism to disability sport and athletes with disabilities. Questions must continue to be asked regarding the relationship among the Olympic Games, the Olympic Movement, and disability sport. Research in sport philosophy and ethics as well as policy and management can examine these questions from theoretical as well as practical standpoints. The status of sport for people with disabilities must continue to be challenged through research and study. The status and place of people with disabilities in sport, particularly relative to Olympism and the Olympic Movement, cannot be ignored.

CONCLUSION

Olympism provides a universal basis for inclusion, diversity, and human rights in sports. As argued throughout this chapter, its tenets clearly apply to disabled athletes. Based on this notion, this group of athletes should not be denied the opportunity to be become and be called Olympic athletes. The Olympic Movement has an opportunity to fully embrace people with disabilities as a vital aspect of the fabric of the Olympic Movement, thus recognizing and legitimating disability sport as sport in its own right. Although there are several challenges and multiple ways to actualize this goal, if Olympism is to be fully served and honored the effort to make this goal a reality is worthy.

REFERENCES

Brittain, I., & Wolff, E.A. (2003, September). *International Olympic Academy: The formation, integration and intersection of Paralympic education within and in connection to Olympic education.* Presented at the International Paralympic Committee VISTA Conference. Bollnes, Sweden.

Coubertin, P. de (2000a). The contribution of the seventh Olympiad. In N. Müller (Ed.), *Olympism: Selected writings.* Lausanne, Switzerland: International Olympic Committee.

Coubertin P. de (2000b). The philosophic foundation of modern Olympism. In N. Müller (Ed.) *Olympism: Selected writings.* Lausanne, Switzerland: International Olympic Committee, 2000.

Craven, P. (2003). *Present and future models of Paralympic structures within Olympic structures.* Presented at the International Conference on Adapted Sports. Spain.

DePauw, K.P., & Gavron, S.J. (1995). Disability and sport. Champaign, Ill., Human Kinetics Publishers.

Fay, T.G. (1999). *Race, gender and disability: A new paradigm towards full participation and equal opportunity in sport. Unpublished Doctoral Dissertation.* Amherst: University of Massachusetts.

Fay, T.G., Hums, M.A., & Wolff, E.A. (2000, June). *Inclusion of sport for athletes with disabilities into non-disabled sport organizations: A comparative analysis of three case studies*. Presented at the 2000 Conference of the North American Society for Sport Management, Colorado Springs, Colorado,.

Fay, T.G., Hums, M.A., & Wolff, E.A. (2000). *Critical Change Factors Model: Understanding the integration process of sport opportunities for athletes with disabilities into National Governing Bodies and the United States Olympic Committee.* Presented at the 2000 Pre-Olympic Congress. Brisbane, Australia.

Fay, T. G., & Wolff, E.A. (2003, November). *Where do I fit? Conflicts of identity and recognition for athletes with disabilities nominated for ESPN's new ESPY Award category recognizing the Best Disabled Athlete of the Year.* Presented at the North American Society for the Sociology of Sport Annual Conference, Montreal, QUE,Canada..

Hums, M.A., & Grevemberg, D. (2002, September). *The Paralympic Movement: Partners in progress with Sport for All.* Presented at the International Olympic Committee Sport for All Congress. Amsterdam, The Netherlands,.

Hums, M.A., & Wolff, E.A. (2003, November). *Sport without disability: Understanding the exclusion of athletes with a disability at all levels of sport.* Presented at the North American Society for Sport Sociology Annual Conference, Montreal, QUE, Canada.

Hums, M.A., Wolff, E.A., & Legg, D. (2003, June). *Examining opportunities for athletes with disabilities within and in relationship to the International Olympic Committee: A case study.* Presented at the North American Society for Sport Management Annual Conference. Ithaca, NY,.

Hums, M.A., Moorman, A.M., & Wolff, E.A. (2000, September). *Integration of Paralympic athletes Into National Sports Organizations: Selected comparative models.* Presented at the 2000 European Sport Management Conference. San Marino..

International Olympic Committee (2004). *Olympic Charter.* Lauserne, Switzerland: International Olympic committee.].

International Paralympic Committee (2003). *Spirit in Motion.*
Retrieved on 1 February 2005 from http://www.paralympic.org/release/Main_Sections_Menu/IPC/IPC_Brochure.pdf

Landry, F. (1992). Olympism, Olympics, Paralympism, Paralympics: Converging or diverging Notions and Courses on the Eve of the Third Millennium? Paper presented at the First Paralympic Congress, Barcelona, Spain .

LeClair, J. & Wolff, E.A. (2002, November). *The unspoken reality in the contested arena of cultural and policy barriers to the development of sport for athletes with a disability: Casey Martin and the PGA.* Presented at the North American Society for Sport Sociology Annual Conference, San Antonio, TX.

Parry. J. (2000). The values of Olympism and sports education for tomorrow. iln *Report on the I.O.A.'s Special Sessions and Seminars 1998* (pp. 521-536). Athens, Greece: International Olympic Academy.

Schantz, O. J. (1996, June). *Olympism and Disability.* Paper presented at the International Olympic Academy Post Graduate Seminar on Olympic Studies, Olympia, Greece.

Segrave, Jeffrey, O. (1998). Towards a definition of Olympism. In J.O. Segrave & D. Chu (Eds.) *The Olympic Games in transition* (pp. 149-161). Champaign, Illinois: Human Kinetics.

Torres, C. R. (2002, April). *The Olympic Movement 2002 – A new chapter?* Presented at the 2002 British National Olympic Academy, Manchester, England.

Olympism and the Olympic Athlete with a Disability

Torres, C. R. (2004, May). *Ethics and Olympic Games*. Presented at the Forty-Fourth International Session for Young Participants of the International Olympic Academy, Ancient Olympia, Greece.

Wolff, E., Legg, D. & Hums, M.A. (2004). *Relationships between International Sport Federations and International Disability Sport Federations*. Boston, MA. Northeastern University's Center for the Study of Sport in Society.

Wolff, E., Legg, D. & Hums, M.A. (2003). *Examining opportunities for athletes with disabilities within and in relationship to the International Olympic Committee: A case study*. Boston, MA. Northeastern University's Center for the Study of Sport in Society.

Wolff, E.A. (1999). *Status of the seven Disabled Sports Organizations within the United States Olympic Committee and recommendations for the future*. Brown University Royce Fellowship. Providence, RI: Brown University.

Wolff, E.A., Fay, T.D., & Hums, M.A. (2000). *Inclusion and integration of soccer opportunities for players with disabilities within the United States Soccer Federation*. Senior honors thesis. Providence, RI: Brown University.

Wolff, E.A., Grevemberg, D., & Hums, M.A. (2001, June). *Integration of Paralympic sport into International Sport Federations: Comparative international models*. Presented at the 2001 Conference of the North American Society for Sport Management, Virginia Beach.

Note

Some of the ideas in this chapter have been previously explored in Torres (2002) and Torres (2004)

17   VOLUNTEERISM AND THE PARALYMPIC GAMES

Pamm Kellett

INTRODUCTION

Event organisers are becoming increasingly reliant on volunteers to perform core event functions from planning to operations (2000p. 228; McDonnell, Allen, & O'Toole, 2002). In the context of mega events, such as the Olympic and Paralympic Games, volunteers have been recognised as crucial in the production of the event itself, and to ensure beneficial social and economic outcomes for the host community (Green & Chalip, 2004). Chalip (2000) suggests that the Sydney 2000 would not have been viable if it weren't for the contribution of over 40,000 accredited volunteers throughout the Olympic and Paralympic Games. He estimates, albeit conservatively, that for every dollar that the Sydney Organising Committee for the Olympic Games (SOCOG) spent on volunteer recruitment and management, over AUS $21 was created in comparative worth, totalling an estimated overall contribution of the volunteer effort to the Games of $AUS109 million.

The use of volunteers to assist in the production of Olympic Games events began in the early 1980s with the Lack Placid Winter Games employing nearly 7000 volunteers (Moragas, de Moreno, & Paniagua, 2000). Since then, volunteer participation has increased dramatically. For example, the 1994 Olympic Winter Games in Lillehammer enlisted 9,100 volunteers (Kemp, 2002), and the Athens 2004 Organising Committee fielded over 120,000 expressions of interest to volunteer for the Olympic and Paralympic Games, of which almost one third were from outside of Greece (Fairley & Kellett, in review). As the Olympic and Paralympic Games events grow larger each year, volunteer participation becomes increasingly necessary for event success. As Juan Antonio Samaranch noted "if we had to pay all the Olympic Movement's volunteers according to the workload and their responsibilities and taking into account the personal expenses they have to bear, we would reach a staggering figure which a government, or an organising committee, would be unable to come to terms with" (Smith, 2001 p. 7). Volunteer recruitment, retention, and management strategies are therefore a core area of focus for host Organising Committees.

The Olympic Games provides the largest volunteer movement in the world. It is surprising that the experience and motives of volunteers in the context of the Olympic Movement (as opposed to other event contexts) has only recently become an area of research in the field of sport management. There is a growing body of research that examines Olympic volunteerism and identifies key differences between the Olympic context and other contexts. For the most part, this literature examines Olympic and Paralympic volunteerism as one and the same. There is no literature that examines the experiences and motives of volunteers in the Paralympic context. It has been assumed that the experience of volunteering in the Olympic and Paralympic Games is congruent, and no consideration has been given to the uniqueness of the Paralympic context from a volunteer management perspective.

The aim of this chapter is to map current literature that examines volunteering in the event context, and in the Olympic context. The chapter will then draw from that body of research in order to develop pathways to provide future direction for managers, event organisers, and scholars to better understand volunteering in the Paralympic contex

VOLUNTEERING AT THE OLYMPIC GAMES

There is a small but growing body of empirically based research that examines volunteering specifically in the context of the Olympic Games (Chalip, 2000; Elstad, 1996; Fairley & Kellett, in review; Green & Chalip, 2004; Kemp, 2002). As noted previously, much of that literature has considered Olympic and Paralympic volunteering to be one and the same. Literature that examines volunteering in the Olympic event context has drawn from previous studies that examine volunteering at events, and mega events.

It has been shown that in general, event volunteer motives are somewhat different to motives for volunteering in continuing or permanent volunteer positions (Farrell, Johnston, & Twynam, 1998; Getz, 1991). Research that examines event volunteering has led to a greater understanding of event volunteer management strategies (Chalip, 2000; Green & Chalip, 2004; Kemp, 2002; Strigas & Newton Jackson Jr., 2003). For volunteers across different event contexts, common factors in volunteer motivation include excitement offered by an event, (Green & Chalip, 1998), prestige (Coyne & Coyne, 2001), social benefits including meeting new friends and experiencing a sense of community (Elstad, 1996; Williams, Dossa, & Tompkins, 1995), the opportunity to help the community or the event (Coyne & Coyne, 2001; Farrell et al., 1998), and learning new skills (Elstad, 1996; Kemp, 2002). Event volunteer recruitment, retention, and management strategies must take the unique event context into account and provide those benefits that volunteers are seeking for successful retention and reacquisition of volunteers for repeat events.

In the sense of being able to offer excitement, prestige, and social benefits to volunteers, Olympic Games events might be considered to be at the pinnacle. In a study of volunteers at the Lillehammer Winter Olympics, Elstad (1996) found that volunteer's experiences of learning about the event, and about other people were key sources of excitement and satisfaction that volunteers attained. Similarly, Kemp (2002) found that the capacity to learn and develop both job specific skills, and social skills was important for volunteers at Sydney 2000. Green and Chalip (2004) further articulated the link between learning and excitement in their survey of over 1700 volunteers across seventeen different work sites at the Sydney 2000 Olympic Games. They found that learning new skills was an important factor in volunteer satisfaction, but that for at least some volunteers, learning about the event itself, and how the event runs was also a source of excitement, and therefore satisfaction.

The importance of learning about the event itself, particularly in reference to the Olympic Games, and the Olympic Movement is demonstrated most clearly thus far by the work of Fairley and Kellett (in review). They have tracked a group of individuals who volunteered at both the Sydney 2000, and Athens 2004 Olympic Games, and have examined their motives for volunteering nationally (in Australia) and four years later, travelling internationally (to Athens) for the Olympic volunteer experience. They found four key motives for volunteering at the Olympic Games – nostalgia; camaraderie, friendship and a sense of community; a connection to the Olympics; and gaining and sharing knowledge.

Interestingly, Fairley and Kellett (in review) found that volunteering at the Olympic Games, for this group, allowed them to feel a connection to the event itself and to learn about what happens 'behind the scenes' which is consistent with previous research in the event context (Elstad, 1996) and the Olympic context (Green & Chalip, 2004). Fairley and Kellett (in review) found that learning for the group of volunteers in their study was more than mere event operations, but also related to the Olympic Movement itself. Volunteers in this study demonstrated a connection with the symbols of the Olympic Movement, as well as the history and culture of the organisation itself. This group sought opportunities to learn about the philosophies of the Olympic Movement, and many of the volunteers in the study reported that travelling to Greece for the 2004 Olympic Games was an opportunity to learn about the history of the Olympics.

Fairley and Kellett (in review) also found that nostalgia was an important motive for repeat volunteering at Athens 2004. Volunteers reported that they wanted to re-live the 'once-in-a-lifetime' Sydney 2000 experience. That experience was linked with the friendships and camaraderie they had made in Sydney at the event, and the continuing friendships they had fostered through their volunteer group. This group met on a regular basis throughout the four years between the Sydney and Athens Olympic Games in order to re-live their previous Olympic volunteer experience, and plan for their Athens travel and volunteer experiences. This group had an appreciation for the sense of community that they had built together, and valued the friendships that they had formed which is consistent with previous research that examines the volunteer experience at Olympic Games events (Elstad, 1996; Green & Chalip, 2004; Kemp, 2002).

What is clear from the discussion thus far, and is consistent with literature derived from event volunteering in general, is that the volunteer experience at the event is crucial for their satisfaction, and continued commitment. This provides us with a useful starting point to consider how the volunteer experience might be different in the Paralympic context. The next section builds upon the knowledge gained thus far in understanding Olympic volunteering and suggests implications for volunteering in the Paralympic context.

VOLUNTEERING AT THE PARALYMPIC GAMES

Although there is no empirical research that has investigated volunteering in the Paralympic context, there is a large body of anecdotal evidence that suggests that the experience of volunteering at the Paralympic Games is different to the Olympic Games. Many of the Sydney 2000 Olympic Games volunteers also volunteered at the Paralympic Games. Some were not intending to extend their volunteer services at the Paralympic Games, however their positive Olympic volunteering experience encouraged them to continue volunteering into the Paralympic events. Indeed, the experience of volunteering at the Olympics and Paralympics was so powerful, that many volunteers have recorded their stories in popular books.

Although there are limited anecdotal accounts of the experience of Paralympic Games volunteers, it seems probable that volunteering at the Paralympic Games engenders different outcomes and experiences for those individuals. For example, one volunteer said "the Olympics may have been thrilling, but the Paralympics were inspiring and humbling"

(Smith, 2001p. 235). When volunteers, particularly those who had never worked with disability groups, the Paralympic volunteer experience was one of great learning. Other volunteers were so touched by their Paralympic volunteer experience that it became their dictum for life. For example, one volunteer thought that the motto of the Paralympics that said it all for him "mind, body, spirit" (Walker & Gleeson, 2001 p. 228).

It has been noted previously that learning has been identified as a factor in volunteer satisfaction and commitment at events, and the Olympic Games events (Elstad, 1996; Fairley & Kellett, in review; Green & Chalip, 2004). Certainly, volunteers at the Paralympic Games had to learn new sets of skills that the Olympic Games experience did not prepare them for. Paralympic volunteers must to learn to deal with logistical matters associated with everyday activities for those with disabilities, as well as specific sport and equipment requirements for elite athletes with disabilities. Olympic Games volunteer participation did not equip them with such specialised skills. In that way, first time Paralympic volunteers must learn a new set of operational skills.

However, anecdotal evidence would suggest that Paralympic volunteers learned more than merely operational requirements for people with disabilities. It is not uncommon to still hear Paralympic volunteers talk about Paralympic athletes as awe inspiring. While conversing with volunteers through the course of the research work that the author of this chapter has been involved in previously, there is unanimous respect for the athletes for a number of reasons. First, is that many of the volunteers had not previously appreciated the elite standards of the Paralympic athletes. Second, the experience of working with many of the athletes and gaining an understanding the difficulties they face in everyday life made many of the volunteers re-evaluate their own personal outlook to hardships they may face themselves. Third, many of the volunteers found Paralympic athletes to be gracious in accepting (or rejecting) their voluntary assistance, and compared this to some negative experiences that they had with Olympic athletes and officials.

It would be easy at this point to draw conclusions about the shortcomings of high profile athletes and their entourages in the Olympic setting. However, this would be erroneous and short sighted. It is possible that the Paralympic Games provide a different experience for volunteers because volunteers might be required to be more centrally involved 'in the action' with athletes in this context. If this is the case, volunteers might feel as though they are assisting to a greater capacity, and that they are indeed a large part of the event. This would be consistent with previous research that identifies those factors as important in volunteer motives (Farrell et al., 1998; Green & Chalip, 2004; Kemp, 2002). In essence, volunteers who report feelings of greater satisfaction with the volunteer experience in the Paralympic setting might be reporting that their motives for volunteering in the first place are being met to a greater level in the Paralympic context.

It is also possible that Paralympic athletes are more familiar and comfortable with a culture of volunteering. Many Paralympic athletes live in environments that require assistance and working with other people, sometimes to achieve menial tasks that able bodied individuals take for granted. In an able-bodied society that values individualism, it is not often that the skills required to politely accept and reject assistance from others are learned, or utilised.

Fairley and Kellett (in review) have found that repeat Olympic volunteers have a thirst for knowledge about the larger context in which their volunteering occurred – the Olympic Movement itself. It is possible that a thirst for learning about the Paralympic Movement, and the associated disability sector might be important to reacquire volunteers for future Paralympic Events.

It has been noted previously that the volunteer experience is crucial to satisfaction, and ongoing commitment. Certainly, Fairley and Kellett's (in review) work suggests that if the experience is a positive one, volunteers are willing to travel in order to repeat the experience. Further, the destination (in their case Athens) was also an important part of the volunteer decision. In essence, volunteering abroad is part of a tourism experience.

The Olympic and Paralympic contexts offer very different experiences of the host city as a destination. For example, the Athens 2004 Summer Olympic Games hosted 11,099 athletes from 202 countries (Athens 2004, 2004a). The Athens 2004 Paralympic Games hosted 3,969 athletes from 136 countries (Athens 2004, 2004b). The Paralympic Games, although facing some logistical challenges of its own, is a smaller event that attracts fewer athletes, events, and therefore officials. It also attracts fewer spectators than the Olympic Games. This provides an important point of comparison for event organisers, in particular reference to the volunteer experience.

Anecdotal evidence suggests that the Paralympic event being smaller is not necessarily negative from a volunteer's perspective. For example, one volunteer rates the most magical moment of his 23 shifts in Spectator Services as an evening working at the Paralympics. He states "the evenings were very quiet at the Paralympics. The school children had left and only the odd spectator wandered the park in between events. This allowed the hosts the opportunity to watch a number of sports during the night" (Walker & Gleeson, 2001p. 204). In the Paralympic context, it is possible that volunteers are able to be part of the event in terms of watching the event themselves as their workload might be lessened, and viewing from different work sites might be less difficult.

Event organisers might be encouraged to further consider volunteer tourism in the context of the Paralympic Games. Fairley and Kellett (in review) noted that volunteer tourism is an important consideration for Olympic event organisers in recruitment of volunteers. It may be even more crucial in the Paralympic context. In informal conversations with volunteers throughout the research in which the author of this chapter has been involved, it seems that there is a growing trend for some volunteers to choose only to become involved at the Paralympic Games, and not the Olympic Games. When asked why this is the case, one particular volunteer noted that volunteer workloads and pressure was not as high as at the Olympic Games. More interestingly however, the volunteer noted that the host city as a destination was more attractive. He noted that air flights were cheaper, it was easier to get around the city, accommodation was more readily available in different price ranges, and tourist destinations within the host city were more accessible and less crowded.

As the Olympic Games and Paralympic Games become more entwined by sharing resources and operational processes, it might be important, at least from the perspective of strategic volunteer management to respect the uniqueness of each event in terms of the kinds of experiences that they each offer to volunteers. Both events are exciting, and opportunities for social interaction, and unity. However, each context provides volunteer satisfaction in very different and specific ways. Event organisers need to be cognisant of the unique factors that Olympic volunteering can provide, and also be aware of the unique factors that Paralympic volunteering can provide. Olympic and Paralympic volunteering can be marketed very differently in order to ensure a future of volunteering for both events. Implications for further research

It seems probable that the experience of volunteering in the Paralympic Games is distinctly different from the experience of volunteering at the Olympic Games. It is increasingly difficult to recruit and retain volunteers in almost every sector of the community; therefore it is imperative that event managers are provided with well developed and effective recommendations regarding volunteer recruitment and retention. In the case of the Paralympic Games, it is crucial that empirical research be focused on understanding if Paralympic volunteering is different to Olympic volunteering, and how.

A qualitative methodology, that allows the stories and experiences of Paralympic volunteers to be elucidated would seem most appropriate for future research in the area of Paralympic volunteering. Methodologies such as the one used by Green and Chalip (2004) that captures the experiences of volunteers throughout the duration of a particular event would be a good starting point. Also, the work of Fairley and Kellett (in review) who have tracked repeat Olympic event volunteers longitudinally might also be appropriate.

In order for events to provide economic and social impacts, events managers are increasingly required to provide a legacy from the event for the host community. Indeed, the International Olympic Committee demands that as part of the Olympic Charter (IOC, 2005). It would be of interest to examine how Paralympic volunteering changes perceptions of disability groups, and engenders interest in volunteering in the disability sector of local communities.

In order to understand leverage of Paralympic volunteering, it would be useful to first understand volunteer perceptions of, and connections with, the Paralympic Games as a social movement. As previous research that understands Olympic volunteering has found that the culture of the Olympics and the Olympic Movement is important for volunteers to identify with, it is possible that similar connections might exist for Paralympic volunteers. If this is the case, it would offer exciting strategic marketing plans for the recruitment and retention of volunteers not only for the Games themselves, but linking to the broader community needs.

If the experience of volunteering is different in the Paralympic Games compared with the Olympic Games, the source of that difference must be examined. It might be interesting to understand the culture of volunteering from the athlete's perspective, particularly in the Paralympic context. It is possible that Paralympic athletes have a different understanding of volunteerism to Olympic athletes. These understandings may influence the way that they interact with volunteers at events, therefore affecting the volunteer's event experience.

Conclusion

The Paralympic Games are recognised as an event that runs in parallel to the Olympic Games. Both events require volunteers for their success, and as a result, the core operation of the volunteer management program is centralised and coordinated between the two events. This chapter has highlighted that from a volunteer's perspective, the experience of volunteering at the Paralympic Games is different than the experience gained at Olympic Games. Whilst there is no empirically based research that understands Paralympic volunteering, it seems that the future of volunteering in this context is positive for volunteers and event managers alike. Paralympic Games event managers must begin to understand Paralympic volunteer motives as subtly different from Olympic volunteer motives, and leverage that knowledge. Empirically based research that explores volunteering in the Paralympic Games is necessary. The Paralympic Movement needs to consider its profile as an organisation and a social movement as a tool to provide a hook for future volunteer management strategies – not only for volunteer recruitment and reacquisition for events, but also as a guide for the development of pathways to move volunteers from high profile events to community level volunteering.

References

Allen, J. (2000). *Event Planning*. Toronto: John Wiley & Sons.

Athens 2004. (2004). Facts & Figures of Paralympic Games. Retrieved 12 February, 2005, from www.athens2004.com/en/ParalympicGames/parahome.

Athens 2004. (2004). Unforgettable Games, Dream Games. Retrieved 13 February, 2005, from www.athens2004.com.

Chalip, L. (2000). Sydney 2000: Volunteers and the organization of the Olympic Games: economic and formative aspects. In Moragas, M. de et al. (Eds.). *Volunteers, Global Society and the Olympic Movement* (pp. 205-214). Lausanne: International Olympic Committee.

Coyne, B. S., & Coyne, E. J., Sr. (2001). Getting, keeping and caring for unpaid volunteers for professional golf tournament events. *Human Resource Development International, 4*, 191-214.

Elstad, B. (1996). Volunteer perception of learning and satisfaction in a mega-event: The case of the XVII Olympic Winter Games in Lillehammer. *Festival Management & Event Tourism, 4*, 75-86.

Fairley, S., Kellett, P., & Green, B. C. (2007). Volunteering Abroad: Motives for travel to volunteer at the Athens Olympic Games. *Journal of Sport Management, 21*(1), 41-57.

Farrell, J. M., Johnston, M. E., & Twynam, G. D. (1998). Volunteer motivation, satisfaction, and management at an elite sporting competition. *Journal of Sport Management, 12*, 288-300.

Getz, D. (1991). *Festivals, Special Events, and Tourism*. New York: Wan Nostrand Reinhold.

Green, B. C., & Chalip, L. (1998). Sport volunteers: Research agenda and application. *Sport Marketing Quarterly, 7*(2), 14-23.

Green, B. C., & Chalip, L. (2004). *Paths to volunteer commitment: Lessons from the Sydney Olympic Games*. In R. A. Stebbins & M. Graham (Eds.), Volunteering as Leisure, Leisure as Volunteering: An International Perspective (pp. 49-67). Oxfordshire: CABI Publishing.

IOC. (2005). Sports. Retrieved 14 March, 2005, from
  http://www.olympic.org/uk/sports/index_uk.asp

Kemp, S. (2002). The hidden workforce: Volunteers' learning in the Olympics. *Journal of European Industrial Training, 26*, 109-116.

McDonnell, I., Allen, J., & O'Toole, W. (2002). *Festival and Special Event Management* (2nd ed.). Brisbane: Wiley.

Moragas, M., de Moreno, A. B., & Paniagua, R. (2000). *The evolution of volunteers at the Olympic Games*. Lausanne: International Olympic Committee.

Smith, L. (2001). *Living is Giving: The Volunteer Experience*. Sydney, NSW: Playright Publishing.

Strigas, A. D., & Newton Jackson Jr., E. (2003). Motivating volunteers to serve and succeed: Design and results of a pilot study that explores demographics and motivational factors in sport volunteerism. *International Sports Journal*, Winter, 111-123.

Walker, M., & Gleeson, G. (2001). *The Volunteers: How ordinary Australians brought about the extraordinary success of the Sydney 2000 Games*. Crows Nest: NSW: Allen & Unwin.

Williams, P. W., Dossa, K. B., & Tompkins, L. (1995). *Volunteerism and special event management: A case of Whistler's Men's World Cup of Skiing*. Festival Management & Event Tourism, 3, 85-95.

18 HERDING CATS: MANAGING AND ADMINISTERING PARALYMPIC TEAMS

Heather Ross

INTRODUCTION

Elite sport has the ability to capture the world's interest, attention and imagination, and the Paralympic Games showcases the highest measures of character, achievement and organization. The Paralympic Games are the second largest sporting event in the world and a growing force in the Paralympic Movement. This type of multi-sport, international competition requires a vast amount of coordination in supporting an athlete's triumph while yielding positive memories for all spectators. I was fortunate to work for the United States Olympic Committee (USOC) in the International Games Division for 6 years. Its mission is to support U.S. athletes by creating the best environment to achieve competitive excellence at the Olympic, Paralympic, Pan-American, Para-Panamerican and World University Games. We supervised all coordination with Local Organizing Committees (LOCs) and its various services such as the administration of the village, sports, transport, accreditation and other services for the delegation. I have observed many changes in the Paralympic movement, both domestically and internationally, during the short time I have been involved and will highlight the management process in the administration of a Paralympic Team in elite, multi-sport competition.

WHAT IS THE USOC?

The paramount goal of the USOC is to support the USA Olympic and Paralympic athletes in achieving sustained competitive excellence. It is a public trust, established by Congress for the purposes set out in the Ted Stevens Olympic and Amateur Sports Act, (l36 U.S.C. Section 2205; 2002). Ultimately, the American public is the ultimate stakeholder in the performance of the USOC. The Stevens Act lists thirteen separate purposes of the USOC. This includes, but is not limited to, establishing national goals for amateur athletic activities and encouraging the attainment of those goals; coordinating and developing amateur athletic activities in the United States, directly related to international amateur athletic competition, fostering productive working relationships among sports-related organizations; exercising exclusive jurisdiction, directly or through constituent members or committees over the participation in the Olympic Games, the Paralympic Games and the Pan-American Games, including representation of the United States in the Games and the organization of such games when held in the United States; obtaining for the United States, directly or by delegation to the appropriate national governing body, the most competent amateur representation possible in each event of the Olympic Games, Paralympic Games and Pan-American Games; and encouraging and providing assistance to amateur athletic programs and competition for amateur athletes with disabilities, including, where feasible, the expansion of opportunities for meaningful participation by such amateur athletes in programs of athletic competition for able-bodies amateur athletes. The complete version of the Amateur Sports Act can be found on the USOC website (www.usoc.org).

In the 25 years since the passage of the Amateur Sports Act (now the Stevens Act), there has been substantial growth and change in the Olympics and Paralympics. The money in sport has increased exponentially and is a big business. The USOC's total support and revenue for the four-year period ending in December 31, 1980 was approximately $55 million; it grew to over $451 million for the four-year period ending in December 31, 2000 (Fehr & Ramo 2003). Direct spending on Paralympic athletes mushroomed from $7.7 million for the 1996-2000 Olympic cycles to $15 million in 2000-2004 with a further funding boost of more than 25% for the period beginning in 2005 (Rocky Mountain News 2003).

Unlike other National Olympic or Paralympic Committees, the USOC receives no government subsidies. A significant portion of the funding of the USOC comes from the USOC's shares of the IOC's broadcast revenues and sponsorship programs – not directly from the USOC's own efforts. For the four years ended December 31, 2000, 46% of the USOC's total support and revenues came from these sources. An additional 10% came from the United States Olympic Foundation, which is a separate nonprofit corporation. Another 18% came from Olympic Games organizing committee revenue related to hosting the 1996 Atlanta Games and the 2002 Salt Lake Games in the United States, which is a source of revenue that will not be available again until 2012 at the earliest (Fehr & Ramo 2003).

INCLUSION OF PARALYMPIC ATHLETES IN THE OLYMPIC FAMILY

The USOC has been supporting, directly or indirectly, America's athletes to attend the Paralympic Games since 1992 providing office equipment, staff and logistical support from the Olympic Games. In preparation for the 1996 Atlanta Games, Paralympic athletes were officially adopted as part of the USOC constitution. In fact, all 45 National Governing Bodies (NGBs), which comprise the United States Olympic Committee, appear to have a small percentage of members who are competing with a disability (Harris Interactive 2004) and 4 NGBs govern Paralympic sport (wheelchair curling, equestrian, wheelchair tennis and sailing). Therefore, the USOC achieves its mission by partnering with and providing select resources and services to the NGBs and Paralympic Sport Organizations (PSOs) in order to obtain the most competent representation in each event of the Olympic and Paralympic Games. It inspires all Americans not by creating or overseeing separate programs, but rather by public awareness of the stories, accomplishments, and performances of Olympians and Paralympians in athletic competition and by public awareness that the USOC and United States athletes conduct themselves in accordance with Olympic ideals.

Even though there is a reference to Paralympic athletes in the USOC Mission, it does not suggest that there should be equal funding of Olympic and Paralympic sports or equal funding among Olympic sports or Paralympic sports. Olympic sport is the primary focus of the USOC. A separate National Paralympic Committee (NPC) for the United States, however, could not generate enough revenue to be self-sustaining in the long run. The USOC is proud to be the only National Olympic Committee (NOC) to take on the responsibility of serving, as a NPC and fully helping Paralympic athletes (Fehr 2003). In 2001, it created a division to manage Paralympic athletes increasing the search for commercial sponsorship, developing expert coaches and established performance-based criteria for athletes to qualify for direct funding and other benefits (Rocky Mountain News 2003).

SUPPORTING TEAMS AT PARALYMPIC GAMES

The study of team administration is the study of team development, team preparation and team management during Games time. In order to properly execute team administration, one must be aware of the organizational complexity of Paralympic Games in post-industrial society. This places wide-ranging planning demands on their organizers in terrains as complex and varied as information technology and telecommunications, town planning, security, transportation, the media, medicine, mass participation and cultural events (De Moragas 1997).

In preparing for a Paralympic Team, planning and coordination begins 4-6 years out with site visits to the host country and meeting with the LOC. The initial visits are starting points to begin building key relationship with the LOCs and familiarize staff where sports venues are in relation to the Athletes' Village. 2-3 years out, the operations team identifies a team processing site for team briefings, apparel outfitting and medical examinations; team training venues; hotel accommodations for satellite staff and sponsors. In addition, village housing accommodations are reviewed. As a side note, factors involved in selecting a processing site are cost, location and space availability. Trips are yearly for the first 2 years of planning and become more frequent in order to discuss logistical and administrative movements as well as coordinate sport entry and accreditation procedures. The USOC sends a survey to the NGB or PSO requesting their team trial dates, ideal team processing dates, arrival dates to and departure dates from the Games site and team staff information. This survey assists the USOC in determining the team processing schedule, airport arrival and departure schedules and housing lists for processing (see attachment A).

Approximately, 1 year prior to the start of the Paralympic Games, a 5-7 day meeting in the host city is held for U.S team leaders, head coaches and team administrators who will have athletes competing in the upcoming Paralympic Games. Representatives from the LOC are invited to present on key issues (i.e., sports and venues, village and transportation) as well as USOC representatives who will manage functional areas relating to games administrations (i.e., tickets, air travel, classification, medical, accreditation, sport entries, delegation quotas, etc.). This is a crucial meeting as USOC operational procedures are shared and negotiations are begun with the various sport representatives to best meet the athletes needs and achieve competitive success. (See Attachment B, C, D and E for an example of materials discussed).

While at this meeting, USA sport representatives have one-on-one time with their venue and competition managers to discuss their specific needs, inspect the competition and training sites as well as build a rapport with their key counterparts. This reduces the chaos during Games time when any and every challenge arises and could cost and athlete an opportunity to represent their country.

GENERAL PLANNING CONSIDERATIONS

Whether one is preparing for a team's participation in the Olympic or Paralympic Games, there are common premises. Team staff and athletes are concerned with adequate facilities for practice; the ability to use identified sports medical staff; the capability to access cutting edge knowledge on nutrition, vitamins, recovery, and sport psychology; the fiduciary responsibilities for shipping equipment; and the development of team selection criteria. Another issue most elite teams face is the need for teams to scout their competitors at competition and training venues. When planning transportation to competitive and training venues, organizers need to allow athletes or teams to stay at the venues to watch other teams and athletes train/compete.

Athletes are not just competitive machines — no matter how much they fine-tune their body. There are concerns on how to support the athlete off the field of play. Not only does there need to be activities related to their competitive performance, there needs to be plenty of services related to relaxation (i.e., coffee houses and kiosks, street entertainment, transportation to local scenes of activity, etc). The Los Angeles' 1932 and Berlin's 1936 Olympic Villages inaugurated this concept perceiving the Villages to be more than a place for accommodation and the definitions of functions to reach beyond providing only room and board (Munoz 1997). The problem of traveling expenses, maintenance, and accommodation for delegations and competitors is one of the main topics of debate on the organizational aspects with regards to getting more and more people to take part in the Paralympics. One of the first solutions was the elimination of participation fees for official delegation members at the 2004 Paralympic Games. This has allowed countries to invest the money saved into improving coaching development programs, providing additional international competition and training opportunities as well as supporting elite Paralympic athletes with performance grants.

The Paralympic Games present unique challenges for accommodating thousands of Paralympic athletes into one location. Most accessibility standards and building codes specify minimum requirements for building constructions. Even most new facilities do not adequately meet the needs of a concentrated number of disabled athletes and officials. When investigating this further, one of the greatest challenges for sport facilities design is wheelchair seating. Historically, wheelchair accommodation was created by removing seats from the back row, which often resulted in seating in less desirable locations as well as often not made for ambulatory companions. The American with Disabilities Act (ADA) design standards specify a minimum number of wheelchair locations that must be dispersed in locations throughout a sport facility. Questions that are not addressed but need to be considered are line-of-sight for a wheelchair user when surrounding spectators stand in a row in front of them during an exciting moment in competition and how much dispersal of wheelchair seating can be practically possible (Beasley 1997).

CHALLENGES AND RECOMMENDATIONS FOR THE FUTURE

There are few competitions more important or richer in tradition than the Paralympics. It has the ability to inspire national pride and provide a sense of identity, in addition to fulfilling dreams of athletes to compete at the highest level. The mission and work of any elite sporting organization must be directed to the ultimate success of our athletes and in turn yield organization growth and success. The Paralympic Movement is still youthful in its development as has the potential to grow dramatically in the coming years. Athletes, coaches and international representatives need to see the value and need to vote in a three-class system (wheelchair, blind and amputee) if the movement is to move forward and be deemed legitimate by sponsors, media and the general public. This would reduce the amount of medals given at Games as well as the number of world records made and increase the level of competitors in an event. In the 2004 Summer Paralympic Games, there were 21 events for the 100 meter and 63 of medals given. It is hard to justify being on the same playing field as the Olympics when only 3 medals were given out for the same distance.

During the Sydney Olympic Games, there were 10,651 participants and 928 medals awarded. For the 2000 Paralympic Games, there were 3,900 participants and 1,657 medals awarded (Bell, 2002). From 1960 until 2000, there have been 79,859 summer Olympians competing for 7,638 summer Olympic medals, or 0.095 medals for each Olympian. During the same period 22,658 summer Paralympians have vied for 13,881 summer Paralympic medals, 0.613 medals per athlete (Bell 2002). If we have a look at the numbers for the 2004 Athens in Athens, there were 1,568 medals for 3,806 Paralympians (0.412 per athlete) and only 929 medals for 10,625 Olympians (0.087 per athlete). It seems that it is getting more difficult to win Paralympic medals, however there are still almost five times more medals to win per participant in the Paralympic Games compared to the Olympic Games. It is important for the Paralympic Movement to increase their pool of talent and the only logical way is to decrease their events thereby increasing their contestants in each event and reducing the number of medals awarded. In conjunction, this would demystify, clarify and simplify classification for to all participants.

Due to the movement's youth, there are idiosyncrasies, shortcomings and interesting concepts in relationship to team administration. Some sport's technical delegates hold fiefdoms and operate out of their kitchen, ergo, running the risk of selecting teams based on national affinity and/or friendships. The current structure may put certain sports/disabilities in jeopardy of making political decisions made for the advantage of particular constituencies of the Paralympic Movement. This in effect becomes a political battleground consisting of representatives of various constituencies contending with one another. This may result in business and operating decisions being made that are often not good for the movement as a whole. In addition, because technical delegates are elected on the basis of constituency-based politics from the volunteer sports network, they frequently do not have the requisite experience to be effective leaders of a complex organization such as the International Paralympic Committee (IPC). This system could also result in constant upheavals among volunteer leadership and an inability to attract or retain first-rate staff. Further, it can fail to recruit or bring to the leadership level of the IPC accomplished individuals who would be universally recognized as able, sophisticated leaders in the for-profit, nonprofits or sports world.

The Paralympic future is extremely bright. The Movement is fortunate enough to learn from the mistakes of its predecessors and has the passion to overcome great obstacles. With the necessary knowledge in communication and management skills, media training, selection procedures, replacement policies for sport and international federation rules, credentialing of athletes and team officials, team management, games scenarios/crisis management, equipment, cultural concerns, security, technical-video analysis it can become an even greater model for other sport organizations to follow.

REFERENCES

Beasley, K. A. (1997). The Paralympic Village: A Barrier-Free City. In *Olympic Villages: Hundred Years of Urban Planning and Shared Experiences*. International Olympic Committee: Lausanne, Switzerland: 105-110.

Bell, D. (July 2002). *Are all Paralympians Elite Athletes?* International Games Archive 1998-2002: 1-12.

De Moragas, M. (1997). Olympic Villages and the major challenges of organizing the Olympic Games. In *Olympic Villages: A Hundred Years of Urban Planning and Shared Experiences*. International Olympic Committee: Lausanne, Switzerland.

Fehr, D. R., de Varona, D., Ebersol, D. & Schiller, H. (19 June 2003). *Report and Recommendation of the Independent Commission on Reform of the United States Olympic Committee*. Library of Congress: Washington, D.C.

Harris I. (December 2004). *USOC National Governing Body Demographic Survey*, Harris Interactive Inc.: Rochester, New York.

Munoz, F. M. (1997). Historic Evolution and Urban Planning Typology of Olympic Villages. In *Olympic Villages: Hundred Years of Urban Planning and Shared Experiences*. Lausanne: International Olympic Committee. 27-80.

"Opinion/Commentary/Editorial" *Rocky Mountain News*. Denver, Colorado Denver Publishing Company. p. 42A, Copyright July, 30. 2003.

19   IT COMES WITH THE TERRITORY: TERRORISM AND THE PARALYMPICS

Peter Horton & Kristine Toohey

INTRODUCTION

This book, in general, offers different perspectives of the Paralympic Movement. The somewhat provocative title questions whether or not the Paralympics can be considered to be representative of elite sport or merely a distraction. The authors of this chapter firmly position themselves with the former classification. In this chapter we look at the Paralympics as a logical extension of the sport development process; a feature, of what Elias calls sportization, in which he parallels sportization to the civilizing process of societies (Elias, 1986, p.129). One feature of the current phase of the sportization process is that it embraces a level of newly endorsed social democratic sensitivity and includes principles of inclusiveness and tolerance that characterise the face of social thought and sport policy making of the current epoch. This emergent 'political correctness' could, in itself, represent an increasing level of regulation and restraint in sport behaviours, attitudes and practices. However, increasing rejection of intolerance towards 'difference' or 'otherness', coupled with increasing levels of legislation regarding inclusiveness, underpins the growth of the provision of opportunities and facilities for sport for both abled and disabled athletes. As sport for those with physical and intellectual disabilities has become less invisible, the figuration of sport has widened.

The Paralympic Games is a mega-sports event involving elite athletes. At the Athens Paralympic Summer Games in 2004, 3,969 athletes (2,763 men and 1,206 women) from 136 countries participated, whilst four years previously, in Sydney, 3843 athletes from 122 countries competed. These figures indicate the games are now significant sporting contests, both in terms of athlete numbers and national representations. Added to this, the Paralympics recent, more formalised association with the host cities of the Summer and Winter Olympic Games, places them even more firmly in the category of mega-sports events.

Sport, particularly in its mediated form, is globally one of the most, if not the most, dominating and pervasive of all social activities. As a significant aspect of elite sport, Paralympic sport must be viewed as part of that dynamic, with all that it implies, both positive and negative. The negative component now includes the risk of terrorism. Sport has long been the target of terrorism (for example at the 1972 Munich Olympics). It has been passé to believe that sport and politics are separate worlds for much longer than politicians would have us believe. The acceptance of the extent of the threat to sport of terrorist attack has resulted in massive increases in the costs and planning for sport all but particularly mega-sport events. The level of security systems, risk management strategies and counter-terrorist overlays associated with any mega-event, such as the Olympic Games and the various World Cup competitions, are complex and expensive. It is thus timely and relevant to consider the nature of the relationship between the Paralympic Games and terrorism.

Sport for disabled athletes at all levels has unquestionably extended the development of sport and has added a new dimension to the sportization process. As Nixon (2002, p.426) states, the Paralympics provide "opportunities for outstanding athletes with physical and sensory impairments to compete at a high level". They are elite sport for elite athletes, athletes with the same instincts, desires, passions and goals (even pecuniary ones) as other elite athletes, except that they are organised by different categories, based on the athletes' level of physical disability. Not only have the Paralympics changed sport, they have changed some peoples' attitudes to the limits of disability and the need for sporting and recreational opportunities for people with disabilities (Nixon, 2002, p.429).

TERRORISM: DEFINITIONS AND LOGIC

Terrorism *per se* really only emerged with the politicization of power. Although there are competing definitions of the term, in essence terrorism is the use or the threat of violence for political purposes (whether socially, religiously or ideologically motivated), by individuals, groups or factions who have no formal political power (Giddens, 1990, pp.361-2). Though the core purpose of terrorism (an expression which has its origins in the French Revolution in the 18th century) has never changed its forms and how it impacts on our lives and our sensibilities constantly alters. As social, political, economic and even environmental factors have altered, terrorism has assumed new causes or accommodated its actions in light of these transformations. The forces of globalization (of which sport is both object and subject) form a critically integral aspect of post-modern culture. They have also provided the ideoscapes and technoscapes (Appadurai,1990) through which the messages of terrorist attacks, such as 9/11, can sweep around the planet almost as soon as the attacks occur.

There now exists a broad international consensus of the key components of terrorism. This enabled the United Nations, in 2004, to establish a set of parameters that define terrorism for its use, but as Whittaker (2000) suggests, that this definition really only reflects the dominant ideology and the motives of the UN itself. For such organisations there is a need to 'define' terrorism to better understand the likely nature of the forms terrorism might take and the precautions that are necessary to prevent it. However, consistent with a postmodernist perception, a definition is difficult to attain, as terrorism involves continually moving and changing forms of social, political, ideological and economic activities. Some critics too feel that without a clear set of descriptors it is impossible to plan or implement any meaningful anti-terrorist measures (Kennelly, 2005). Others, such as Gearson (2002), insist that there are many terrorisms and a preoccupation with attempting to come up with a working definition could detract from understanding terrorism's consequences. No single definition can adequately delimit terrorism (Jenkins, 2001); there is, in fact, not a single form of terrorism, nor can we safely believe that a single counter-terrorist strategy can accommodate it. Who of us had imagined that two passenger jets piloted by terrorists could be flown into the World Trade Center? Is it any more unlikely that elite Paralympians could be targeted? Despite the fact that some critics dismiss the fixation with the definition of terrorism, the more that sporting event organisers know about terrorists' motivations and capabilities, the better the chance they have of implementing appropriate preventative measures.

Until recently it was believed that the nature of terrorist activity and, the clandestine environments that terrorists worked in, meant that they would operate in small cells and use mainly conventional means of plying their trade. Thus, anti-terrorism systems and strategies have historically been similarly conservative. (Merari, 2002) Reflecting upon: 9/11; the sarin nerve gas attacks in the Tokyo subway by disciples of the Aum Shirikyo cult; and the slaughter of school children in Beslan by suspected Chechen separatists; it can be seen that it is folly to make this assumption. Not only have terrorist groups globalized, they now also embrace state of the art technology and communications systems, for example, they now use the internet to propagate their messages and images of their terror, as witnessed by the online footage of the execution of hostages by insurgents in Iraq in 2004. In general terms and unfortunately for terrorists, advances in communication technology and transport have overcome the tyranny of distance. Consequently, targets have become more accessible to terrorists, and ironically the same advances have made it harder to monitor and regulate these terrorists.

So Why Sport?

Why has sport become a target for terrorists and how is this a part of the development of sport? The links between globalization and sportization are clear and apparent (the ever increasing levels of interdependency in most dimensions of our lives have essentially 'compressed' the world) Maguire (1999, pp.77-88) has linked the sportization process with the phases of globalization as coined by Robertson (1992). Maguire's description of the current phase, the fifth global sportization phase, in his analysis of the global sports formation (pp.75-94), suggests that there is a hint of the decentring of the West in the control of sport (pp.86-7). The increased involvement of stakeholders from non-Western countries demonstrates an extension of the figuration of sport. More non-Western people and new sports are increasingly part of the figuration of global sport (p.86), thus this phase embraces a challenge to the dominant hegemony (ibid). It also involves the widening of the acceptance of ethnicities, non-Western sport forms and the emergence of new sports and extreme sports. Whilst Maguire does not specifically refer to the emergence of the Paralympic Movement during this phase of development, it is fair to include sport for the disabled as an extension of the development of the growing figuration of sport: and the Paralympic Movement and its Games represent the elite dimension of this aspect of the emerging global sports formation.

Sport was arguably one of the major cultural influences that precipitated the emergence of a global culture. Sport, particularly the mega-forms such as the Olympic Games, and now by definition, the Paralympics, has become a central feature of the global media. Because mega sport events are politically, ideologically and culturally prominent: they have 'terrorism capital'.

How has this relationship occurred? Sport it would seem has no direct conceptual links with terrorism (Atkinson & Young, 2000, p.54), yet its prominence, social and cultural significance, and the simple fact that it attracts large crowds, presents it as an 'excellent' target. However, this suitability is far more complex and sophisticated.

Elite sport is characterized by a high level of media interest which is symbiotically linked to its economic and commercial potential. Sport has political significance and has been appropriated by nationalistic motivations. It has historically been a tool of ideological movements. The Ancient Olympics were politically as well as religiously motivated, with the competitors, many of whom were elite professional athletes, competing as representatives of the various city states. Sport was utilized as an ideological 'weapon' in the Cold War in the 20th century and today it is one of the most powerful driving forces of the global media-commerce engine. The social, economic, political and cultural pre-eminence of elite sport indicates it has enormous socio-cultural capital and, as such, this makes it attractive to terrorists, just as it is to politicians and profit driven organizations and individuals.

Is there something special that makes sports events, as the Olympic Games and the myriads of World Cups, targets for terrorists? Or is the appeal based upon the perceived significance of such mega-sporting events to Western cultures? The 9/11 assaults on the World Trade Center and the Pentagon attacked not only the heart of American finance and military command but also the symbols of the nation. As the aim of terrorists is not necessarily to kill the victims but to frighten those watching, an event such as the Football World Cup final, with an audience of 4 billion people, presents an unparalleled opportunity for the terrorists to make their point to terrify and destabilize as many people as possible.

ARE THE PARALYMPICS TARGETS FOR TERRORISM?

Two identities that mark Paralympians dominate this discussion; one that of them as disabled individuals who are involved in sport and the other is that of Paralympians as athletes. These essentially underpin the 'no' and the 'yes' sides of this argument. To believe that the Paralympic Games are not a potential terrorist target is not only naïve but also unwise. The belief that terrorists would not perpetrate an attack on Paralympians or Games' venues, because of the potential repugnance an attack on 'disabled' victims would create, demonstrates a complete lack of understanding of the nature of terror, terrorists and terrorism. Here Paralympians are positioned as individuals with disabilities. This attitude also reflects the hierachizing of vulnerability and value of lives. Paralympians are, in this case, positioned to be less significant and more vulnerable than Olympians, not because of the lack of security measures in place for their sporting competitions but because of the perception of their disability. This argument is at best elitist and at worst illogical. Terrorism is seen in this context, almost as a sport itself, with nothing to be gained from beating a weak opponent. It suggests that there is an optimum extent of capital, based on ableness, in the human lives that terrorists seek to exploit. Yet, terrorism is not, in essence, a physical form but a "form of psychological warfare" (Hoffmann, 2002, p.314), in which there are no innocent victims. In fact, for the fundamental Islamic terrorists, who preoccupy the consideration of Western governments particularly post 9/11 and the Bali bombings, would disabled elite athletes, who are complicit in the 'Western, capitalist economic, political, social, cultural religious hegemony' really be considered innocent? This proposition clearly positions Paralympians as being athletes.

Terrorism is about the creation of fear and the subsequent de-stabilization or propaganda effects promoting a movement's or an individual's cause it is not about the ableness of the victims. This is demonstrated by an incident that occurred on the day of the first post-'liberation' election in Iraq. Insurgents captured a 19 year old Down syndrome sufferer,

Amar, who had a mental age of a four. They fitted him with an explosive device and led to him to an election booth in the Baghdad suburb of Al-Askan. The bomb he was wearing exploded prematurely as Amar detonated it before he reached the election booth. He was killed. The fact that this incident causes such a visceral reaction is indicative of its 'success' as a terrorist act. That is the nature and logic of terrorism. (McGeugh, 2005, p.8)

To accept that the Paralympics will not be a target of terrorism is based heavily upon the notion that the disabled sports movement is outside the 'mainstream'. Yet, ironically, the Paralympic movement's history is steeped in the outcomes of violence. The Paralympic Games, as we know them today, have their origins in the games/activities conducted at Stoke Mandeville Hospital in Surrey, England post World War II as part of the rehabilitation of military casualties. So war and the injuries/victims of terror have never been strangers to the Paralympic movement. At the 2004 Athens Olympic Games many of the athletes that took part were victims of land mines. Even now some of the motivation for the Movement is a direct attempt to confront and deal with the violence and inhumanity that still pervades our World. For example part of the International Paralympic Committee's (IPC) mission is 'to promote Paralympic sports without discrimination for political, religious, economic, disability, gender or race reasons" (International Paralympic Committee, 2003).

As the Paralympic movement seeks and gains: more credibility; less marginalisation; more community acceptance; greater exposure; more funds; more media attention; more commercial potential; more political clout; and more academic consideration, such as this text, the prospect of the Games becoming a possible terrorist target increases. All such changes firmly place the Movement in the mainstream of not only sport, but of society in general. The IPC itself states that it wants 'a high level of international recognition' (International Paralympic Committee, 2003). As the Paralympic Games have now moved into the 'big' league they are up for grabs. Paradoxically with their acceptance, the celebration of sports for athletes with a disability may become a more attractive target for a terrorist attack.

It is difficult to accept a logical argument that supports the notion that the Paralympics are not potential targets for a terrorist attack. One thing we can glean from recent world events is that terrorists fully appreciate sentiment and exploit it expertly. All major sporting competitions that attract global media attention can be considered as being prospective targets for terrorist attack.

THE IMPLICATIONS

The Paralympics have lost their sporting innocence. As Craft (2001) suggested, they have matured and, as such, they have appropriated some of the most desirable aspects of 'mainstream'. However, he also noted that: "there were the less desirable signs of maturation-evidence of banned drug use, increased security precautions, and the shake out of less glamorous sports in favour of the flashy ones that sell well".

Paralympic events have now assumed a level of competitiveness akin to that of the Olympic Games; they have also acquired some of its more distasteful elements. The quest for glory and medals in the Paralympics has reproduced the unseemly side of sport, leading to instances such as the disqualification of the 2000 Spanish men's Basketball Gold medal team in the Intellectual Disability (ID) category because some team members were not intellectually disabled. This form of deception was also evident in the Spanish ID table tennis, swimming and track and field teams where some athletes were also not actually intellectually disabled. (McDonald, 2000) This example of systemic sporting fraud evokes memories of the steroid abuse at the Cold War Olympic Games by both sides of the political divide.

Today athletes and their entourages may be motivated more by profit than ideology. Despite the ever-advancing sophistication of drug testing, the doping continues. For example, 11 of the 643 drug tests at the Sydney Paralympic Games were positive, (which was four times the rate of Sydney Olympians). A potential reason for this is illustrated by the fact that some Paralympians can now be financially rewarded for medal success; for example, Chiang Chih-chung, a blind javelin thrower from Taiwan, received US$58,000 for winning his event at the 2004 Athens Paralympic Games. The Mexican team at the same Games also had some tremendous incentives to win medals. A Mexican billionaire offered them US$17, 000 for a Gold medal, US$8,600 for a Silver and US$4,300 for a Bronze (Incentives, 2004).

The Paralympics now have political (as well as politically-correct) currency. Nations are investing in sport development programs to increase their medal count: witness the efforts of the Chinese team at the Athens 2004 Paralympic Games to head the medal table with 63 Gold medals and 141 medals overall, after placing 6th in Sydney with 34 Gold medals and 72 medals overall. Clearly, the significance of the Paralympics, whether it be political, economic or sporting, ahead of the Chinese hosting of the Olympic/Paralympic Games in Beijing, in 2008, has precipitated a high level of motivation for their team to win medals, as undoubtedly was the case for the Australians in Sydney 2000.

The 'maturing' of the Paralympic Games is apparent, and so, with this mantle, the logistics needed to counteract terrorism implicitly become part of their reality. For example, the security overlay for the Sydney Paralympics was, with some additions, exactly the same as that of the Olympic Games. The design and implementation were conducted in tandem, with the chain of command and operational structures being the same for both events. The NSW Police Commissioner, Peter Ryan, continued his role throughout both competitions. The Key Deliverables embraced the same goals and the scope of the work and operational concepts shown below were also the same. (See Appendix 1).

This security planning and infrastructure lead-in to the Sydney 2000 Olympic and Paralympic Games began in 1994 with the creation of a State Olympic Security Working Committee (OSWC) by the Premier of NSW. The OSWC formed 12 working parties to look at various security concerns ranging from accreditation to biological responses to terrorist attacks. Within a year eight fulltime planning officers were in place and in 1997, after witnessing the systems at the Atlanta Olympic Games, a separate police command, the Olympic Security Command Centre (OSCC) was established. Links were made with the Department of the Prime Minister, Australian Defence Forces (ADF), the Australian Security Intelligence Organisation (ASIO), the NSW Fire Brigades and the NSW Ambulance Service

(IOC Official Report of the XXVII Olympiad, Vol. 1, pp. 191-5). One recommendation of the Sydney Paralympic security planning was that future Games organisers 'do not underestimate the scope and scale of the security operation' (Sydney 2000 Paralympics Post Games Report).

CONCLUSION

To date there has not been a terrorist attack at the Paralympic Games. While it is hoped that this record remains intact, the security prevention measures taken at 2004 Athens Games indicate that authorities believe that the probability of such an eventuality is too high to ignore. Equality and inclusiveness in elite sport is a two-way street; it certainly implies access and acceptability, but it also means that those involved are not immune to prevailing geopolitical forces such as terrorism; it comes with the territory. The Paralympic Games is now an accepted feature of the mega sporting event calendar, and, as such, must be fully equipped to face all economic, political, technological, environmental and social issues and controversies that could possibly befall it.

Unfortunately the threat of terrorism, in its many forms, has now to be faced. This threat, however, is far more multifaceted and far more complex than a simple 'us and them' notion could qualify. The heightened level of awareness of terrorism and the media's preoccupation with it, serves not only the motives of the terrorists but it also serves to maintain the status quo by reinforcing the established political hegemony. In 2004 both the USA Presidential election and the Federal election in Australia were won by conservative parties which used the threat of terrorism as major planks in their campaigns. However, the threat of terrorism to people, institutions, practices and symbols of a culture may stabilize rather than destabilize dominant political hegemonies and, as we saw in 2004, are avidly exploited by politicians and their policy makers. This is the territory of political reality, this is the territory of all major social gatherings; this is now the territory of the Paralympic Movement.

REFERENCES

Atkinson, Michael and Young, Kevin. (2002). Terror Games: Media treatment of security issues at the 2002 Winter Olympic Games. *Olympika: the International Journal of Olympic Studies 9* (53-78).

Appadurai, A. (1990). Disjuncture and difference in global cultural economy, *Theory, Culture and Society, no. 7.* 1990, (295-311).

Craft, A. (2001). Impressions from Australia: the Sydney 2000 Paralympic Games, http://www.palaestra.com/sydneyparalympics.html; sourced 1/02/05.

Chalk, P. (1999). The evolving dynamic of terrorism in the 1990s. *Journal of International Affairs, 53*(2), (151-164).

Elias, N. (1986). The Genesis of Sport as a Sociological Problem. In *Quest for Excitement: Sport and Leisure in the Civilizing Process*, E. Dunning and N. Elias (Eds.), (p. 129). Oxford: Basil Blackwell.

Gearson, J. (2002). The nature of modern terrorism. *Political Quarterly, Suppl. 1*, 73(4), 7-24.

Giddens, A. (1990), *Sociology*, Cambridge: Polity Press, (361-2).

Hoffman, B. (2002). Rethinking terrorism and counterterrorism since 9/11. *Studies in Conflict and Terrorism, 25*, 303-316.

International Paralympic Committee, (2003), Vision and Mission, http://www.paralympic.org/release/Main_Sections_Menu/IPC/About_the_IPC/Vision_and_Mission/, accessed 24 February, 2005.

Jenkins, B. M. (2001). Terrorism and beyond: a 21st century perspective. *Studies in Conflict and Terrorism, 24*, 321-327.

Kennelly, M. (2005), [no title yet] unpublished honours thesis, University of Technology, Sydney Nixon, 2002, (426).

IOC Official Report of the XXVII Olympiad, Vol. 1, pp. 191-5.

Incentives for Mexico's Paralympic teams, September 9, 2004, sourced from, http://www.internationalgames.net/paralympsummer.htm. 08/02/05.

McDonald, M. (2000). *The XI Paralympic Games.* (2000 Paralympic Games Olympic Review, August-September, 2000, sourced from http://www.internationalgames.net/paralympsummer.htm, 08/02/05.

Maguire, J. 1999. *Global Sport: Identities, Societies, Civilizations*, Cambridge: Polity Press, (75-94).

McGeugh, P. (2005). Down syndrome youth used as a suicide bomber, The Age, Wednesday, 2 Feb. 2005, (8).

Merari, A. (2002). Deterring fear: Government responses to terrorist attacks. *Harvard International Review, Winter*, (26-31).

Sanan, (1996) Barcelona Olympics: Counter-terrorism success. In, A. Thompson (Ed.), *Terrorism and the 2000 Olympics*, Canberra: Australian Defence Studies Centre. (139-145).

Sydney 2000 Paralympics Post Games Report, 2001, http://www.gamesinfo.com.au/postgames/pa/pg000384.htm, accessed 25 February, 2005.

Whittaker, D. J. (Ed.). (2001). *The Terrorism Reader*. London: Routledge.

APPENDIX 1

Traffic and Transport	Intelligence
Bomb Management	Olympic Volunteers In Policing (OVIP) Training
Specialist Training	Rostering
Rail Incident Response	Counter-Terrorist/High Risk Coordination
Emergency Management	Protocol
Communications	Training
Aviation Security	C3 Orders
Villages	Accreditation
Procurement	Human Resources
Marine Security	Dignitary and Athlete Protection
Crime Management	Common Domain
Logistics	Security Personnel Accommodation
Torch Relay	Forensic Services
Public Order	Volunteers In Policing
Information Technology	Finance
Olympic/Paralympic	Risk Management
Family Hotels	Guidelines and Products
Media	

SECTION 4

CULTURAL DIVERSITY AT THE PARALYMPICS

This section reviews the concept of how some countries have developed their Paralympic Movements. For example the Eastern European countries of Slovenia and Kosovo are quite different in their establishment from New Zealand, African countries and those of Asia. This chapter then highlights the great need to establish research in individual countries into the development of sport and more importantly the development of Paralympic sport within the separate regions.

20   PARALYMPIC SPORT AND NEW ZEALAND: THE JOURNEY

Trish Bradbury

INTRODUCTION

This chapter provides an overview of the development of disabled and Paralympic sport in New Zealand. The content focuses on written documents and publications in addition to anecdotal evidence from athletes, coaches, and managers. Furthermore, as Assistant Chef de Mission responsible for Games Operations at the 2000 Sydney Paralympics I offer my own personal interpretations and experiences to supplement the data.

THE HISTORY OF PARALYMPIC SPORT IN NEW ZEALAND

Paralympics New Zealand (PNZ) was known as the New Zealand Paraplegic and Physically Disabled Federation from its naissance in 1968 to the early 1990's. From then until 1998 it was known as ParaFed New Zealand. The final name change to Paralympics New Zealand was made in 1998. The organisation had always been responsible for athletes with a disability and Paralympic sport. The final name change came about in order to increase public awareness and the profile of disability sport, and to reflect on the national sport organisation's (NSO's) main purpose – to prepare teams to compete in disability sport at an elite level and more specifically for the Paralympic Games. This is now the main emphasis and raison d'être of Paralympics New Zealand. However, this emphasis is not clearly delineated in PNZ's mission statements which have seemingly evolved over the years without much consistency. In their Introduction to the Organisation of Paralympics New Zealand (2001) document their mission as stated was "… to be a high profile and professional organisation enabling people with disabilities to achieve their potential in sport" (p.4). In their 2003 Sport Information and Reference Guide the mission was described as, "To provide and foster sporting opportunities and competition for people with disabilities who meet International Federation minimal disability criteria" (p.3). However, in their Organisation Overview (2005) and Strategic Plan 2005 – 2008 it was respectively written as, "To provide World Class coach, athlete and administration systems that support and enhance all levels of athlete elite performance" (p.2) and as "Inspiring disabled athletes to become successful Paralympians" (p.3). And finally, their web site, www.paralympicsnz.org.nz accessed on the 2 February 2005, says their mission is to encourage and support people with disabilities from the club developmental level through to international competition levels.

Their mission seems to have progressed towards elite level sport over the years. Initially it was to help people with disabilities to achieve in sport. It then superseded this to be concerned with people with disabilities but only those who met IPC disability criteria. More consistency came in the Organisation Overview and Strategic Plan documents when the focus was more on elite sport. The February 2005 website mission included developmental to elite level sport.

Your average New Zealander would not analyse or even review PNZ's mission statements. A couple of lines from the Alice in Wonderland story demonstrate mission and vision statements well.

> Alice asks, "Would you tell me, please, which way I ought to go from here"? "That depends a good deal on where you want to get to," said the Cat. I don't care much where..." said Alice. "Then it doesn't matter which way you go," said the Cat.

It is necessary that PNZ knows their purpose and where they are going. If they do not know, or care like Alice, they will have a difficult time getting there and achieving their set aims. PNZ's first foray into international competition was at the British Commonwealth Paraplegic Games in Perth, Australia in 1962. These Games were replaced by the Far East and South Pacific International Competition (FESPIC) Games after New Zealand's turn at hosting them in 1974 in Dunedin. New Zealand elite athletes have regularly competed in these Games and other IPC events since this time. There are two main differences between PNZ and any other NSO as PNZ is both a NSO and a National Paralympic Committee (NPC). First of all, most NSOs are responsible for one sport or one derivative of that sport. PNZ is responsible for 14 sports as follows below.

Alpine skiing	Sailing
Athletics	Shooting
Archery	Swimming
Boccia	Table tennis
Cycling	Wheelchair basketball
Equestrian	Wheelchair rugby
Powerlifting	Wheelchair tennis

Secondly, Paralympics New Zealand is a member of and is recognised by the International Paralympic Committee (IPC) as the National Paralympic Committee in New Zealand. No other NSO in New Zealand has this dual responsibility. PNZ performs similar roles to the New Zealand Olympic Committee (NZOC). This mainly includes the preparation of teams to attend the Paralympic Games as the NZOC does for the Olympic and Commonwealth Games. PNZ is supported by a network of ParaFed Associations located regionally throughout the country as well as by NSOs, regional sports trusts, sport clubs, coaches, volunteers, and athletes themselves. The first Regional Parafed Association was formed in Auckland in 1965. Their main purpose is to encourage people with disabilities to participate in sport, recreation, educational, or vocational opportunities. The Parafed's focus should be on increasing the mass participation levels of people with disabilities and developing athletes to progress to elite level competition. This should not be a responsibility of PNZ.

In 2003-2004 PNZ established a High Performance Panel (HPP). Its purpose was to ensure that the best possible preparation was available for Paralympic athletes to achieve international success. The programme offers advice, support, vision, ideas, initiatives, debriefs and evaluations on all aspects of training and competition preparation. This corresponds with PNZ's 2005 version of their mission statement which has the aim to enhance the preparation of athletes at the elite level. Prior to the High Performance Panel

PNZ supported a Paralympics Squad Programme (PSP) that was initiated in 1999 to assist athletes, both financially and administratively, who were attending the 2000 Paralympics in Sydney, Australia. Its role was to support PNZ's athletes to compete and achieve at the highest level possible. In addition, a developmental squad programme was activated at this time to support and build a base of future Paralympians. Eligibility for the Programme was performance–based. Athletes had to show commitment and performance results to be selected as part of the Programme. The High Performance Panel is a positive progression of the Paralympic Squad Programme.

Another one of PNZ's foci is on including and integrating athletes with disabilities (AWD) into programmes of NSOs that currently only cater for able-bodied people.

INCLUSIVENESS AND INTEGRATION: TO BE OR NOT TO BE

Inclusiveness, or inclusivity, is a debatable consideration for all athletes with a disability and for all people involved in the development and promotion of sport in New Zealand. Indeed, PNZ describes an inclusive environment as, "Events where both able bodied and AWD compete in the same competitive environment, utilising the same venues, equipment and officials. AWD events may be conducted separately from able bodied events" (Parkinson, 2003, p.3). PNZ also defines inclusion and integration. Inclusion refers to AWD participating in sport and active activities at their preferred level and setting (Parkinson, 2003). Integration is defined as preparing the AWD to possess the physical and social skills to participate in community activities including sport and active activities (Parkinson, 2003). PNZ has been collaborating with NSOs to provide inclusive sporting opportunities for their athletes. They have been very successful in these efforts in such sports as athletics, basketball, cycling, shooting, and swimming. They are not settling here and are pushing the envelope further. Firstly, they are working with NSOs encouraging them to offer opportunities for athletes with disabilities to participate wholly in the particular sport. Secondly, they are encouraging the NSOs to become an Affiliate or Principal member of PNZ. This means that the NSO will have direct affiliation to PNZ and therefore their athletes will as well providing that the athlete has a membership with a Parafed organisation, a club, or sport-specific group affiliated to the NSO.

Their successes to date are part and parcel of their drive to work with Sport and Recreation New Zealand (SPARC) to revise and emphasise the "No Exceptions" policy. The No Exceptions policy was developed for the period of 1998-2001 with the aim of enhancing the physical sport and recreation experiences of people with disabilities. SPARC, a new government entity created in 2001 replacing the Hillary Commission, reviewed this policy in 2003. The updated version of the No Exceptions policy, now termed strategy, and the implementation plan for the No Exceptions strategy is to be released in 2005 (www.sparc.org.nz, accessed 22 March 2005). PNZ's role in promoting this strategy will assist their efforts as well as SPARC's.

It must be considered and understood that many Paralympic athletes feel that inclusion and integration are part of the answer but not the total answer in itself to the question of the "sport for all" theory. It is felt that a disabled forum such as the one that PNZ provides would still be required even if inclusion and integration became prevalent so that issues important to them would not be suffocated and could still be addressed "in-house". Organisations such as PNZ, the Parafeds, and the Halberg Trust, who created the role of the Sport Opportunity Officer to promote and further the development of sporting opportunities for people with disabilities, will always be needed to act as lobby groups for the disabled community. It can be fairly stated that 'Inclusion and integration are just one of the challenges that PNZ and athletes with disabilities face'.

PARALYMPIC ATHLETES AND THEIR CHALLENGES

A challenge can be defined as a demanding or difficult task (Allen, 1991). Paralympic athletes have various challenges and many are the same as their able-bodied counterparts experience. Some of these challenges include lack of trained sport specific coaches (and those that understand disability sport); the geographical location of New Zealand and the expense to travel to gain quality competition; financial support in general; under resourcing of organisations that support disability sport; and a recruitment, development and succession programme for younger athletes and those with acquired disabilities. Wheelchair racer Gavin Foulsham believes the most difficult aspect is to access coaches with experience in coaching people with disabilities. Mainstream coaches in sports such as athletics or swimming can assist disabled athletes quite easily but in sports where there is no actual comparison such as boccia it is much more difficult. Occasionally a coach comes along who commits tremendous amounts of time and effort into coaching athletes with disabilities but the problem is that they are coaching the athletes – which is not a problem in itself – but there is no succession planning or development of younger coaches to fill this person's shoes when they move on. More coach development and training is a definite requirement. One of the bigger challenges seems to be the introduction of people with a disability, and especially an acquired disability, into the sporting fraternity. The main queries appear to be: how do I find out about disability sport and where is the first port of call? Anecdotal evidence has it that most people find out about sporting opportunities by "bumping" into a mate or through a friend of a friend. The questions to be asked and resolved are: How can these athletes be better identified? How can they be introduced to disability sport? How can they be educated as to the available options? If the pool of athletes is to be increased, identification of these potential athletes must be considered and a strategy for implementation developed.

Even though one of the aims of PNZ is to integrate athletes with disabilities into able-bodied sporting opportunities this could evolve into a dilemma for PNZ. The more integrated the athletes become the less avenues are available to identify potential athletes for the Paralympic Games. This challenge was identified during conversations with ex-Paralympians. It also identifies a bit of a catch 22 situation. Athletes with disabilities should be given the opportunity to partake in daily life and sporting activities with the able-bodied. I say this could evolve into a dilemma as it is an aim of PNZ on one hand while it must be realised that disabled athletes still want the opportunity to compete in an arena only available to disabled athletes. Can this be considered as having your cake and eating it too? Should disabled-athletes be granted these options? Foulsham has a viewpoint to this query which will be discussed in the final section of this chapter. There are other challenges that deserve recognition here but one that irks many Paralympic athletes, those with disabilities, their supporters, and management is media coverage.

MEDIA AND RECOGNITION OF DISABLED ATHLETES' ABILITIES

One of the on-going challenges that PNZ faces is gaining the recognition of the New Zealand media and public for the achievements of Paralympic athletes' successes nationally and internationally. Paul Holmes, PNZ's patron since 1996, wrote in the foreword of Gray's 1997 book on the experiences of New Zealand Paralympic athletes.

> Paralympic athletes who train for years for the big event can't understand why full recognition in the sports departments of radio and television stations around the world is held back. It's as if the commentators quite willfully don't make the leap (p. 8).

Gavin Foulsham believes the disability aspect must be taken out of the equation. It's the athletic performance that must be considered. The athletic endeavour is the same as any able-bodied athlete. The preparation, mentally and physically, is the same as is the attitude and desire to win when in the athletic circle. This is what the media should be educated to do.

Lack of coverage on the sports pages of our print media has long been a thorn in the side of Paralympic athletes and those that support and manage Paralympic sport and sport for athletes with a disability. These athletes train with commitment and intensity for hours a day and multiple times a week. They are supported by sport nutritionists, sport psychologists, sport scientists, and coaches with experience and qualifications. They have rigorous training schedules and set goals with aspirations of being Paralympic champions. They deserve to be treated with respect and admiration as any elite athlete should because that's what they are – elite athletes. They have earned their way to the Paralympic Games through International Paralympic Committee championships, and regional or zoned qualification tournaments such as Oceania, the zone in which New Zealand and Australia compete. Interestingly, many disabled athletes feel that they are as competitive as able-bodied athletes and have as much desire, commitment and dedication. Why shouldn't they be considered as elite athletes and given the recognition and coverage that their able-bodied counterparts receive? Gray (1997) has summarised their plight well. "Their aim is to come off the human interest pages and onto the sport pages, to be recognised as sportspeople" (Gray, 1997, p.13). Many times Paralympic athletes' achievements have been read about on page three of the newspaper and not in the sports section where it rightly deserves to be and community reporters and not sports reporters are sent out to cover the events. Why aren't athletes with disabilities given their due recognition?

Glenda Hughes, media consultant and former Olympian, was quoted in Gray's 1997 book about her views of Paralympic media coverage. She may have the answer to the above question. She said,

> There are two types of people involved in sports in New Zealand. There's what we call the tribal sportsgoer who is totally performance-oriented... . Then there's the theatergoer – and the Paralympians are theater. Unfortunately, most of the people who write about sports in the media or decide what's going on television are tribal (p.13).

This is a good analogy and a good example of a situation where education, attitude change, and awareness building are required. Elite disabled athletes have said that they do not only have to meet challenges in the athletic field of play but in many aspects of their daily lives to make it to the training or competition field. So why it is that these elite athletes are rarely recognised in the sporting news with their able-bodied counterparts? Dave MacCalman, multi-medal athletics field star, believes that the average individual is not aware of or does not understand disabled or Paralympic sport, and therefore feels this is why there are human interest stories abound (D. MacCalman, personal communication, 1 March 2005). He wants these stories to be in the sports section. He feels that perhaps the general public is not ready to accept disabled athletes' achievements. Able-bodied people may not be able to comfortably relate to people with a disability and need to be educated in this respect. It is curious to note that when an athlete in a wheelchair is interviewed the camera does not show the wheelchair and therefore not the disability. This can be interpreted in two ways. Firstly that the production team also feels that the general public is not comfortable with disability and therefore not does display it or secondly, that they are trying to portray that the athlete as just that, an athlete. They do not want the public to focus on the disability and just the achievement.

There needs to be a gradual change of attitudes and exposure to athletes with disabilities. Again, some feel that PNZ should be responsible for enhancing this exposure, the change in attitudes, and education of the media and the general public. It was also suggested that organisations like PNZ should work with their athletes to educate them on their role of educating the media. Foulsham feels that the athletes themselves must be more pro-active in building relationships with the media. He says,

> Media is the key as it strongly relates to marketing and sponsorship opportunities as well as to the exposure given to our athletes. It must be an on-going activity to keep Paralympic sport in the public eye and not only every four years at Paralympic Games time (G. Foulsham, personal communication, 28 February 2005).

He also believes that the "full" story must be told to ensure credibility is gained and kept. The "full" story includes informing the public about those competitions where gold medals and world records were attained but in a sport or class where there were few competitors. The truth must be told to be credible and to encourage further media coverage.

Paralympic sport gained some of this deserved recognition at the inaugural 2004 Freedom Air Peoples' Choice Sports Awards. The Awards provided a chance for New Zealand's public to vote for their favourite sporting heroes under six categories: Sports Team of the Year, Coach of the Year, Paralympian of the Year, Sportswoman of the Year, Sportsman of the Year, and International for non-New Zealanders. There was also an overall Peoples' Choice Supreme Award. Five Paralympic athletes were recognised as were the Wheel Blacks (rugby), the 2004 Athens Paralympics Gold medal team. They were selected as a Sports Team of the Year contender. Peter Martin, captain of the 2004 Paralympics Team, world record holder, and multi-medallist who has competed in three Paralympic Games, won the Paralympian of the Year Award. The Wheel Blacks came up short in their division but at least they made it as a finalist in the category. This exposure and recognition helps the cause of increasing awareness and hopefully attitude change. Through the efforts of one gentleman, Chas Toogood, all came to fruition at the 2004 Paralympic Games. These were the first Games where PNZ athletes received deserved television coverage. Executive producer Toogood has covered New Zealand at Paralympic Games since 1996 but this is the first year that the Team gained such exposure. Three high profile sports interviewers attended the Games and fronted 12 one hour highlight packages. This was a major increase on previous coverage at any Paralympic Games. For the first time ever Television New Zealand (TVNZ) fully funded the production costs. The overall sentiment was that the New Zealand public felt the coverage to be outstanding and captured the personalities of the athletes and values of the Paralympic ideals. The amount of media coverage and recognition of Paralympic athletes' achievements is slowly changing. Questions must still be asked: What more can the Paralympic movement do to educate and entice sports reporters to provide coverage in the sports pages? How long will it take for Paralympians' athletic feats to be recognised as an athletic achievement of great heights? More effort needs to be placed on getting New Zealand's successes realised in the sports pages of our local print press instead of on page three as a human interest story. Once again these athletes are committed elite athletes and compete in their chosen sport as able-bodied athletes do. Some tell us why in the next section.

I DID IT FOR NEW ZEALAND

"Doing it for New Zealand" implies to me that those people, and in this case athletes that do "it" for New Zealand, do "it" for their country and not for their own personal passion or benefit. Two athletes interviewed did not comply with this viewpoint of "doing it for New Zealand" even though they were proud, patriotic, and honoured to represent New Zealand. The honour was considered to be no different than anyone else representing New Zealand whether it is in a sporting, arts, or cultural context. For example, Gavin Foulsham thought it was a very personal thing. In 1996 he missed out on selection for the Atlanta Paralympic Games. At that time he felt people expected him to do "it" and he did "it" but not because he wanted to but because they wanted him to. He believes that sport is a selfish endeavour, especially an individual sport as he competes in. He does not do "it" for New Zealand per se but when he is out on the field of play, he is a proud, patriotic Kiwi who enjoys wearing the silver fern, New Zealand's national sporting emblem. It's about him partaking because he enjoys "it" and doing "it" because he wants to. He concluded by saying, if athletes report that they do "it" for their country and not for themselves personally, then they are naïve and are not being truthful to themselves and the public.

Dave MacCalman has an acquired disability gained through a swimming accident while studying and playing university basketball in the United States of America. Like many Kiwi lads, he had a boyhood dream to represent New Zealand in his chosen sport, which as an able-bodied athlete was basketball. After Dave reached a certain level of recovery and rehabilitation his determination to be independent was strong. He spent hours preparing himself for his day and spent much time in occupational therapy to gain the strength he needed to perform independently personally and as an athlete. Dave discovered the javelin and spent hours throwing and retrieving his javelin. He visualised himself as the best javelin thrower in the world. It took him 15 years to realise this goal but he did it! One of Dave's proudest moments was in 1989 when he was named captain of the FESPIC Games team. Finally, he saw himself as an elite athlete again. Dave did "it" for New Zealand but as well his personal achievements fulfilled his desire to be the elite athlete he once dreamed of. There is no question that MacCalman satisfied his passions to represent his country and felt proud, patriotic, and honoured. He did "it" for himself as much as he did "it" for his country.

There are many New Zealand Paralympians who deserve special mention and discussion in a book such as this but one there is one who stands out. This individual was awarded a Member of the British Empire (MBE), participated in the Olympics, the Paralympics, the Commonwealth Games, FESPIC, and a world championship event. Gold medals were won at the Commonwealth and Paralympic Games. This person is Neroli Fairhall, an archer. She was selected to both the 1980 and 1984 New Zealand Olympic and Paralympic teams and the 1982 Commonwealth Games team. She won a gold medal at the 1982 Commonwealth Games. She was the first person with a disability ever to compete at an Olympic Games. New Zealand joined the USA led boycott of the 1980 Olympic Games hosted by Russia in Moscow. Neroli did not get to participate in these Games because of this. She competed in the 1984 Olympic Games in Los Angeles but not the Paralympic Games as there was a date clash in the Olympic and Paralympic Games with the timing of her events. Neroli's desire to compete and "do it for New Zealand" was never questioned. She was an athlete who excelled and achieved in her sport and gained many accolades like her able and disabled comrades.

PARALYMPIC AND WORLD RECORD ACCOMPLISHMENTS

New Zealand has a reported population of 4,084,200 as of the 31 December 2004 (www.stats.govt.nz/top-20-stats, accessed 1 April 2005). Of this total population, 743,800, one in five, have an impairment (http://www.sparc.org.nz/whatwedo/pdfs/ NE_issues_themes.pdf, accessed 22 March 2005, p.5). For a small country 1500 kilometres from north to south with 1/8 of the population eligible to compete in Paralympic sport, New Zealand performs extremely well in Paralympic Games and international events providing world rankings.

Below Tables x.1 and x.2 respectively indicate New Zealand's medal history at Paralympic Games since 1988. New Zealand generally competes in the following sports: alpine skiing, athletics, boccia, cycling, equestrian, powerlifting, sailing, shooting, swimming, wheelchair rugby, and wheelchair tennis. New Zealand also boasts many world records gained at Paralympic Games, IPC events, and other international and national competitions.

These statistics show that the New Zealand public should be proud of the successes the Paralympians have gained considering the resources and number of athletes PNZ has to work with. In some years the Paralympic Team has performed better than the Olympic Team. One tool that Paralympic athletes have over Olympic athletes is the use and impact of humour on their team environment.

Table x.1: New Zealand Summer Paralympic Games Results

	NZ athletes	Gold	Silver	Bronze	Medal totals	Medal table placing	Countries competing	Athletes
1988 Seoul	17	2	4	11	18	30th	61	3053
1992 Barcelona	18	5	1	0	6	23rd	82	3020
1996 Atlanta	34	9	6	3	18	19th	103	3195
2000 Sydney	41	6	8	4	18	25th	123	3843
2004 Athens	36	6	1	3	10	26th	136	3969

Table x.2: New Zealand Winter Paralympic Games Results

	NZ athletes	Gold	Silver	Bronze	Medal totals	Medal table placing	Countries competing	Athletes
1988 Innsbruck	2	0	1	0	1	13th	22	350
1992 Albertville	4	2	0	0	2	11th	24	475
1994 Lillehammer	5	3	0	3	6	10th	31	1000
1998 Nagano	4	4	1	1	6	11th	32	571
2002 Salt Lake	2	4	0	2	6	10th	36	416

PARALYMPIC ATHLETES' SENSE OF HUMOUR

There is definitely humour in the lives and relationships of athletes with disabilities. I was interviewed for the Assistant Chef de Mission position for the New Zealand team participating in the 2000 Paralympic Games. Part of my interview focused on my ability to work with and comprehend the needs and lives of our Paralympians. I was quite confident in my ability to carry out the required duties and functions. Little did I realise the role that humour played and how it might affect my duties and functions, at least in the lives of the athletes I worked with. The interview was a success and I was appointed to the management team.

Paralympic athletes have a tremendous sense of humour which at times may make able-bodied people feel uncomfortable. Early in my tenure I had one of these experiences but quickly got over it. While enroute to a meeting with wheelchair track star Ben Lucas I was caused some discomfort. As we exited the lift to the meeting room I started to say "walk this way". I stopped myself mid-sentence. No, it was actually mid the word "walk". Ben continued my thought and made a joke out of my awkward statement. It was a small faux pas but it got me over the hump and I often tell the story to various groups of people. Perhaps this is not considered humour per se but it was one of those awkward situations that able-bodied people may experience. Ben found it amusing, and then so did I.

A story that I have been told which I think is quite funny involves a coach and a blind athlete sharing a room while away at a multi-sport competition. For a couple of nights in a row the coach heard a scratching noise about 2:00 in the morning. He thought that it might be a rat and hoped it was in the walls of the room and not in the room itself. Finally, gaining some confidence to check out the sounds, he turned the light on. Sitting in the bed next to him was his "rat". His room mate was reading his book – in Braille! After the final day of competition, the coach being the character he is, moved all the furniture around in the bedroom. When his room mate came back to the room, of course he bumped into everything. They, and the team, had a good giggle at this.

One athlete, when discussing the use of humour, described that athletes with disabilities can call themselves crips but able-bodied athletes, or people in general, can not. It was described like a "club", in a silly sense. It is seemingly the same as for some other cultures or nationalities. They are comfortable naming themselves with a term that can be interpreted as derogatory or non-politically correct but if you are not part of "the club", culture of nationality, it is not acceptable.

Foulsham says the humour can be incredibly funny but some of it is better kept in-house. Lots of things go on but they are stories that the "club" shares. People with disabilities are laughing at people with disabilities and it is acceptable to the "club". They can laugh at themselves. He says you just don't take the mickey out of someone unless you know and understand them. A touch of realism is always there for them. Some of these athletes, especially those who have an acquired disability, gain a philosophical attitude towards life and finally have to just get over it and get on with it. Humour helps them to do this and adds a lighter side to the tension and pressure that athletes experience while competing in elite level competition.

CONTINUING THE JOURNEY

Where to from here? What must the management, athletes, supporters, and people in the lives of people with disabilities do to aid their sporting, and life, journeys? It is clear that the breakdown of attitudes towards people with disabilities must continue. The Commonwealth Games Organisation and the International Olympic Committee have been proactive in promoting athletes with disabilities by having demonstration events at their international competitions. Both have held competitions in some sports and classes for athletes with disabilities. This is providing the needed exposure to the mass media and numerous viewing audiences discussed earlier. Foulsham talked about his experiences while he and Ben Lucas competed in wheelchair racing at the 1994 Commonwealth Games. It was a highlight of his career at that time because he was able to learn a lot from his team mates and be part of a team that meant a lot to New Zealanders. This opportunity provided dual benefit. Both Gavin and Ben had a great experience personally and athletically. Also, as noted above, not only were the mass media and viewing audiences exposed to athletes with a disability but so too were the able-bodied athletes. The occasion provided opportunity for able-bodied athletes to realise the feats and athletic abilities of athletes with disabilities. These experiences aid in the attitude change, the awareness raising, and education efforts noted as definite requirements for disability sport earlier in this chapter. Foulsham says it is time for a cross over between Olympic and Paralympic sport and athletes with and without disabilities.

As noted earlier Foulsham has a viewpoint of sporting integration. He strongly feels that wheelchair racing in an open class could become a Commonwealth and/or Olympic Games event and still remain a Paralympic event. There is nothing to stop anyone from getting into a chair and becoming a wheelchair racer. Able-bodied kids who have parents in wheelchairs are getting into their chairs and giving it a go. There is no reason why these kids do not continue "playing" in a wheelchair or pick up wheelchair racing as their chosen sport. He realises that some people may have major issues with this idea but he doesn't. He believes others feel it could damage disability sport or that athletes with disabilities would give up Paralympic sport instead of competing in both arenas. If inclusion and integration are to be realised this is step in the right direction.

In 1992 one of New Zealand's Paralympians was on the IPC Athletes Representative Committee. At this time they were discussing the idea of having athletes with intellectual disabilities included in IPC events. The Committee was afraid that their inclusion would tarnish their image and cause more attitudinal problems. They did not want to lose the ground they had already secured. They then realised that they themselves were being hypocritical, as they had felt some able-bodied people were towards the disabled community. Why would the Athletes Representative Committee reject them when they realised that's what they themselves as athletes with disabilities were experiencing? They rejected their initial thoughts and were open-minded towards the athletes with intellectual disabilities. Open-mindedness must continue within and outside the disabled community for the cause to grow.

Each of these efforts will further the Paralympic movement. On the international scene, the IPC now has a President who is a paraplegic. He has helped integrate wheelchair basketball into the Federation de Basketball Association (FIBA) and is currently seeking to be an ex-officio on the IOC Board to promote further integration. It really does not matter that he is a paraplegic except for the fact that perhaps he better understands the movement's needs and therefore the direction that the journey has to take. This is a good sign for the future of Paralympic sport.

REFERENCES

Allen, R.E. (Ed). (1991). *The Oxford Concise Dictionary*, New York: Oxford University Press

Cockburn, R. (2003). No Exceptions: Issues and themes.
http://www.sparc.org.nz/whatwedo/pdfs/NE_issues_themes.pdf, accessed 22 March 2005.

Gray, A. (1997). Against the odds: New Zealand Paralympians. Auckland, New Zealand: Hodder Moa Beckett Publishers.International Olympic Games, www.olympic.org, accessed 1 April 2005.

Paralympics New Zealand (2001). *Introduction to the organisation of Paralympics New Zealand*. Auckland, New Zealand: Paralympics New Zealand.Paralympics New Zealand (2005).

Strategic Plan 2005-2008. Auckland, New Zealand: Paralympics New Zealand.

Paralympics New Zealand, www.paralympicsnz.org.nz, accessed 2 February 2005.

Parkinson, A. (2003). *A guide to inclusive event management*. Auckland, New Zealand: Paralympics New Zealand.

Sport and Recreation New Zealand, www.sparc.org.nz, accessed 2 February 2005.

Statistics New Zealand, www.stats.govt.nz/top-20-stats, accessed 1 April 2005.

21   THE RISE OF PARALYMPIC SPORT IN SLOVENIA

Mojca Doupona Topic

INTRODUCTION

In Slovenia, different terms are in use when dealing with sports activity of people with special needs, such as: sport for the disabled (disability sport), sport for persons with special needs, rehabilitation sport, therapeutic rehabilitation, sport for the locomotory impaired, adapted sports activity, Paralympics, Special Olympics, etc. By means of the said terms, we try to define the diverse, complex and demanding developments in the field of involvement in sports associated with various types and levels of impairment in individuals. Some historical background

Before the Second World War, only the deaf and hearing impaired were organised in terms of sports in Slovenia, as was the case across the rest of the world; they had their federation. As regards other disabled people, their organised sports activity began after the Second World War, which left behind 150,000 war invalids. Similarly as elsewhere in the world, rehabilitation institutions (Institute for Rehabilitation of the Disabled in Ljubljana) played a special role. The initiative to launch organised sports came from the ranks of military war invalids in 1949. They set up a commission for sport which was in charge of the promotion of disability sport. Support for such efforts was also provided by social security and by the Physical Culture Association of the RS.

In 1955, the Sports Federation for the Disabled of Slovenia was established as a result of an agreement between the Disabled War Veterans Association of Slovenia and the Slovenian Sports Association. In 1964, B. Hrovatin began to develop, within the Institute for Rehabilitation of the Disabled, disability sport among paraplegics during their rehabilitation. In the early period, Miro Vesel and Bojan Hrovatin (Vute, 1999) had a decisive impact, especially among the amputees and paraplegics. The Slovenian Sports Association had a pioneering role on the Yugoslavian scale, as, based on its experiences, sports activities for the physically impaired were also launched in other regions and republics of the former Yugoslavia.

Within the Federation for Sports and Recreation of the Disabled of Yugoslavia, both the republic and regional federations for sports and recreation of the disabled were eventually combined. In the Federation, emphasis was placed on ensuring the inclusion of the impaired into sports activities, ensuring professional and planned work, promotion of sports for the physically impaired, cooperation with international organisations that bring together the impaired, and management and coordination of competition sports at the federal and international level. Until the beginning of the 1990s, the federation had undergone many phases of development. At the beginning, sports of a purely recreational nature had prevailed, while later competition sport began to dominate, and most recently, top-level sports.

In the 1990s, 10 national disability organisations decided to establish a new Sports Federation for the Disabled of Slovenia (ZŠIS). Thus, from the Federation of Disability

Sports Societies it became the Federation of National Sports Societies. Slovenian disabled athletes participated for the first time at the fourth Summer Paralympic Games held in 1972 in Heidelberg. From then on, they participated in the national representation of Yugoslavia, and since 1992, they have been taking part in all international competitions as the national representation of Slovenia.

For the Slovenes and their sports history, especially the paralympic sports history, the following milestones are, without doubt, important:

1992 - Barcelona: first gold paralympic medal for independent Slovenia: Franjo Izlakar (track-and-field: discus and shot put) and bronze medal: Dragica Lapornik (track and field: shot put);

1996 - Atlanta: Slovenian athletes won one silver and three bronze medals;

2000 - Sydney: Slovenian athletes won two silver and two bronze medals;

2004 - Athens: Slovenian athletes won one gold, two silver, and one bronze medal.

Today, the Paralympic Games are an elite competition both as regards organisational and competition-related aspects. The interest in them is increasing from year to year and even if we look at the statistical data, we can see how the number of athletes - and also the number of states from which they come – is constantly increasing. In the first Paralympic Games held in 1960 in Rome, 400 athletes from 23 countries participated, while in the last summer games held in 2004 in Athens, 3806 athletes from as many as 136 countries participated. The interest of the media is constantly increasing as well: the games in Athens were very well covered by the media. It was possible to watch events on the television and the internet. Therefore the Paralympic Games are now far from being merely a sports gathering. The life of paralympians is becoming more and more similar to that of professional athletes. As an example, the competition in track and field has become so large that competitors have to train twice a day if they want to keep pace with the world's best. For example at the last games in Athens, 304 new world records were attained. However, the majority of paralympic sports are divided into categories depending on the various levels of physical impairment and physical problems of the athletes. At the Paralympic Games, however, only the so-called elite can compete, that is the ten best in each category. The leader of the team departing for Athens, Branko Mohorko, said: In fact, more than 20,000 athletes could have competed in Athens if the standards were not so strict. Indeed, the standards were so high that even an achieved (A) standard in track and field was not enough for participation. The organisers imposed limitations because they did not wish to finance a large number of competitors. For example, only 6 teams could participate in the sitting volleyball: the first three teams from the world championship and three best teams from individual regions. However, there could have been considerably more teams. If (A) and (B) standards had been taken into account, Slovenia would have had a much larger national representation.

The Slovenian representation in Athens was the largest in number up to now, as 29 athletes participated. The whole team together with coaches, medical team, a press representative and the leader comprised of 43 members. The expectations were high, although only few dared to think about medals. Slovenian athletes competed in sitting volleyball, goalball, track and field, cycling, swimming, table tennis, and archery. Altogether, they were competing to win medals in 27 disciplines.

The games in Athens were very successful for the Slovenian paralympians, as the team of 29 members won four medals. Gold in wheelchair table tennis was won by Mateja Pintar, only 19 years old; and the most successful Slovenian competitor, with two medals, was Tatjana Majcen, who won bronze in shot put and silver in javelin throw, where for some minutes, she even held a world record. A silver medal, already for the third time in succession, was also won by the veteran Franc Pinter. The number of medals won could have been even larger with a little luck, since our paralympians also won four fourth places.

ORGANISATION OF DISABILITY SPORT IN SLOVENIA

The Sports Federation for the Disabled of Slovenia is considered to be a non-profit organisation. The non-profit nature is stipulated in the Act on Societies and in the Act on Disability Organisations. The management of the organisation consists of the assembly of the federation (the highest body), consisting of two representatives from each disability organisation. The assembly meets once a year and also when necessary. It adopts all important decisions, programmes, reports, it decides on real property, etc. Within the assembly there operates a management board, carrying out the conclusions of the assembly and performing operational tasks between two successive assemblies. Within the management board there is a commission for competition sports. Special bodies are also the monitoring committee and the disciplinary board.

The organisation is governed centrally. The disabled can become involved in the organisation through their parent disability organisations. The organisation only partly covers recreation of the disabled, i.e. in the counselling and professional field, while the implementing tasks are within the scope of individual disability organisations. Clubs and societies are not directly included in the organisation. The organisation has four regular employees (expert service). In addition, 30 coaches, assistants and individual programme leaders – coordinators are engaged in the organisation. Among them there are no regularly employed disabled persons; however, the disabled are among the heads and individual functionaries. It also directly covers youth sport and competition sports, while by projects it covers the individual organisation of large events on an international scale and participation in official competitions. No government body is directly responsible for organisation of disability sport; however, they disability sport does come under the aegis of the Ministry of Education and Sport and Ministry of Labour, Family and Social Affairs. Within the Ministry of Labour there is a directorate for the disabled. The financing of the organisation is provided by the Ministry of Education and Sport, mainly by the Foundation for financing Disability and Humanitarian organisations (FIHO) and only a smaller part of funds is obtained through donations and sponsors. No financing is obtained from the European funds.

Each disability organisation receives the same share of money. Disability organisations can raise money separately from sponsors, donors and branch federations. Organisation of competitions is left to the disability organisations and branch federations. Each disability organisation takes care of its sport. The athletes are reimbursed for the expenses incurred by participation in competitions. An accompanying team (physician, physiotherapist, psychologist, coaches and non-professional companions) is sent to international competitions. The competitions are covered by a reporter who describes the competition events. Some larger events are broadcast by television, thus contributing to the prominence of disability sport in Slovenia.

In preparing for the Olympic and Paralympic Games, they have until now mainly not been directly involved with the Olympic Committee; only in some minor protocol-related parts (dispatch of the team, partial equipment, etc.). Competitions are organised and financed by societies and federations. At competitions, qualifications take place. The number of competitors at competitions depends on the respective sport. Annual participation in all national championships is approximately 1300 athletes and approximately 130 disability athletes in official competitions. This means from 8 to 9% of all disabled in the country. The disabled athletes are reimbursed for the expenses incurred due to their participation in competitions. To international competitions, an accompanying team is also sent (physician, masseur, psychologist, coaches, experts and non-professional companions). At individual competitions, psychologists are also involved, mostly in individual cases.

The representatives of the federation have assessed that the conditions as regards the sports facilities at competitions are good; however, they have no sports centres of their own for the disabled. Slovenia has no separate status specifically applying to the disabled athletes. Also the process of regulating this status is very slow. The Sports Federation for the Disabled of Slovenia organises various international competitions and, in the longer run, also European competitions. The Sports Federation for the Disabled of Slovenia is a member of the National Olympic Committee (NOC) (associate member, however, the status is not regulated). Their (NOC's) attitude towards disability sport was assessed as poor. The attitude of the Sports Federation for the Disabled of Slovenia to Deaflympics and Special Olympics was assessed as very good.

At the moment, they are faced with a number of issues, including the regulation of the status of a disabled athlete, insufficient professional staff; cooperation with the University or Faculty of Sports, Paedagogical and Medical Faculty is not good; there are no suitable sports facilities, there is a lack of sports equipment; very poor response from the media and the organisation is in contact with branch federations only in some cases. They also are responsible for youth disabled sport by including the young into their programmes; thus enabling them partial purchase of equipment, and send them to competitions. Cooperation with schools is not satisfactory. They point out that experts from the medical sport field are not sufficiently included in the organisation. No marketing experts are involved in the organisation. Concerning the involvement of public relations experts, they say that such persons were included in the past, but no progress or personal ambitions could have been observed (B. Mohorko, personal interview on 11 March 2007).

PROPOSAL OF THE MODEL OF ORGANISATION OF DISABILITY SPORT IN THE FUTURE

In order to comply with the directive from November 2005, Slovenia will have to reorganise disability sport. At the assembly of the International Paralympic Committee (IPC) it was, required that disability sport should be renamed into the National Paralympic Committee or include the word 'Paralympic' into the name of the Federation (Sports Federation for the

Disabled of Slovenia). Therefore, instead of the Federation of Disability Sport, the name Sports Federation for the Disabled of Slovenia – Paralympic Committee has been used since 2007. Regrettably, only one part - the Paralympic Committee - has been added to the name of the organisation, while the organisation of the federation has not changed. The National Paralympic Committee of Slovenia is a non-governmental, non-profit organisation which is managed centrally and is included into an umbrella organisation (Sports Federation for the Disabled of Slovenia). The members of the umbrella organisation are: the National Paralympic Committee, Deaflympics, Special Olympics. These are the main branches of the Sports Federation for the Disabled of Slovenia .

Each of the three disability organisations works independently. It would be more appropriate if, instead of the present 15 national governmental organisations, three disability organisations were organised (National Paralympic Committee, Deaflympics, Special Olympics). The main advantage of the latter division is seen in the different allocation of funds obtained from the state and the distribution functions which the organisations included in the National Paralympic Committee should perform. Such an allocation of the funds would be more appropriate because it would allow each disability organisation to assess by itself which of its members needs, at a given point in time, a greater share of money for its projects.

One of the major issues in Slovenia is that disabled athletes do not have the status of a top-level athlete and hence also do not have any benefits or rights arising from that status. In the majority of the described countries, the status of a disabled athlete is regulated and equal to that of the status of an able-bodied athlete. This status entitles the athletes to enjoy certain benefits and rights and thus facilitates their preparation for competitions. In order to place disability sports at a higher level in our country as well, it is mandatory also to introduce the status of a top-level athlete for the disabled, which status should, however, be equal to the present status of a top-level able-bodied athlete. The criteria for obtaining the status of a disabled athlete should be the same as the present criteria for obtaining the status of a top-level able-bodied athlete.

In Article 38 of the Act on Sports, the following is laid down: 'The title of a top-level athlete can be obtained by a citizen of the Republic of Slovenia who attains a top-level sports result of an international class'.

The criteria for top-level sports achievement referred to in the first paragraph and the duration of the title shall be stipulated by the expert council on the proposal from the Olympic Committee of Slovenia, or from the competent national sports federation. The title from the first paragraph of this article is awarded by the Olympic Committee of Slovenia on the basis of criteria referred to in the second paragraph of this Article (Act on Sports, 1998). A change in determining the status of a disabled athlete is also seen in that the title of a top-level athlete is proposed by the Olympic Committee of Slovenia and the National Paralympic Committee, which also lay down the criteria for acquiring the title of a top-level athlete.

As regards sports for young people, there are provided various activities (one type of disability at each school, Disability Sports Day), increased cooperation with schools, help for purchasing the equipment and fastest possible involvement of children in sports and recreation. It is necessary to provide for the preparation of various projects – development of various sports (swimming, track and field, table tennis etc.). It would also be necessary to set up better cooperation with Slovenian universities and high schools, as well as with competent institutions in order to elaborate educational programmes with the contents that raise the level of knowledge of sports and sports education in people with special needs. Due to the size of Slovenia (only 2 million inhabitants), it is possible to build our own disability sports centre that would serve as a rehabilitation centre for the disabled or as a space for training the competitors, or also as the space for recreation of the disabled. In the centre, various experts form various professions (suitably trained) would work in order to help the disabled.

PARALYMPIC COMMITTEES IN THE WORLD – SOME EXAMPLES

Data on the situation in the field of paralympic sports in individual countries have been obtained by surveying questionnaires. The main findings can be summarised as follows:

It has been found that Scandinavian countries can be ranked among the most developed countries in terms of disability sport. In these countries, disability sports play an important social role. All these countries have very well regulated legal provisions and equality between the disabled and the non-disabled. Among European countries, Spain also stands out; it has the largest number of representatives on the International Paralympic Committee. It can be concluded from the data obtained that the founders of Paralympic Committees are non-profit organisations.

In the majority of countries, all types of disability are included into their organisations. They usually exclude from their organisations only the deaf-mute as these usually have their own organisations. As regards financing, it was noticed that the majority of organisations are financed from both public and private funds; only some of them are financed either only from private or only from public funds. Organisations in Finland, Serbia, Bosnia and Hercegovina, and China are financed only from public funds, while organisations in the United States of America are financed only from private funds. When we speak about financing, we must also mention that the issues most often given in the replies are those associated with the raising of funds and with the premises, which points to financial difficulties.

All countries - except Finland and Austria, which have not provided replies, and Bosnia and Hercegovina, in which the status of the athlete is the same for all athletes - have a special status for disabled athletes, yet this status is being equalised with that of non-disabled athletes. German, Dutch, Swiss, Belgian and Serbian Paralympic Committees are members of national Olympic Committees in their countries, while Paralympic Committees in all other countries (Finland, Austria, Greece, China) are not members of national Olympic Committees; however, their relation with national Olympic Committees is described as good in the majority of cases. In the USA, there are no separate national Olympic Committee and Paralympic Committee; they all fall under the National Olympic Committee.

In the majority of countries they connect with branch federations and provide for youth sports. They most often take care of youth sports through various projects, special development programmes, youth camps and by promoting sports in special schools. In all countries, except in Serbia and Greece, they are connecting with various experts (from the medical and sports field, psychologists). In Serbia and Greece, they cooperate only with experts in the sports field. Marketing and public relations are also provided for in different ways in different countries. Some have their own marketing agencies, some cooperate with external agencies.

Sports centres for the disabled also proved to be problematic, since we can find that only in Belgium, the Netherlands, Switzerland, and in China they have sports centres of their own for the disabled. In other countries, they help themselves in various ways. As evident from the analysis of individual countries, the majority of countries have these issues resolved. Some countries distinguish between the status of a disabled athlete and that of an able-bodied athlete. We are of the opinion that this distinction is not justified since in the both cases we have to do with top-level athletes who attain top-level results at the largest competitions.

COVERAGE OF PARALYMPIC SPORTS BY THE MEDIA

Development of sport for the disabled depends partly also on how public relations are handled. The coverage of disability sports by the media also falls under these relations. The media have several reasons for giving coverage to disability sports. Many sports are, in themselves, interesting for the public. Many disabled athletes achieve, at international level, results that are comparable to the results of able-bodied athletes. Even more, the results of the progress of the disabled are, compared with other sports organisations, unique in terms of sociological, psychological and physical readaptation. Why aim for publicity?

- because it directs the public towards the events involving the disabled;
- because it encourages the disabled to engage in sports and thus attain faster readaptation;
- because it praises the results attained as a result of diligent training of the disabled (Milanović, 1996)

In general, the media are not favourably inclined to presentation of disability sports, and mainly argue that such events are not interesting for them. For such an attitude, the managing personnel in disability sports are also partially to blame because they are actually the ones who should send reporters to disability sports events. Therefore, the responsibility for the publicity of disability sports is very wide, and cooperation between institutions and media must be on a professional level to ensure that articles, reports and all other materials on the development of disability sports, as well as on competitions and the results attained are published. All of these should contribute to placing disability sports, from the sociological point of view, in a completely different light than is perceived by many at present. Also the Paralympic Games, the most elite sports event for the disabled, is given negligible coverage by the media in comparison with the Olympic Games. Golden made some interviews with sports commentators at the Olympic Games in Sydney and at the Boston Marathon and came to the conclusion that they do not see disabled athletes as 'valid' (Golden, 2002, v http://physed.otago.ac.nz/ sosol/v7i1/v7i1_1.html). This is also confirmed by the following statement of some reporter: 'They cannot compete on the same level as the athletes at the Olympic Games, and hence this is only a 'bone' offered to them in order to make them feel better'. He went on to state that:

'It is not a real competition and I do not see why I should ever report on it? (http://physed.otago.ac.nz/sosol/v7i1/v7i1_1.html

That disability sport is not accepted as equal in Slovenia as well is reflected in the statement by Joïe Okorn after appearance of the Slovenian wheelchair basketball team, which was ranked in group A in '1996 Ljubljana Games': 'We expect more understanding from the state; it should provide money for the development of – and should, of course, better listen to the needs of ? top-level disability sports. There still prevails the thinking that disability sport is something inferior, yet this is not true. It was exactly at the championship in Ljubljana that we could best see that this is not so, when our matches were watched by a large number of basketball friends (Glavonjić, 1996)'.

Mateja Pintar, a table tennis player, also commented after receiving the award as female athlete of the year 2005: 'We, disabled athletes, also work very hard to attain results, which, regrettably, are not sufficiently valued by the public, the media and also by the governmental and sports organisations, which still look on us as recreational athletes. I sincerely hope that this situation will be resolved and that we will also be able to obtain the status of a top-level athlete, which will enable us to be given equal treatment with other athletes' (Lipovšek, 2006).

The largest problem of the disability sports is that the state and sponsors are not willing to cooperate. This is also the consequence of the fact that disability sport is not promoted in the media. Mihorko, the head of the organisation committee of the 8th European Wheelchair Table Tennis Championship (EPINT 2007), which took place in 2007 in Ljubljana, said that the costs of the championship were 800,000 €; however, the state did not contribute 1 € for this event. All sponsor funds were raised by private capital. The national TV of Slovenia directly broadcast the majority of final matches, which is the first time in the history of disability sports that the national TV (TVS) included direct broadcasting of disability sports in its programme scheme. The reporter who commented on the final matches directed much of his attention, above all, to the promotion of disability sports in terms of the importance of involvement in disability sports. (Too) often he invited potential disabled viewers to think about becoming involved in sports activities, since this should have a remarkably positive impact above all on the psycho-social feeling of a person with special needs. In Slovenia, the media only rarely decide on presenting the results or showing sport events of the disabled, and consequently lack the necessary experiences to do so.

Nevertheless, it is necessary that into the subconsciousness of some there should penetrate the fact that through their persistent training, participation in large competitions (Paralympic Games, World Championships, European Championships and World Games)

and winning of medals the disabled can also become top-level athletes. Finally, despite their specific disabilities, with their greatest successes they do promote the Slovenian state in the same way as the able-bodied athletes. Slovenian disabled athletes do not lack the will to work and the wish to succeed; however, better and more frequent media attention would give them even greater impetus for work in the future.

POSITIVE MOVES IN SLOVENIA

In Slovenia, the first steps towards the knowledge of and popularity of disability sports, e.g. disability swimming, has begun. The proof of this is the project of development of disability swimming in Slovenia. The project material gives some guidelines for the development of this sport among the disabled, and it would be appropriate to follow this in other sports (table tennis, track and field) as well. This can be achieved only by top-quality, competent personnel and by interdisciplinary cooperation between them. Regrettably, we have in Slovenia very few professionally competent personnel in this field.

Steps have also been made towards the recognition of disability sport, since in June 2007, the Federation arranged the Disability Sports Day for the first time. People with special needs are not known to the wider public and people tend to avoid what they do not know. By holding an event such as the Disability Sport Day they will help to ensure that people and media will accept different individuals.

REFERENCES

Act on Sports. Uradni list RS 22/1998. (1998). *Zakon o sportu*. Ljubljana: Republika Slovenija.

Glavonjić, M. (01.08.1996). *Težave športnikov invalidov. Dolenjski list, 31*, p.13.Hardin, M. M. & B. Hardin (2004). The 'Supercrip' in sport media: Wheelchair athletes discuss hegemony's disabled hero. sosol 7/ 1
(http://physed.otago.ac.nz/ sosol/v7i1/v7i1_1.html),

Lipovšek, V. (2006). Pintarjeva, Pinter in gluhi košarkarji. *Športnik*, n. 2, p. 16-17.

Mesaresc, P. (2007). Model organizacije Športov invalidov na primeru v Sloveniji. Diploma thesis. Ljubljana: Faculty of Sport.

Milanović, A. (1996). *Evropska Povelja o sportu za sve: hendikepirane osobe*. Sarajevo.

Mohorko, B. personal interview on 11 March 2007.

Vute, R. (1999). *Izziv drugačnosti v športu*. Ljubljana: Debora.

22   KOSOVO'S ATTEMPTS TO JOIN THE WORLD STAGE

Barbara Petri-Uy

INTRODUCTION

Sports for the disabled – elite sport or side show? The question is quite blunt, but in the context of post-conflict Kosovo, its pertinence is all but uncontested. This chapter will aim to answer this question considering Kosovo's specific situation as a territory **when** under UN administration, and also attempt to go beyond a simple description of the programs and policies of sports for the disabled in Kosovo. What follows is a quick background on the socio-political particularities of the new country of Kosovo. The first section of the chapter presents the historical background of Kosovo and aids the reader in understanding the role of the United Nations Interim Administration Mission in Kosovo (UNMIK). The second part of this chapter is more descriptive than analytical and is devoted to the recontextualization of what is termed the "Handisport Policy" of the Department of Sports (DOS) in the Ministry of Culture, Youth and Sport (MCYS)[1]. The conclusions in the chapter support the arguments of the short socio-political analysis of the development of sports for the disabled in Kosovo. It concentrates on the "instrumentalization" of sports, or, in this case, of sports for the disabled. Using the sociological ideas and principles of the Bourdieu school of thought, this final part illustrates how the appropriation of the positive representation of sports is specific and intrinsic to each organization. In this case study the challenge is to evaluate the developmental process of sports for the disabled in this area of Southeastern Europe, considering its specific political and social conditions.

To summarize, the body structure of this chapter will develop the following three points:
1   Historical glance of Kosovo sports institutions
2   Sports for the disabled in Kosovo – a special project
3   Political stakes of the development of disabled sports

A BRIEF INTRODUCTION TO THE HISTORY OF KOSOVO

Kosovo is a small provincial new state located at the heart of former Republic of Yugoslavia. During the Cold War period, sports were highly developed in communist countries, contributing to an indoctrination of the masses, but also serving the political and ideological disputes of the opposing Eastern and Western blocks. For example, in 1974, some autonomy was given to Kosovo sporting institutions and concretized under the "League of Sports", which was managed under the umbrella organization of the Yugoslav Federal Government.

---

1 *To dilute all kind of misunderstanding, the appellation "Handisport Policy" should be solely understand with the perspective that the author of this chapter, at the time, Policy and Program Adviser of the Provisional Institution Self-Governance Department of Sports was simply inspired by the denomination of sports administrative infrastructure for the disabled in France. As such, it is unnecessary to start a polemic on the "politically correctness" of the term. There is neither any social, nor political orientation induced in this title.*

The year of 1989 represents a second benchmark in the modern sports history of Kosovo. This date coincides with abrogation of limited independence by former President Slobodan Milosevic. Consequently, conflict flared in Kosovo between the two principal communities, the ethnic Serbs and Albanians[2]. As institutions were highly Serb-dominated and discrimination against Kosovo ethnic-Albanian. Were not common, the Albanian community had decided to boycott Milosevic's politics and created their own parallel institutions, mirroring all administrative and social structures. As a consequence, the Kosovo sports system, among others, was also deeply affected, not only in terms of athletic performance, but also in terms of sports culture, sports infrastructures and sports politics. It became a system characterized by a lack of transparency and was largely male dominated.

UNMIK'S MANDATE AND ORGANIZATION

On 10 June 1999, the Security Council of the United Nations adopted Resolution 1244 authorizing the then UN Secretary General Kofi Annan to establish a unique peace-keeping mission, giving birth to the United Nations Interim Administration Mission in Kosovo. At the time of its creation, it was the biggest mission ever put in place by the United Nations, and was consequently designed and conceived with a very unique structure that enabled other multilateral organizations to work in close cooperation with the United Nations while under its leadership. Four "pillars" were created:

Pillar I: Police and Justice, under the control of the UN[3]
Pillar II: Civil Administration, under the direct leadership of the UN
Pillar III: Democratization and Institution Building, under the control of the Organization
            for Security and Cooperation in Europe (OSCE)
Pillar IV: Reconstruction and Economic Development led by the European Union

The first internationally-designated "governor" of the province, the Special Representative to the Secretary General (SRSG), Bernard Kouchner, signed the Administrative Regulation 2000/41 into power on 10 July 2000, establishing the Department of Sports. This Regulation was followed by the signing, on 17 August 2000, of the Administrative Direction 2000/18 setting out the basic framework of the new administration of sports in Kosovo. This Administration Direction regulated sports associations, federations and committees in Kosovo and for the development of sports in Kosovo in order *"to promote sports in the spirit of tolerance and Olympic ideals of peace, solidarity, friendship and fair play"*[4]. Administrative Direction 2000/18 also made it mandatory that 30% of all sports associations' members be women, and 10% representatives of minority communities.

With the establishment of the Provisional Institutions of Self-Governance (PISG) by UNMIK, the DOS would be brought under the umbrella of the Ministry of Culture, Youth and Sports

---

2 *The terms "Serb" and "Albanian" are used here primarily to indicate two of the major ethnic communities in Kosovo, and should not be necessarily taken to mean actual citizens of Serbia and/or Albania.*
3 *During the whole emergency phase and until May 2001, Pillar I was for Humanitarian Assistance led by United Nations High Commissioner for Refugees (UNHCR). It then became the pillar of Police and Justice, under the direct leadership of the United Nations.*
4 *UNMIK, Administrative Direction 2000/18, Bernard Koucher, 17 August 2000*

(MCYS), headed by a Kosovo Minister and a UN employee called the Principal International Officer (PIO). Each department was created along this bilateral organization, joining efforts of both local and international staff in policy making and programs organization in respect of the principles set by Resolution 1244.

THE DEVELOPMENT OF SPORTS FOR THE DISABLED: A SPECIAL PROJECT

The organization of the 1st International Seminar on Sports for the Disabled was not the unique idea of single actor, but mainly the consequence of a cascade of different circumstances. A brief background of the policy which rules the activities of the DOS and a quick description of some of the major projects are indispensable elements to grasp the special project related to the development of sports for the disabled in Kosovo.

[1] Background of the project; the Laws on Sports

One of the primary responsibilities of the UNMIK Policy and Program Adviser of the Department of Sports was to organize an international seminar preliminary to and around the drafting of the Laws on Sports. In February 2003, experts from the Council of Europe were invited by the DOS; and supported by the Council of Europe which can be regarded as one of the most active international organizations in international legislation, especially in fields related to sustainable development and human rights issues. Through this perspective, particularly in a post-conflict era, the introduction and the playing of sports can be utilized as a very strong and helpful instrument for the development of peace and reconciliation among communities[5]. In this context, it is interesting to note that all the three Council of Europe's experts originated from recently independent Eastern European countries. These experts were all the more equipped to comprehend not only the post-Communist era, but also the post-conflict era, the conditions inherent in the social fabric of Kosovo at this time, and to better position the discussions of the sports laws in this respect.

It is fundamental to highlight that the purpose of such a seminar as it fulfilled one of important UNMIK objectives to ensure capacity building among locally-employed staff. The purpose of this seminar was to give its working groups the opportunity to discuss different points of view with experts and to share analytical thought on the core text of the laws. Although the experts' function was to raise questions and propose appropriate solutions, the drafting of the laws was the sole responsibility of the local actors involved in this project. As a result, the current adopted text can be characterized as inwardly turned, reflecting mainly local concerns, and cumbersome, providing for Communist-era ultra-centralized power structures and holding an idealistic conception of sport solely for the able-bodied masses

[2] The DOS "Handisport Policy"

Sports for the disabled remained an area virtually unaddressed; only a handful of projects had been funded by the DOS budget in the previous years. Following the recommendation

---

5 An excellent and fruitful cooperation is maintained between UNMIK officials of the DOS and the office of Mr. Adolf Ogi, Special Adviser to the Secretary General on Sport for the Development and Peace.

of the European Charter on Sport for All and the Council of Europe's Recommendation on a Coherent Policy for People with Disabilities[6], the Program and Policy Advisor presented a project to add an appropriate policy in the DOS yearly program devoted specifically to the development of sports for the disabled to both heads of the MCYS, the UNMIK Principal International Officer and the Kosovo Minister. The project proposal procedure is fairly simple technically but requires navigation of several political and cultural obstacles. For example each policy is granted a budget line only after a proposal by the Program and Policy Adviser who, with the approval of the PIO, must seek its approval and signing by the Minister. It is necessary to keep in mind that this project might be confronted with cultural prejudices it may face. Although the idea of this chapter is not to confront the cultural representation of the issue of disability and handicap, it is a point which shall not be neglected as it directly involves the success of new projects in this field.

It is also interesting to remember that in a post-conflict phase, different stages scale across international activity. In the first phase of emergency and humanitarian aid, the DOS's activities were ruled by eight policies[7], each of them linked to a specific budget to finance the projects initiated directly by the DOS itself or by NGOs which followed project proposal procedures. At the beginning of year 2003, another peace-building phase was reached in Kosovo, leading to long-term sustainable development programs and followed almost simultaneously by a transfer of power to the local authorities. At this stage, in political terms it is of the utmost importance to seek for wider cultural awareness. Albeit this point is further developed in the analysis of the program's implementation of sports for the disabled, this issue has reached a critical dimension as non-governmental organizations would then be invited to play a role in its achievement. In the context of peace building, the logic of development espoused by government may not coincide with the logic of humanitarian action and the short-term goal-seeking often targeted by NGOs. As such, the main objective of the Program and Policy Adviser was to invite the main representatives of the biggest local NGOs dealing with the issue of disability to the working groups editing the new Sports Laws.

A second phase was to consolidate a Kosovo-wide network as it became quickly apparent that major internal and intergroup conflicts were hampering development and collective progress. With the logistical assistance of the largest international organization for the handicapped, the French organization Handicap International, a survey was made among almost forty Kosovo associations active in this field, both in Albanian areas as well as minority enclaves. The DOS contacted the leaders of those associations and organized visits on the field. All programs and projects were catalogued in order to form a more accurate idea of the needs of disabled persons in Kosovo in the field of sports. This work was necessary to adjust the implementation of the new DOS "Handisport policy" appropriately and to adapt the text to the field's requirements with proper cultural awareness.

---

6 *Recommendation of the Committee of Ministers to Member States on a Coherent Policy for People with Disabilities, No R (92) 6, Council of Europe, Committee of Minister, 474th meeting of the Ministers' Deputies, April 9, 1992.*
7 *In numeric order: Women in Sports, Sports Medicine, Summer Camps, Internationalization of Sports, International competitions in Kosovo, Multiethnic Sports, Sports Infrastructure, Capacity Building.*

This study concluded that most organizations were organized according to specific social and handicapped criteria such as the War Invalids (with a majority of Serbian members), Deaf and Blind, etc. The only real ethnically-heterogeneous groups were the two international associations, the French Handicap International (HI) and the Vietnam Veterans of America Foundation. (VVAF). Both of those international associations were working according to different strategies. HI's purpose was to create and sponsor the local NGO Handikos which had become the largest Kosovo association, independent and politically very active. The goals set by VVAF were to disperse projects supporting a large variety of sports activities, without any discrimination of handicap or disability. VVAF was also very active in minority enclaves, while simultaneously causing much friction with other local and majority NGOs, as it was using a fundamentally sensitive issue as a proper "marketing asset" in order to attract governmental and international financial support.

However, the implementation of the "Handisport Policy" was to surpass those cleavages and negotiations in order to create a coherent lobby. In the spring of 2003, the Department of Sports organized the Third International Half-Marathon of Pristina, one of the largest sport events in Kosovo, attracting approximately 1500 participants, among them a group of a dozen of international professional athletes. Negotiations were launched by the Policy Advisor to convince both PIO and Minister of the MYCS to allow a symbolical participation of disabled athletes. The idea was to bring together those who were interested in sports and bridge the gap over the usual conflicts separating the largest organizations in order to promote better coordination. The International Half-Marathon of Pristina required enormous logistical support to provide the necessary security for all athletes and enjoyed vast media coverage, as the event was transmitted live by a local media to European countries such as France and Switzerland, where Kosovo's diaspora receives and views Albanian satellite channels.

In the harsh reality of present-day Kosovo, where deteriorating roads are unfit for cars and pedestrians alike, security difficult to assure, and prejudices deep-rooted and unchanging, convincing officials of the Organizing Committee to allow disabled and untrained participants to run together was a daunting task, to say the least. However, forty athletes with various disabilities took part in the event, running a special loop and enjoying huge media coverage. The Minister gave the trophies to the winners of the different categories. Part of the social gap separating disabled persons from the rest of the Kosovo society was bridged.

From then on, the following stage of the "Handisport policy" was to be launched. After long and serious discussions between representative groups, the DOS, in close cooperation with the Olympic Committee of Kosovo (OKK), decided to organize the First International Seminar on Sports for the Disabled. The seminar was scheduled to be concluded with the founding of the "Handisport Federation of Kosovo", automatically recognized by the OKK. A panel of five international experts answered positively to the invitation sent by the DOS. Professor Otto J. Schantz (who previously worked as a consultant in Kosovo in 2000) and Professor Keith Gilbert, renowned scientists in the research area on sports and disabled responded to the call, as did Mr. Ole Ansberg, a full-time consultant in the Danish Sport Organization currently working on large projects with Handikos, and Ms. Beatrice Hess, famous international Paralympic athlete, accompanied by Ms. Muriel Schreiber, who herself very active in the French Basketball Federation.

The First International Seminar on Sports for the Disabled spanned over five days and ten different sessions, each of them with simultaneous translations in Albanian and Serbian. An average of forty participants attended each session of the seminar. The goal of the seminar was to alternate between practical and theoretical sessions in order to develop a sense of community among the participants and stress the idea of the necessity to create an appropriate federation to meet their specific needs and requirements as athletes.

Why create a federation? In sports organization, the federation is the highest sports body responsible for the administration of sports at all levels of the state or territory. Falling into the category of NGO according to the Kouchner Administrative Regulation 2000/41, it has a non-political status with respect to the government in power and aims generally at developing mass to elite sport activities. At the level of the Department of Sports, a specific federation would have had the main goal to democratize sports for the disabled in the Kosovo society and permit the socialization of the disabled youth. Independence of Kosovo disabled athletes under the umbrella organization of a federation empowers and gives symbolical recognition to athletes, strengthening the validity of their interaction with other social groups and its own internal dynamic, its specific rules and balance of power.

From a purely logistical standpoint, the organization of the seminar was a definite challenge, truly reflecting the difficulties disabled athletes meet. We discovered that sports infrastructures in Kosovo are not adapted to disabled athletes' needs and the new projects funded either by private, municipal or governmental resources do not meet any appropriate standards for their use either. In the political arena, previously held conflicts re-emerged with even more tension as the seminar was closing with the adoption of the statute of the "Handisport Federation".

This statute had been written by the Policy Adviser in cooperation with the President of the OKK. The text was edited in the three official languages, English, Albanian and Serbian, by the translators of the DOS and sent to each of the organizations of the new network for comments, critics and adaptation so as not to merely reflect the perceptions of a single, foreign UN employee, but to meet the needs and expectations of the persons with disability in Kosovo as they themselves perceived them. Already, the VVAF, the OKK and the rest of the working groups had already reached compromises among themselves concerning this statute. Indeed, the VVAF, having participated in the Special Olympics organized in Dublin in 2003, insisted that the federation should allow a fair representation of mentally handicapped participants. Although this issue is an long-standing conflict between Special Olympics and the Paralympic Movement, all local representatives made the conscious decision not to fight over this old international dilemma, potentially aggravating local internal conflicts which could undermine the whole project. However, due to strong objections raised among the different groups, it was decided that the DOS representatives (both local and international), as well as Olympic officials, would not get further involved in what was considered an internal conflict between Handikos and smaller organizations. A tentative schedule for the elections of the "Handisports Federations" representatives had to be aborted, and due to the transfer of power from UNMIK to local structures in civil administration, the Policy Adviser was not mandated to go beyond her legal field of actions. As such, it was decided with the PIO, the Policy Adviser and the international experts to proceed to the creation of a working group elected among the participants. This working group would then be responsible for the final edition of the statutes and the organization of the elections.

The conclusion of this project remains to be analyzed. However, it is important to mention a few changes to the organizational presence in Kosovo. Shortly after the international seminar, international VVAF staff closed their mission in Kosovo, leaving their local staff and various teams in disarray, with little technical, moral or political support or guidance. Handikos and ex-VVAF groups nevertheless monopolized the debate, disregarding the voices of smaller organizations, in particular those from minority areas. Several meetings were organized by the working group to proceed to elections; each of them had to be aborted as they did not meet the standard procedures set by DOS policies for the recognition of a new federation.

However, some very positive points ensured greater representation for disabled people in the Kosovo society, as the original seminar served as a catalyst for several other meetings and projects to be launched and funded. In one example, the DOS policy adviser was asked to participate in a round table and advise the Prime Minister office on some issues related to the social and economic situation of handicapped in Kosovo. Further actions were launched by various organizations to request proper financial treatment of their pensions and annuities and special handicapped parking places, a common sight in many other countries, were finally allocated. Though much work remains, the initial mediatization surrounding the participation of disabled persons in the half-marathon or the international seminar laid solid cornerstones to construct a more viable future for this type of sport. Each local actor will have to find their own pace and orient their projects and goals according to their specific local needs while surmounting internal strife.

SPORT FOR PEOPLE WITH DISABILITIES IN KOSOVO: ELITE SPORTS OR SIDE SHOW?

To conclude this chapter objectively, it is necessary to proceed to the interpretation via an epistemological perspective. Quick references can be made to Bourdieu's theories in order to keep distance with empiric experiences. Indeed, as referred in the introduction, the concept of the field is defined by Bourdieu as a space in which agents and actors have their own goals and compete to accumulate different forms of capital to dominate. Each field can be invested by social agents, with its own history and within its own limits. The chronological description of the implementation of the DOS policy is an excellent example of the theory, demonstrating that the field of handicapped in Kosovo has its own history, but is not really independent, as there are numerous interactions, and interpenetration with other fields such as the sports field, political field, and economical field. However, the field of disability in Kosovo showed signs of evolving despite its internal battles among different actors and associations, simultaneously revealing each parties' specific interests and the existence of a certain balance of power internal to this field. Although disregarded by the Policy Adviser, and consciously or unconsciously denounced by international NGOs active in the field, these are however the basic conditions of existence of a particular sociological field. Although the author of this chapter did not aim to proceed to a real rupture with the ascendancy of her personal motivations, it aimed to determine some distance with this empiric experience, especially because the results expected (creation of the Sport for people with disabilities Federation) were not met at a time scheduled. It was therefore necessary to proceed to construct a reflexive analysis, and not be a victim of what Bourdieu called in the text ethnocentrisme de classe.

To conclude this chapter and answer the original and main question asked in this book, it would be very hard to rationally state that sports for the disabled in Kosovo is on its way to elite sports. This might be seen as a very harsh comment, but one must keep in mind that it does not mean that sports for the disabled in Kosovo is following a static development curve. There was an attempt at evolution, which could be analyzed as relatively positive.

Although it may be intellectually risky to refer to "field" as in the Bourdieu's theory of the field when referring to sports for the disabled, this sociological concept is a convenient tool to assist in understanding the conflicts among actors generated by the will to dominate this specific field. Whether these be international or local organizational bodies, it is regretfully apparent that the political stakes in this positioning went beyond the simple goal of the well-being of disabled and handicapped persons in Kosovo.

The purpose of this joint project of the DOS and the President of the Olympic Committee of Kosovo was to give a chance for an isolated population of Kosovo society to fully take part in the development ongoing in the recent years in Kosovo. In this sense, it is possible to say that all the projects representative concrete and positive achievements.

Working as an adviser has presented interesting opportunities to convince local government staff to accept and develop new ideas and concepts, and to propose new solutions to recurrent problems. The additional status and responsibility of "monitor" carries with it an equal part of frustration, especially if one is only results oriented as are most Western ideas of project management. It is necessary to keep in mind that if the seed is planted, it is already a success; plants need time to achieve maturity! We shall therefore conclude that, at this stage, the development of sports of the disabled in Kosovo is a Side Show, and victim of its potential success. However, it will hopefully develop in the following years, due to the geo-political situation of this small territory. Kosovo's disabled athletes will not access the international level in the near future if recent history is any indication, but their role is closely linked to the political status of the Olympic Committee, and, generally speaking, to the political status of the territory. Although the political situation is too unclear at this time in 2006 to give any prognostics on this issue, it is to be hoped that the seeds planted by all actors in the handicapped field will bloom and offer disabled, impaired and handicapped persons of Kosovo a chance to occupy a their place as part of Kosovo society.

REFERENCES

Boniface, Pascal (Dir), (1998) *Géopolitique du football*, Ed. Complexe, Bruxelles.

Bourdieu, Pierre, (2000) *Propos sur le champ politique*, Presse Universitaire Lyon, Lyon.

Bourdieu, Pierre, (1984) *Questions de sociologie*, Editions de Minuit, Paris.

Centre Universitaire de recherches administratives et politiques de Picardie (CURAPP), (1992), *La Solidarité: Un Sentiment Républicain* ? PUF, Paris.

Galtung Johan, (1971), A structural theory of Imperialism. *Journal of Peace Research, 8* (2), 81-117.

Houlihan, Barrie, (1994) *Sport and International Politics*, Harvester Wheatsheaf, New-York, London.

Rufin, Jean-Christophe, (1991) *L'empire et les nouveaux barbares: Rupture Nord-Sud*, Pluriel, Paris.

23   THE PARALYMPIC MOVEMENT IN THE AFRICAN CONTEXT

Roger Noutcha

INTRODUCTION

The objective of this chapter is to bring to light the constitution process of the Black Africa Paralympic movement. The development of this chapter takes its foundation from a social context (which is in this instance refers to the notion of perpetual evolution) and will emphasize the consequences of acculturation. Acculturation in the context of the chapter can be perceived in our work as a concept closely related to cultural anthropology. Indeed, the core-field utilized in this chapter, is the definition given in a Memorandum of the Social Science Research Council which defines acculturation as being:

> ......the whole of the phenomena resulting from the direct and continuous contact between groups of individuals of different cultures with subsequent changes in the original types of culture from one group to the other groups.
>
> Bastide (1998)

Throughout this chapter we will not put forward any value judgments on the benefits that Black Africans would have by giving up their social traditional models in order to take up the model of modernity which has materialized in the emergence of physical activities and sport in favour of disabled individuals. Thus, we consider the role of modernity resulting from colonization from the same perspective as Balandier (1986). This theory argues that there is a   complex diffusion of cultural elements such as sport, or   sport known as Handisport (sport for people with disabilities) and that these elements act like a tool of transformation within the receiving society. In other words, sport could be utilised in terms to build the relationship building between cultures and different civilizations that are generating the phenomena of acculturation.

In various fields like in the field of the disability, education, health, sports, etc. the modern African evolution as a true social dynamic has pushed the social actors to change and adapt to the modern culture which is symbolized by new practices. This social transformation has been seen to have an effect on the traditional cultural practices dominated by magic, sorcery, fetishism, etc. We can understand some of this witchery when referring to the writing of Caulerick (1981), who argues that disability in the Sub Saharan Africa finds its origins in the African curse, and through offences made to the gods.

In developing countries, in addition to these cultural conditions, political and economical reasons will influence the practice of adapted physical activities and the possible participation in future Paralympic Games.

METHODS

Our working hypothesis for the study which underlines this chapter is that in Africa physical and sporting activities are used initially as a therapy, thereafter as a means of integration, insertion and reintegration of people with disabilities into society. However, the representations which the Black Africans have about the causes of the disability and ensuing poverty still constitute an obstacle to the development of physical and sporting activities, even when it comes to the Paralympics movement in the sub Saharan region. In order to demonstrate this assumption, a qualitative methodology based on discussions with some Black African sportsmen concerned with the handisport programme proved to be essential. Indeed, telephone talks were conducted with athletes from the Ivory Coast, Cameroon and Burkina Faso.

The analysis and the interpretation of the information collected by this technique of data acquisition made it possible to partly develop the history of the Paralympic movement in the African context.

THE EMERGENCE OF AN AFRICAN PARALYMPIC MOVEMENT

After their independence, the African countries which had been colonized by France, adopted a model of sport management and physical education based on the public utility of sport in Black Africa, (Dikoumè: 1989). This kind of sport management made it possible for the State to control the sporting movement from its roots to its summit. This control appeared in the political definition and the financing of African sport, has materialized by the granting of the subsidies to structures which manage sport on a daily basis. It is an example of the power of national sporting federations and mostly of the support of various countries in developing sporting infrastructures.

When it comes to sport for people with disabilities, two major factors have supported its emergence in Africa. These are, the creation of the first structures of assumption of responsibility by the missionaries with the example of the national center of rehabilitation of people with disabilities of Etoug-ébé, a suburban area of Yaounde in Cameroon in 1970 by the Canadian cardinal Léger Paul Emile, and importantly the diffusion of the French law of orientation of the people with disabilities which was proposed in 1975.

It is essential to point out the construction of the center of Etoug-ébé here, because it was conceived on the basis of the Canadian architectural model, i.e. which integrates the various sporting infrastructures such as swimming pools, basketball fields, athletic tracks, (Noutcha 1997). From these infrastructures, disabled sport is practiced under medical and leisure aspects in a single structure in the central and Western African regions, which follows the original medical model espoused by Guttmann.

With regard to the repercussions in French-speaking Africa of the French Law of Orientation (1975), it is instantly recognizable that the majority of African countries such as Cameroon, Ivory Coast, Gabon, and the Central African Republic, initiated laws in favor of the integration of individuals with disabilities into sports. Cameroon's constitution for disabled sport for example was adopted early in 1983. In Cameroon then, sport is presented not only as a tool of functional rehabilitation, but also as a tool of integration, leisure, social insertion and reintegration of its people with disabilities. This law was preceded by the Charter of Sports and Physical education in 1996, which granted access to sports for all people with disabilities, and was enacted by the creation within the Ministry for Youth and Sports of the adapted sports programme. It is interesting to note that in 1990, a democratic opening on the political level which had effects on the sporting plan with the liberalization of the sporting federations. It is under these conditions that the majority of the sporting federations were developed in favor of the people with disabilities. This immediately gave them links and affiliation with the supranational, continental and other world sporting structures for people with disabilities. Therefore as early as 1995 there was the emergence of the African sport in favor of disabled individuals at the time that the first championships of Africa were held in Harare in Zimbabwe. Starting from this championship in Harare the African Paralympic movement was born. However, the obstacles to the development of the African Paralympic Movement have remained of a cultural, political and economic nature.

The obstacles related to democratization of the Paralympic movement in Black Africa

The African representations of the handicapped

The social representations that Africans have south of the Sahara about disability do not support the disabled individuals when it comes to the practice of adapted physical activities. For example we understand by adapted physical activities, that the definition means 'the various physical and sporting activities adapted to the nature of each handicap'. (The representations that Africans have about the handicapped, even if it is physical, physical or mental, play a paramount part in this practice.) The same is argued by Koné when referring to the representations that people have of his handicap states that: ....people told in my entourage that I had this handicap because either my mom was a witch, or because I was a wizard.

It is interesting that disabilities like madness, infirmity (amputees, lame, etc.) in Black Africa are constructed pathologies, i.e. society argues that it is society which makes people insane, it is society which makes the handicapped. 'Since society accepts that society is responsible for this otherness, one cannot speak about individuals with disabilities'. It is then advisable to note that the people with disabilities are regarded as a personal punishment. 'It is for this reason that one tries to hide the handicapped body', (Noutcha 2004). If it is hiding or being looked after, out of sight, it is because one does not want to show to society that the family sanctions the problem. This is also one of the reasons why there are a deficit of disabled players in Black Africa. It is thus necessary that we consider the social causes of the handicap to understand why adaptive centers for people with disabilities, regarded as centers of salvage, are not full.

Independently of the country involved and their policies, to place the person with disabilities in the central position is to make public the misfortune which has overcome the family. Indeed, it is as if they shun that member of the family, it is also seen as the exposition of the "monster" Stiker (1982), and it is finally a way of losing the meaning of the African social linkage which is the family solidarity and which implies full devotion of the healthy people toward those who are not.

The different religions and the treatment of disability

In Black Africa, there are basically three religions which are in contact. These are: animism, Christianity and Islam. However, it is not the purpose of this chapter to develop a history of these religions, but rather to show the relationship that they maintain when it comes to the social treatment of the handicapped. This is achieved in order to show the obstacles which could emerge by those who are in charge of sport for people with disabilities and those who are also in charge of training the future Paralympic teams for possible participation in the Paralympic Games.

Animism as an obstacle to the practice of adapted physical activities in Black Africa

As previously mentioned animism is an ancestral practice which has always existed in Africa even before the diffusion of Islam and Christianity into society. Animism thus allows an individual who is a victim of misfortune (accident, etc.) or to the family of misfortune, to ask the ancestors while worshipping for their protection, happiness, a cure, etc. It allows them to understand the origins or the factors of the handicap through spiritual awareness.

As argued by Mrs Tsanga:
> ... as a whole, you know that in the African customs, a person with disability, is either a wizard, or his/her parents did something...

> Tsanga in Noutcha (2004)

From experience, in many instances, the development of individuals thinking about people with disabilities is generally of a social nature. Betsama for example, who had walked until 4 years old then became paralyzed. According to the soothsayer priest's diagnosis or of the "Megni-Nsi", Betsame became paralyzed because it had been about 17 years since his mom had gone to the local village to make sacrifices on cranium of her late father. This example supports the logic of animism which is the worship of the ancestors and induces treatment for the perceived problem by the practice of sorcery. With this in mind it was noticeable that the link to animism and people with disabilities supports a multiplication of traditional healers' dispensaries in Cameroon. This multiplication drew the attention of the State to their role in the social treatment of disability. It explains why in Africa, whatever the place of residency (rural or urban), the consultation of the "Megni-Nsi", the marabouts, the "nganka", etc, is still a large part of Africans custom and life. Such consultations take place within the framework of a precaution for the future of anamism, within the framework of a "shielding" against the bad fate, within the framework of a treatment or an enchantment and are a product of African mythology.

Animism and the social representations of disability

In comparison with the social mechanism, animism is the religion which governs the interactions between the visible and invisible forces, and they claim that the person with disabilities could be either carrying a capacity treatment or care, or be impregnated with some kind of bad fate.

In general, any person with disabilities, since his youth, is initiated to fetishism because of the members of their "religion", and because of this difference, is endowed with supernatural power which comes from the supreme power. This part played out by the majority of the people with physical disabilities in Africa expresses a social context which supports their integration in society.

As for the people with intellectual deficiencies within animism, they are generally regarded as victims of a bad fate or of a divine punishment. Unfortunately they are excluded in the society to which they should rightfully belong.

When it comes to the relationship between the physical and sporting activities, animism is supposed to induce the negative representations of people with disabilities and does not support the practice of sport because animism preaches the exclusion or especially the maintenance or the hiding-place of the person with disabilities in his/her residence. This is one of the reasons which could explain the lack of democratization of the physical and sportive activities. Indeed, of the Paralympic movement in the majority of the African countries, whereas Olympic national committees can be found everywhere. The following countries however provide positive role models to the other countries these are: Cameroon, Burkina Faso, Ivory Coast. However it can be fairly stated that there is an absence of disability sporting structure and the lack of sports management in the Paralympic sports in these countries suggests the lack of interest of these States toward the Paralympic movement.

Importantly for this chapter the majority of athletes questioned within the framework of this work raised the notion of a lack of interest from politicians for sport played by people with disabilities, and particularly for the Paralympic movement. In other words (no one really cares). However people with disabilities themselves, are exceeding the representations that politicians, the population, families and friends have about the handicapped, and are mobilizing in order to practice the sporting activities in spite of the many barriers provided by the animism.

Islam in Africa and its social representation of the sportsperson with disabilities

Islam covers almost all of West Africa and the North side of Cameroon. It is a religion which preaches charity and especially giving. It is one of the reasons why most beggars are in the geographical areas occupied by the Muslims. To better appreciate Muslims relationship with the handicapped, we will retain begging as the major element which explains the positive vision of people with disabilities by Islam. Islam as it was conceived in Africa aims to reduce the barriers between non-disabled people and people with disabilities (considered as victim of a fate). It is one of the reasons why 'giving' is encouraged in these places. What then led us to think that the act of begging would facilitate the integration of the people with disabilities within this religion? We were amazed to find that Islam has become a refuge for many individuals with disabilities. The gifts coming from the wealthy are limited and the distribution remains governed by the social principles defined in the Islamic settings in Africa, i.e. to give to the most unfortunate and poorest, among whom people with disabilities are to be found.

Contrary to Christianity and its humanitarian corollaries which invest a lot in the care and the assistance of these individuals, they have little social and cultural impact. Islam on the other hand gives little but is better structured and more and more the society of Cameroon benefits from the Islamic ideals. In this religion, we realized that the social treatment of people with disabilities is more structured in the Islamic setting because of the representations of the people which are positive rather than the vehicle of Islam. So there is more chance to initiate the strategies put in place for taking charge of the physical and sportive activities for Muslims with disabilities than in the settings of animism where representations of the people with disabilities are negative. This could also explain the development of the physical and sportive activities in the countries linked to Islam for example Nigeria, Senegal and Burkina Faso. By way of example, Nigeria which is an Islamic country gained 12 of the 21 medals of the countries of the Black Africa in the last Paralympic Games. However, it is interesting to note that Black Africa obtained only 21 medals out of 98 gained by the entire African countries at the Games.

ECONOMIC AND MATERIAL OBSTACLES

Since 1990, Black Africa has been confronted with an economic crisis brought about by the devaluation of the CFA frank, and the fall of the wages in the various national public offices, etc. This crisis has imposed a program of structural adjustment by the international financial institutions for the example the World Bank, the International Monetary International Monetary Funds, etc. The objective of this program was not only to reduce the expansive lifestyle of African states, but more especially to support the privatization of the societies of the State. This reduction of lifestyle has had effects on the social plan of the states. Thus, the branches of industry related on health, education, rehabilitation, etc have experienced a reduction of treatment in the various subsidies which are allocated to them. Moreover, we noted an absence of legibility and visibility of the various concrete actions of the State by the means of the ministries charged to promote or develop adapted physical activities. In this regard Betsama argues that:

> ......the policy of the State is almost non-existent when it comes to sports for disabled people. Once more, I raise here the problem of materials and financial means of the State. Cameroon is in economic crisis since approximately 1990, when you pose a problem about sports activities and leisure for handicapped people, one answers you that wages of the fonctionnaires already have difficulties, and that problems of handicapped people are not a priority in their process.

There are other African countries with financial problems for example the Ivory Coast. Koné Oumar highlights these difficulties which are encountered by the population:

> Difficulties of the practice of the sport in the Ivory Coast are much related to financial problems. You see, the State does not assist us in spite of the results which we bring back, if I compare my results with the result of other Paralympic champions in their respective countries.

These two examples reinforce the idea that in Black Africa, sports for people with disabilities and the Paralympic movement have major difficulties to survive. This problem is partly due to a lack of political good-will from the States. This lack of will leads to other problems. For example the one of the suitable sporting infrastructures, and in particular of the high cost of the specific training material. At the time of our investigations on the ground, the president of the Cameroonian federation of sports for people with disabilities stated that with 500 players, one counts only 25 competition wheelchairs, the others being obliged to use their own wheelchairs to practice tennis, basketball or athletics. This lack of suitable resources and material due to the cost, clearly affects the sportsperson with disabilities in Black Africa.

Another important obstacle of the Paralympic movement emergence in Black Africa resides in its structural organization. This movement for its effectiveness would gain in prominence if it were structured on the same basis as the Olympic movement. This would mean cohesion between the National Paralympic Committees which would integrate with the Higher Council of Sports in Africa. However, we realize that many African countries are not even equipped with an National Paralympic Committee because it does not form part of their countries or sporting priorities. This last point explains the non participation of the Cameroonian athletes at the last Paralympic Games. Since they do not have a National Paralympic Committee, the Olympic and sporting national committee gave up the selection. On this subject, Betsama stated strongly that:

> For the good development of the Paralympic Games, it would be necessary that in all the countries, for national Paralympic committees to be installed, which will be able then to relay the problems of the athletes to the level of the International Paralympic Committee. Also, it would be necessary to give assistance to the countries in the process of development, and finally help the athletes of these countries with mutual aid funds allowing them to take part in the various competitions.

The above athlete like the many of the others who were questioned felt supportive of the Paralympic movement which is viewed by many as a contribution to the development of sport in favor of people with disabilities in the various countries that are concerned.

CONCLUSION

Even with all of its problematics and difficulties this work enabled us to understand that a real emergence of sports in favor of the disabled and the Paralympic movement in Black Africa is possible in spite of all the obstacles. Indeed, some of the solutions are possible if individuals, governments and politicians realize that a better understanding by Africans on the people with disabilities, sports for people with disabilities, the reduction of poverty, and the implication of the politicians, families, and the International Paralympic Committee have to be combined to provide a solid platform for success.

As a matter of better understanding the problem it is about using information and the sporting structural formation in order to make Black Africans acquire various understandings of the athlete with disabilities and disability itself. We argue here that disability should be seen as the result of a deficiency which creates incapacity, (Ebersold 1992).

As soon as this is completed, we can move forward and think about the development of a truly global African sporting policy in favor of people with disabilities while understanding the real reasons behind disability and the needs of the athlete with disabilities. Individuals with disabilities will stop being hidden like monsters, but will be placed in already existing adaptive centers, and consequently will be able to discover the practice of physical and sportive activities in specialized situations, then go forward in groups or in the clubs advocating the Paralympic movement.

One of the major problems encountered by the sportspeople with disabilities of Black Africa is recognition. The media, their policies, and even the Olympic and Paralympic structures do not give them recognition for their sporting deeds. What causes the athletes themselves to argue for equal treatment (e.g. equal premiums and medals) during both Paralympic and Olympic Games. This statement is supported by the following athlete comment:

> What would need to be changed, is to give the same price to the various medals: that the gold medal to the Olympic Games has the same financial value as the gold medal to the Paralympic games... It is time that these organizers consider the disabled as any other athletes taking part in the Olympic Games. As long as they regard us as handicapped people, it will be normal that these ideas also come to handicap our practice of the sportive activities.

Some of the athletes interviewed also supported the integration of the Paralympic Games within the Olympic Games, whereas others requested an inversion of the calendar for a better Paralympic visibility and a better mediatization of the Games.

> .....what it would be necessary to change, is that the Olympic and Paralympic institutions agree on the representativeness of the sponsors at the time of the great appointments, with the agreement to cover the Olympic Games as well as the Paralympic Games... That Paralympic Games proceed over the same sites, but this time before the Olympic Games with the sponsors retained for the Olympic Games. In short it will act of an inversion of the calendar .

This final insightful comment by an athlete regarding representativeness highlights the plight of the Black African nations Paralympic development.

REFERENCES

Balandier G.(1986) *Sens et puissance : les dynamiques sociales*, PUF, Paris.

Bastide R. (1998) *Acculturation*, in Encyclopedia Universalis.

Dikoumè F. (1989), *Le service publique du sport en Afrique Noire: le cas du Cameroun.* Dalloz.

Ebersold S. (1992), *L'invention du handicap.* CTNERHI, Vanves.

Gaulerick E. (1981), *Les enfants handicapés, dépistage, intervention précoce et éducation spéciale in Bulletin de* l'UNESCO, Paris.

Noutcha R. (2004), Des œuvres missionnaires au traitement social du handicap au cameroun. Du protectorat à la république, thèse de doctorat en STAPS, Université Marc Bloch de Strasbourg2.

Noutcha R. (1997), Le traitement social du handicap au Cameroun : l'exemple du centre national de réhabilitation d'Etoug-ébé, mémoire de DEA, Université de Strasbourg2.

Stiker J.H. (1982), *Corps infirmes et sociétés.* Aubier, Paris.

Tsanga in Noutcha R. (2004), *Des œuvres missionnaires au traitement social du handicap au cameroun. Du protectorat à la république,* thèse de doctorat en STAPS, université Marc Bloch de Strasbourg2.

24 THE PARALYMPICS: A MALAYSIAN PERSPECTIVE

Abdul Hafidz Omar & Norazman Abdul Majid

INTRODUCTION

Firstly it must be clearly stated that in Malaysian society able bodied individuals have come to the aid of the people with disabilities and secondly in Malay society we believe that having a disability does not and should not stop individuals from excelling in different fields, more especially in sports. However, this cannot be achieved unless individuals with disabilities are assisted by the government, society or the private sector. Indeed, we believe that people with disabilities should not be seen as alien to the rest of society as they are part of the society which further adds to the variety and nature of the world we live in. Individuals with a disability did not ask to be born disabled. In Malaysia we believe that people with disabilities can develop just like any of us if they are given the opportunities to progress. Disabled individuals we have taught possess the interest and motivation to study, play, to be involved in sports, work and have a family just like the able bodied individuals.

In Malaysia, the individuals with different ranges of disability have recently received special attention from people in society in general and more specifically from the government through various efforts and contributions made by the public as well as the private sectors. In the seventies, references to people with disabilities attending sports competition were rarely heard of in the Western world. As early as the sixties and seventies, the government began establishing classes in regular schools to cater for the students with disabilities. Currently specially trained teachers and counselors are available in most schools to provide specialized services to these groups of students. Indeed, at present, the individuals in our society with disabilities receive special privileges and conveniences from the government and society supports them in many different ways. For example society provides:

1   Special sports for people with disabilities
2   Cultural and Arts Activities for people with disabilities
3   Educational privileges
4   Special Access to Building Facilities
5   Facilities and Encouragement - Tax Cuts
6   Public Transportation Facilities
7   Exemption for Medical Services
8   Exemption of Traveling Document Payment
9   Job Opportunities
10   Convenience to Purchase Cars or Motorcycle
11   Special Pension
12   Small Business Grant
13   Incentives to People with Disabilities Programmes
14   Telecommunication convenience
15   Special Insurance Coverage under 'Takaful Malaysia'

Apart from the above-mentioned privileges and in keeping with the spirit of Islam to help the people with disabilities to excel and develop in their unique ways, the government has declared the 3rd of December of every year to be the National Day for the People with Disabilities, conforming to the United Nations Resolution on the National Day for the People with Disabilities. The objectives of the national day for the people with disabilities in Malaysia are:

- to create awareness in the society that people with disabilities as members of society have their own rights in the society and the normal people cannot look down at the people with disabilities as useless.
- to increase the awareness among the society that the responsibility they have towards the people with disabilities and to push the community to increase the facilities for the people with disabilities.
- to increase the ability, capability, affordability and skills of the people with disabilities towards excellent performance and at the same time benefiting the progress of the country.
- to increase the connection between the government, the NGOs, the corporate sectors and the community in providing various facilities for the people with disabilities.
- to expose the general public to the various services and facilities made available by the government and NGOs for the people with disabilities.

MALAYSIAN PARALYMPIC COUNCIL

With the intention to further stimulate the progress and development of the people with disabilities, the Malaysian Paralympic Council (hereafter MPC) was established on the 18th of May, 1988. The formation of the MPC was recognized by the government under the Ministry of National Unity and Community Development and under the patronage of the Ministry of Youth and Sports. As a foundation, which sees the development and progress of athletes with disabilities, the MPC has determined several objectives, which would further develop its cause. The following are among the objectives put forward by the MPC: to set up the State's People with Disability Sports and Recreational Council (MASRON).
- to elevate Malaysian Paralympic Sports as the product of MPC with vision, by developing twenty different sports.
- to increase the performance of MPC management as the organizer of international sports such as the FESPIC Games.
- to conduct systematic training sessions for the country's athletes and technical officers in preparing them to perform successfully at the 2008 Paralympic Games, and establish and encourage MPC planning for the next ten years.
- to carry out outstanding programmes for sports excellence and sports for all (people with disabilities), by establishing a Malaysian Paralympic Academy, and
- to improve the MPC management, assets and property

MPC VISION

The MPC has a vision to develop the society for the people with disabilities, which are progressive, productive, confidence, competitive, relevant, and integrated within the Malaysian society through the advancement of Paralympic sports. In addition, the mission of the association is dedicated towards achieving excellence in planning, services and the execution of the Sports for All and High Performance Sports for the benefits of the quality of life of Malay people with disabilities. In order to achieve its vision and mission, MPC has created its own philosophy, which believes that only through synergy and collection of resources from all quarters will they produce mentally, physically and spiritually dynamic individuals. This philosophy was born out of several manifestations, which include the participation of the people with disabilities to be a catalyst towards achieving the vision 2020 through MPC, and also the willingness of the private and corporate sectors in supporting the advancement of the MPC and the profusion of volunteer services among the society, youth and professional groups in MPC.

THE UNDERLYING PRINCIPLE AND CONCEPT OF STRUGGLE

The underlying principle driving the progression of the MPC revolves around a footprint that includes all categories of people with disabilities in the country. This principle covers two primary approaches that represent the pinnacle of struggle for the MPC, which is Sports for All and Sports Excellence. The principle was established based on the rational concepts that oversee all planned and implemented activities representing a part of self-development programs and healthy living for all people with disabilities, and that all people with disabilities will receive equal and fair recognition, respect and encouragement similar to the ones given to those able individuals. What follows explains these concepts further.

SPORTS FOR ALL

To help meet the goal to serve the people with disabilities, the MPC has emphasized the two approaches mentioned above: Sports for All and Sports Excellence. Sports for All signify the efforts taken to involve the people with disabilities in sports activities. The approaches for Sports for All refer to the sports and recreational activities organized by the MPC for the purposes of encouraging and en masse participation of the people with disabilities. The primary aim of the Sports for All is to instill a sports culture in the life-style of the people with disabilities in general. Amongst the other elements being planted in the people with disabilities are health values, vigorous and active life-style, and integration within the Malay society. Indeed, in Malaysia the history of the 'games for people with disabilities' began in 1977 which was organized by the Department of Community Welfare - Malaysia and the Malaysian Council for Convalescence. The objectives of the 'games for people with disabilities' are:

i. to encourage and increase the activities and quality of sports among the people with disabilities;
ii to help and accelerate the integration process for people with disabilities into the society;
iii to create awareness and responsibility in all quarters of the convalescence efforts and services to the people with disabilities;
iv to identify talent and ability of people with disabilities in various fields of sports to represent the country at international level such as FESPIC and Paralympic Games.

SPORTS EXCELLENCE

The approaches for Sports Excellence refers specifically to sports activities that involve competition following the rules and regulation stipulated by the International Paralympic Committee, the FESPIC Federation or other recognized international sports body. The planning and training approaches and exposure prepared by the MPC are to ensure the athletes or teams are successful without sacrificing the Fair Play principles. The important elements being developed are that all athletes with disabilities would have the competitive spirit, be skillful and able to understand teamwork and knowledge about sports science.

In this manner 'Sports for All' and 'Sports Excellence' are related and mutually supportive of one another. The sports development process is based on the concept of a pyramid, which sits on a solid and stable base facing all kinds of obstacles and challenges but with continued efforts to generate excellence in all kinds of sports. Nevertheless, the basis that acts as the catalyst for the commitment is the athletes with disabilities themselves. They are the targets which the regular sports have supported and made the basis for self-development of positive-minded people with disabilities, which acts as an important asset for the nation. In other words, the MPC sports program is recognized as an effective mechanism towards the development of people with disabilities, in terms of physical, mental, spiritual, emotional, social, cultural, political, and economic. It is hoped that through 'sport-cultured living'; people with disabilities will be more confident, competitive, productive and possess high self-esteem.

It is the MPC's mission and hope that all categories of people with disabilities all over the country would support all the efforts and planning drawn within the sports development programs for the people with disabilities, and would work together with confidence that the MPC would make it happen.

ASSOCIATIONS UNION

So far, the MPC has different member organizations from different associations such as the National Council for the Blind of Malaysia, the National Council for the Association of Spastic Children of Malaysia, the Malaysian Association for the Blind (MAB), the Selangor and Federal Territory Association for the Mentally Retarded Children, the Malaysian Association for the Handicapped, the Malaysian Sports Federation for the Deaf, the Malaysian Association for the Welfare of Dwarfs, and the Malaysian Chinese Handicapped Association.

Planning
Through different meetings and discussions, the MPC has come up with its planning of activities and events for the decade starting from 2001 until 2010. The MPC's ten-year planning activities include:
* establishment of the States Sports and Recreational Council,
* establishment of Sports Excellence Centre,
* Paralympiad Malaysia,
* to be the host country for international events,
* human resource development,
* preparation of national athletes,
* sports-friend program and Paralympic support programme,

- solidarity fund,
- motivational schema,
- construction of the Paralympic tower,
- establishment of sports academy, and
- quality management recognition through ISO 9000 certification.

The Organizational Structure

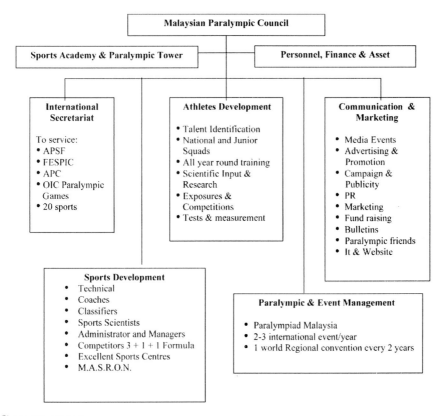

CONCLUSION

In conclusion, the formation of the Malaysian Paralympic Council was established with its people with disabilities in mind. The government is intrinsically interested in helping the people with disabilities to progress and benefit from the development of the country just like the other normal people, so that they are not marginalized from the mainstream activity of the country. Nevertheless, this is not an easy task to do as it needs the support and commitment of the whole of Malay society, the NGOs and private sectors to work together hand in hand with the government to ensure that this group of special people would remain in the centre of the activities. Different measures and actions have been taken to help the people with disabilities and there are many more actions that need to be carried out to improve the lives and the conditions of the people with disabilities. However, plans are in place to support our young disabled athletes.

SECTION 5

FUTURE DIRECTIONS OF RESEARCH INTO THE PARALYMPIC MOVEMENT

This section of the book reviews ideas in relation to future research and the use of critical theory and research into other aspects of the Paralympic Movement.

25   CRITICAL THEORY AND THE PARALYMPIC MOVEMENT

Allan Edwards & James Skinner

INTRODUCING CRITICAL THEORY TO SPORT PRACTICE

Critical theory dates back to the time of Socrates whose approach consisted of upholding the reality of ideas or forms over the reality of appearances. Over the millennia this debate on interpretation and representation became the intellectual foundation of philosophy, communications and education. The continuing debate that has occurred within academic circles highlights that critical theory asks us to identify and critically examine the discourses, practices and relationships of our practice worlds in order to determine the extent to which they encompass hidden elements of power and domination that fail to serve interests that we would wish to acknowledge as legitimate. This chapter argues that critical theory and the Paralympic movement are synonymous with the theoretical assumptions required to develop research in the Paralympic domain.

Critical theory also claims to promise us the possibility of coming to understand our worlds in an empowering way. Critical theory therefore offers us the challenge of reconstructing our social worlds in ways that are less distorted by relations of power and domination; of finding for ourselves new, less oppressive, more just ways of structuring our existence. In this light critical theory promises us the possibility of subjecting existing sporting practice social orders to critical scrutiny and provides us with some of the conceptual tools to do so. The sporting world itself is a social construction not an object; it is shaped by people who bring to it their own understandings of the world. It is not something that exists external to people and their interactions with one another. As a consequence of acknowledging this it becomes clear that we should consistently subject to critical scrutiny our understandings and actions of sport and the ways in which we shape and are shaped by our sporting worlds. We need to subject to scrutiny our sporting practices and relationships, noting particularly the interests that are served by maintaining the status quo.

Academics and practitioners involved in sport must come to accept an ongoing evolution or even revolution in our understandings and practice of sport both at personal and collective levels. In our ongoing search we should seek to expose, understand and overcome the contradictions and frustrations that others and we experience - in so doing critical theory has the opportunity to influence the sport praxis. The concept of praxis has been introduced into literature largely since 1970 when Freire's *Pedagogy of the Oppressed* was published in English. Freire (1972, p.28) was using praxis to refer to: "reflection and action upon the world in order to transform it". Thus, in the process of liberation, praxis becomes central, in the dialectical relationship between thought and action. This distinguishes theory for its own sake on the one hand, and pure action or activism on the other.

In sporting practice, a critical praxis can facilitate freedom for elite athletes to question what is elite sport, how we know and who provides the evidence of elite sport practice.

Habermas (1971) contended that critical theory helps to uncover what ought to be done in order to create and to support self-reflection. Without critical reflection, patterns of communication and socialization are reproduced and inevitably determine the theoretical and research traditions that are perpetuated without being challenged. By analysing how and why embedded assumptions guide theory development, research and practice, elite disabled athletes can begin to describe and explain oppressive effects. Habermas (1981a/1984) contended that researchers have a responsibility to identify constraining circumstances in society and to assist in liberation from oppressive structures. Determination can be made as to whether goals can be achieved through critical praxis and self-reflection. The process of critical reflection is praxis, because the ends and the means are directed toward transformation. Critical approaches promise us the possibility of examining our sporting worlds in terms of moral and political as well as simply technical concerns. In accepting the political, interested nature of our activities we are provided with the conceptual tools to theorise our sporting practice, and to reconstruct it.

It would be accurate to suggest that critical theory has not been a dominant mode of thought that surrounds the practice of sport. However, the impact of critical theory is increasing and critical theoretical approaches to conceptualizing sport are gaining greater momentum (Chalip, 1996; Frisby & Crawford, 1994). It would appear that critical theory is a fertile ground for understanding the practice of sport.

CRITICAL THEORY AND THE PARALYMPIC MOVEMENT

The Paralympics has initiated change within our current sport system demanding a paradigm shift in thought processes, practices and strategies of sport managers. These changes are seen to be better because they offer enlightenment and emancipation for athletes in the sport environment. Emancipation, consciousness raising and enlightenment are directly applicable to the circumstances surrounding the Paralympics. Luke (1991) acknowledges the role of critical theory and the importance of emancipation and enlightenment as needing to:

> ...adopt the goal of guiding human behaviour actions to realize greater emancipation and enlightenment in the lives of people today...refining peoples thinking abilities and moral sensibilities...should equip individuals with a new consciousness of what must be done and how to do it (and) move away from currently held beliefs that embody elements of domination and exploitation.
> (Luke, cited in Wexler, 1991, pp. 21-22)

Such realization he says: "....advances the process of human emancipation by lessening the victimization that people impose on themselves from within or that is forced upon them from without" (Luke, cited in Wexler, 1991, pp. 21-22). The promises of critical theory that are either implied or made explicit relate to the nature of critical theory as a philosophical position and as a process of theorizing. There is libratory intent in using radical critiques to transform the existing restrictive social order and conditions within the status quo into those that are based and enacted on the principles of equality, freedom and justice. The emancipatory critique of critical theory relies on systematic reflection and promises freedom from the distorted understandings communication and activities of pre-existing social structures, giving possibilities for new ways of being and acting within them.

Critical theory then, in its concern with the ways in which human beings are not only shaped by the circumstances of their own existence but actually shape them promises to move our understandings of the practice of sport beyond a socio-historical determinism. This move is away from the reification of social constructions; away from the portrayal of existing social orders relationships and practices as 'natural' 'inevitable', 'immutable' - the only 'logical' way of ordering our existence.

Critical theorists alert us to the notion that knowledge and human beings' construct forms of social existence and hence that they are interested, that is they serve particular, identifiable human interest (Habermas, 1971). They also alert us to the possibility that the very means of interpretation and communication may be dominated by particular groupings in a given social order. As such the interests of dominant groupings may be maintained at the expense of the interests of others not only by direct coercion but also by the force of intellectual and moral leadership. Thus, providing the basis by which people may come to reclaim the power to interpret and give meaning to, and hence to structure their social existence is perhaps the most important offering of critical theory.

Critical theory allows for the emancipation of Paralympians. It is concerned with exploring the tensions between the give (what exists, or what we understand exist) and the possible. That is between the ways in which life worlds are presently constructed and ways that they could be constructed. Critical theory encourages movement beyond the dominant social order, to a reconstruction of the life world in just and liberating ways. Its theory is suited to the quest for emancipation of athletes with special needs as knowledge, freedom from oppression, rationality and communicative action endeavour to create societies and sporting practices that are free from domination. Societies where all members have an equal opportunity to contribute to the production systems that meet human needs and lead to the progressive development of all, as Landman (1977) states:

> The individual can only achieve self-fulfilment in a society that is liberated from wants and from the oppression of man by man (sic), that is, in a society in which conditions for dignified human existence are established (Landman, cited in Tar, 1977, p. vii).

Critical theory exposes to us our power to shape rather than simply be shaped by our social forms of existence. It is concerned with exploring the tension between the given (what exists, or what we understand to exist) and the possible, that is between the ways in which our lifeworlds are presently constructed and the ways that they could be constructed. Critical theorising then promises us the opportunity to come to a cognitive understanding of our worlds particularly our social existence, and in so doing move beyond the dominant social order, to reconstruct our worlds in just and liberating ways.

Critical theory asks us to identify and critically examine the discourses, practices and relationships of our sporting practice worlds in order to determine the extent to which they encompass hidden elements of power and domination that fail to serve interests that we would wish to acknowledge as legitimate. It also claims to promise us the possibility of coming to understand our sporting worlds in an empowering way. Critical theory therefore offers us the challenge of reconstructing our social worlds in ways that are less distorted by relations of power and domination; of finding for ourselves new, less oppressive, more just ways of structuring our existence.

CONSCIOUSNESS RAISING TOWARD PARALYMPIC SPORT

Consciousness raising involves the recognition of social, political, economic and personal constraints of freedom, and it provides the forum in which to take action to challenge those constraints. Freire (1972) suggests that consciousness raising involves dialogue between those with theoretical analysis of oppression and those who are oppressed. By engaging in critical and liberating dialogues, individuals can uncover the hidden distortions within themselves that help maintain an oppressive society and as such, consciousness raising encourages social and individual change to occur. In light of the Paralympics consciousness raising brings forward Habermas's theory of knowledge and interests and more specifically the concepts of lifeworld and rationality. Consciousness raising is simultaneously an individual experience of empowerment that can contribute to psychological change for the individual and social transformation for society and communities. In relation to the Paralympics consciousness raising is a vital factor in the emancipation of the lifeworld of athletes with special needs. The theoretical diagram (Figure 1) demonstrates that the outer constraints of society (the lifeworld) can impact on Paralympic sport. The impact of society on the sport lifeworld of the disabled athlete can be discussed from two tangible elements: the general public or community and the sport environment.

Raising consciousness of the general public towards the rights of athletes with special needs and the establishment of a sport system within a society that fears concepts of 'taking away from the whole'. Consciousness raising as a means to better understand the placement of disabled athletes in the elite sport environment is pertinent to the success of enlightening sort communities and in particular disabled athletes. Thus sport communities and environments are a viewed as a type of 'life world' to the disabled athletes because sport provides hope and opportunity. They are places where these elite athletes should be free of all form of rationality and colonisation from 'external' life worlds. Importantly, the consciousness raising of sport managers regarding special needs athletes generally takes the form of 'knowledge' from a theoretical and practical perspective. However, in terms of critical theory, consciousness raising affirms the self as the knower of one's condition and critiques the conditions that have created what one is. Thus, when lived realities (experiences) are linked to the objective of realities (theory), gaps may exist between the distinction of knowledge labelled 'theory' and knowledge labelled 'experience'. While they are separate aspects they need to go hand in hand if emancipation is to follow. Fonow and Cook (1991) emphasise the importance of personal and political outcomes of consciousness raising: "emotional catharsis, academic insight and intellectual product, and increasing politicization and activism" (p. 31). As such, transformation of perceptions and ideologies via consciousness raising can be a critical principle involved in the unification of rationalised society. Consciousness raising occurs in a process of enlightenment, empowerment and emancipation.

ENLIGHTENMENT

Enlightenment is the experience of communicating to see oneself in a radically new way by engaging in a dialogue that is a process of self-reflection and theorising. In critical theory enlightenment seeks to explain why thing are the way they are. New theory is created out of this dialogue as individuals come to see the links between their own struggles and those of others and to create their own explanations. In Paralympic sport enlightenment occurs for both the sport manager and the disabled athletes. Enlightenment for the sport manager is reached when they foster philosophies and become aware of ways to facilitate athletes with special needs in their sport. And enlightenment for the special needs athlete is being accepted into a sport community that offers hope and opportunities. Along with enlightenment comes empowerment.

EMPOWERMENT

Enlightenment itself however is not enough to bring about liberation for the athlete. To transform the existing social order, individuals and groups must become their own mobilising force. Empowerment is the process by which a group of individuals become galvanised to act on their own behalf. It is also a state of feeling empowered and having ability to affect others and change social institutions. Empowerment is an inter-personal and intra-personal experience, with each contributing to the other. In Paralympic research individuals become empowered to explore the links between the inequities in society and their own impaired sport systems and to take action where these links are uncovered providing and emancipatory condition.

EMANCIPATION

Emancipation is both the process of becoming liberated and the state of being liberated. Emancipation is the state of being in which people come to know who they are and have the collective power to determine the direction of their existence. The nature of emancipation is dynamic. Because human beings are not inseparable from their social and historical context, reality is not a static entity, but a process – a transformation. By engaging in acts of enlightenment and empowerment, human -beings become liberated – and more fully human. Thus Paralympic sport needs to encourage people to embrace emancipatory actions, moving beyond coping and adaptation.

CONCLUDING COMMENTS

Critical theory philosophy provides hope and opportunity to athletes with special needs. It affects all parties involved in the well being of disabled athletes. Critical theory recognises an emancipatory society is one in which human beings actively control destinies. This is achieved through a heightened understanding of situations and circumstances which surround the preceding future. It encourages self-criticism and continuing critique through a praxis method, which implies emancipation from ideological dogmatism leading to the transformation of authoritarian systems through democratic processes. Emancipation is a dynamic state of being in which self-knowledge (enlightenment) and self-advocacy (empowerment) are connected to knowledge and advocacy for others. Emancipation is accomplished by engaging in enlightening and empowering experiences and it takes place in concert with enlightenment and empowerment. Consciousness raising is the meeting ground of theory and practice and is both a method of achieving the goal and the goal itself.

REFERENCES

Chalip, L. (1996). Critical policy analysis: The illustrative case of New Zealand sport policy development. *Journal of Sport Management,* 10(310-324).

Fonow, M. & Cook. J. (1991). *Beyond Methodology: Feminist scholarship as lived research.* Bloomington, Indiana: Indiana Press.

Freire, P. (1972). *Pedagogy of the oppressed.* New York: Seaview.

Frisby, W. & Crawford, S. (1994). *Journal of Sport Management,* 8(1).

Habermas, J. (1971). *Knowledge and human interest* (J. Sharpiro, Trans.). London: Heinemann.

Habermas, J. (1981). Modernity versus Postmodernity. *New German Critque,* 22(Winter), 3-41.

Habermas, J. (1984). *The theory of communicative action: Reason and rationalisation of society.* (T. McCarthy, Trans.). (Vol.1). London: Heinemann (Original work published 1981a).

Tar, Z. (1977). *The Frankfurt School: The Critical theories of Max Horkheimier and Theodore Adorno.* Canada: John Wiley & Sons.

Wexler, P. (1991). *Critical Theory Now.* London: Falmer Press.

26   Breaking the Chains!

Keith Gilbert & Otto J. Schantz

Empowerment or side show? The question we posed as the title of this book remains unanswered! Indeed, even after we brought together a variety of perspectives: personal experiences, descriptions, analyses and scientific papers we have not been able to solve the complex question. Certainly, none of these papers could give a definitive answer to our question. However, as mentioned in chapter one this was not the purpose of the book and we consider this volume of selected papers as a modest starting point which will open the way to new horizons. The different contributions raised a multitude of themes, problems and questions, which need further investigation and discussion. It is clear from the chapters and data in this text that it's not by repeating a naive discourse claiming that the Paralympics contribute to the empowerment of people with disabilities that we help them to get out of the margins of society. Indeed, serious research calls for an epistemological rupture in order to transcend common sense and previously taken for granted opinions. Every perspective has its blind spots, only a critical and self-reflective position can help us to be aware of this matter of fact. What we need within the Paralympic movement is further critical social analysis to deconstruct the marginalising discourses, and to unveil the disabling power structures and mechanisms which exist outside but also within the movement. The chapter on Critical Theory from Allan Edwards & James Skinner presents a possible research paradigm for such kind of research.

Quite a number of chapters in this book support the idea that sport and competitive sport may contribute strongly to the empowerment of people with disabilities. Nevertheless, we feel that there are some reservations about this statement in that we should be blinded neither by the emotive discourses of athletes nor by the enthusiastic propaganda of the Paralympic leaders and oversee the fact that categorizing people as Olympians and Paralympians has as result in a binomial order where the one elite group is on the top and the others, the Paralympians, on the bottom. Indeed, the very notion of the categorization means to include and to exclude. In fact as viewed from the outside and from a critical perspective there appears to be an enormous gap between the official Olympic discourse of non-discrimination and the discriminating reality.

Further to this statement we believe that the existing structures of competitive sport promote an extremely, quasi-Darwinist selection by norms and rules which favour abelist standards of function and presentation of the human body. The Paralympic management by copying this selection process also produces and is driven to attempt to promote exceptional athletic performances; however, these performances do not always fit the standards of the body cultures of our societies and even less their body cult. We agree that even though many of the Paralympic performances are exceptional, they could also be perceived as to be exceptional in the sense of curiosities rather than in the sense of human sport performances or by pushing the limits of the human body. They inspire empathic admirations, they are worthy to be mediated as "supercrip" stories, but in the field of sports they are relegated to the side show arena, whereas the main show room is occupied by the dominating Olympics.

Paralympic athletes have been and still are excluded from mainstream sport competitions for reasons of disadvantage. If they are able to compensate for these disadvantages by perhaps utilising technology they are excluded because the powers at be state that they are advantaged. Society is never short on arguments justifying exclusion. The case of the South African athlete Oscar Pistorius is a good illustration of these disabling control mechanisms. Hard training, pure talent and artificial legs made him able to compete with the very best quarter-milers in the abelist world. But narrow biomechanical and physiological investigations almost destroyed his dream to be an Olympian. After a medical definition of normality and abnormality (cf. Canguilhem 1966) we now have to face a biomechanical definition of normality. The question in the Pistorius case should not be whether a prosthesis gives back more energy than a natural leg, which is just one single factor contributing to the overall complex performance of a 400-m dash. The question should be whether the 400-m performances of these runners are comparable in term of the goal of this competition, i.e. go run as fast as possible around one lap of the 400-m track, allowing an interesting and exciting competition, where the outcome is not clearly predictable. The idealistic discourse stating that "sport brings people together" lacks credibility as long as rules are made to create barriers instead of rendering sport accessible without discrimination of any kind.

Further social research in the field of Paralympic studies should contribute to finding possibilities to change sport in order to render it inclusive. The fact to prepare and to train people with disabilities according to the logic and to the demands of existing abelist sports does probably not add to their empowerment and their equality, but will end up in categorizing and exclusion. Shouldn't we try to find solutions and try to improve accessibility and inclusiveness for athletes at all levels, to ensure the right to practice sport together? Serious, independent, self-reflective, and critical research should contribute to reach these new horizons of emancipation in the field of sport and help to construct a fairer and more human world of sports. As Nietzsche argues, to improve dancing in chains or to try to break them? That is the most challenging question for future research in the discipline of Paralympic studies.

REFERENCE

Canguilhem, G. (1966). *Le normal et le pathologique*. Paris: Presses Universitaires de France.

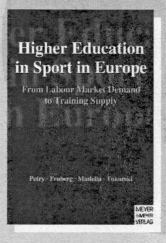

Roland Naul
Olympic Education

Olympic Education is not only a book for students and teachers in sports education as well as for course instructors and coaches in children's and youth sports, but also for executives in sports federations. It explains what the term "Olympic" really means in the broader context of a great variety of different sports. Olympic Education is an educational mission that is relevant for all children and youths, in schools as well as in sports clubs.

About 160 pages, b&w
13 photos and illustrations
Paperback, 6¹/2" x 9¹/4"
ISBN: 978-1-84126-254-3
$ 24.95 US
£ 14.95 UK/€ 19.95

K. Petry, K. Froberg, A. Madella, W. Tokarski
Higher Education in Sport in Europe
From Labour Market Demand to Training Supply

Academic and professional aspects of sport programs in higher education and the labor market are covered in this book. Supported by the project AEHESIS (Aligning a European Higher Educational Structure In Sport Science), the European Education Policy, the Bologna Process and the Tuning program are explored in detail.

c. 200 pages
some illustrations and tables
Paperback, 6¹/2" x 9¹/4"
ISBN: 978-1-84126-230-7
$ 19.95 USN
£ 14.95 UK/€ 18.95

MEYER & MEYER SPORT

The Sports Publisher

MEYER & MEYER Sport